Living at the Crossroads

An Introduction to Christian Worldview

Michael W. Goheen
and Craig G. Bartholomew

Baker Academic

a division of Baker Publishing Group
Grand Rapids, Michigan

© 2008 by Michael W. Goheen and Craig G. Bartholomew

Published by Baker Academic
a division of Baker Publishing Group
P.O. Box 6287, Grand Rapids, MI 49516-6287
www.bakeracademic.com

Printed in the United States of America

Library of Congress Cataloging-in-Publication Data
Goheen, Michael W., 1955–
    Living at the crossroads : an introduction to Christian worldview / Michael W. Goheen and Craig G. Bartholomew.
        p.   cm.
    Includes bibliographical references and indexes.
    ISBN 978-0-8010-3140-3 (pbk.)
    1. Christianity—Philosophy. I. Bartholomew, Craig G., 1961– II. Title.
BR100.G643 2008
230—dc22   2008017898

To
Pieter and Fran Vanderpol
John and Jenny Hultink

In appreciation for their commitment to Christian scholarship

Contents

Preface

Our Stories

Life is—or should be—about knowing God deeply. This book emerges out of the journeys we have been on since God turned our own lives upside down by drawing us to his Son.

Mike grew up in a Baptist church. The gospel that was preached there was one of individual, future, and otherworldly salvation. It was all about going to heaven when you die. Nevertheless, that church was a place where God was at work through the gospel; people loved the Lord, and their faith was alive. Mike remains grateful for much in this tradition—for example, its earnest commitment to reading Scripture, to prayer, and to evangelism; its stress on the importance of individual holiness and morality; and its emphasis on the personal relationship that we have with Jesus. These remain important issues for every Christian, and Mike is thankful for this early training. Yet it had little to say about the broader, public life of Western culture—politics, economics, scholarship, education, work, leisure, entertainment, and sports.[1]

During Mike's seminary years he began to see that the gospel that Jesus preached was a gospel *of the kingdom*. The good news is much bigger than Mike had been led to believe: God is restoring his rule over all of human life in Jesus and by the Spirit. Further reading during those seminary years in literature that explored the Christian worldview began to open up the implications of this scriptural insight for a Christian approach to the public life of culture. It was exciting, akin to a second conversion! The gospel had something to say about all of human life.

Doing his doctorate on the work of Lesslie Newbigin, one of the greatest missiologists of the twentieth century, Mike found his conviction deepened and strengthened. Having served as a missionary in India for most of his adult life, Newbigin was concerned in the last years of his life to bring the gospel to bear on the public life of Western culture. Newbigin shared many of the convictions that Mike had embraced during his seminary days. But Newbigin also had fresh emphases and critiques that were important in Mike's worldview development.[2] Mike got to know Lesslie Newbigin well, and his influence helped Mike to see the integral connection between mission and a Christian worldview.

For the better part of the last two decades, Mike has taught numerous worldview courses to undergraduates and graduates of varying denominational backgrounds in various parts of the world. But the importance of worldview for living has moved beyond the classroom for Mike. It moved him and his wife, Marnie, to struggle with the implications of the gospel for education and to undertake the home schooling of their four kids with the intention of shaping their education with the gospel. This change affected numerous areas of life, but it has especially opened up the arts, literature, and music. Marnie shared and participated in the same "worldview conversion" that Mike did. Her new appreciation of the arts as God's gift was passed along to her family. Their four kids became an accomplished string quartet and devoted themselves to the study of literature, music, and the other arts. It has led on to graduate studies in the arts and music for several of them up to the PhD level. Mike and Marnie's life is still filled with concerts, now at a professional level, in which their children play. This is only one way that a broadening worldview has affected Mike and his family, but it shows that one's view of the gospel does have consequences.

For Mike, worldview is about opening up the wide-ranging scope of the gospel and the church's mission to embody that gospel. Few things excite him as much as helping Christians to see the length and breadth and depth of God's love for us and his world.

Craig grew up in South Africa during the era of apartheid, by which every aspect of South African life was structured along racial lines. He went to a whites-only school, lived in a whites-only neighborhood, and enjoyed all the "benefits" of being a white South African. Craig was radically converted to Christ in his teens through the evangelical youth group of the Church of England (into which he was eventually ordained as a minister). Like Mike's Baptist church, Craig's Anglican church was evangelistic and alive but had nothing to say about the oppressive, racist social context in which they lived. Really committed Christians went into "full-time ministry" (as pastors or missionaries); it was better to stay away from politics, since, after all (so it was reasoned from Rom. 13:1–7), the government had been appointed by God!

Craig has a great love for horses, and when he left high school, his choices were between becoming a vet and studying theology. He went to Bible college in Cape Town, where he was exposed to Reformed theology and the worldview thinking of Francis Schaeffer (though this was never explicitly brought to bear on the South African situation). Later Craig began to think through Schaeffer's work, and he realized that if the gospel is a worldview, then it applies to all of life, *including* politics—a dangerous insight to have at that time in South Africa.

While working as a pastor in South Africa, Craig made contact with Afrikaner Kuyperian[3] Christians in Potchefstroom, and together they developed the Christian Worldview Network, which held annual conferences and published a *Manifesto on Christians in the Arts* and a quarterly magazine called *The Big Picture*.[4] Craig believes that what South Africa went through then, and the general failure of evangelical Christians to relate their faith to the realities of South African life, have a great deal to teach us now about the vital importance of understanding the gospel as a worldview. We now know from the Truth and Reconciliation Commission what terrible injustices were perpetrated in South Africa during the apartheid years under its "Christian" government. How was it that evangelical Christians could not see the evil right in front of them? How was it that, on the whole, evangelicals ended up reinforcing this evil rather than challenging it?[5] One important answer is that they lacked a coherent Christian worldview. How different might the history of South Africa have been if evangelicals there had combined their "passion for souls" with a sense of Christ's lordship over all of life!

As Craig's thinking about a Christian worldview developed, he began (under the influence of his Kuyperian friends) to see the importance of philosophy for Christian scholarship, and this led him to Toronto for a year of philosophical study and then on to the UK, where he completed his doctorate on the book of Ecclesiastes. Craig's current research deals with the ways in which the gospel as a worldview shapes academic biblical studies.

A Christian worldview gets you interested in everything. Craig loves reading novels and listening to music; he makes crafts and sells jewelry, has two chinchillas as pets, and enjoys teaching philosophy and religion. A Christian worldview also helps you to meet interesting people. Several years ago Craig and Mike met in Canada and then again in England, and they discovered a mutual commitment to mission and Christian worldview. Out of this friendship came, first, *The Drama of Scripture: Finding Our Place in the Biblical Story* (Baker Academic, 2004), and now this book.

Lessons We Have Learned

Both of our stories have underscored a number of things that are important to what we hope to share with our readers in the chapters that follow. First, Christianity involves a personal relationship with God through Jesus. In this respect, we remain grateful for the Pietist tradition that has deeply shaped English-speaking evangelicalism in general and both of us in particular. We believe that this tradition often has unfortunately narrowed the true scope of the gospel, but we also believe that it has emphasized some aspects of biblical truth that are of the utmost importance, such as the need for a personal relationship with Christ, a high view of the Bible as God's Word, and the importance of evangelism.[6]

Second, the gospel as recorded in Scripture is as broad as creation. Since the church has been sent to make known this good news in all of life, in actions and in words, the church's mission is, likewise, as broad as creation. Indeed, our deepest concern in this book is to give expression to the gospel of the kingdom and the cultural mission of the church that follows from this. Our hope is that the readers of this book will be interested in relating their own faith to every part of God's good creation.

Herman Bavinck has expressed these first two emphases in a helpful way. He quotes the well-known preacher J. Christian Blumhardt, who said that a person "must be twice converted, first from the natural to the spiritual life, and then from the spiritual to the natural." This is a truth, Bavinck believes, that is "confirmed by the religious experience of every Christian and by the history of Christian piety in all ages."[7] The first conversion is to God and is expressed in the sigh of the psalmist, "Whom have I in heaven but you? And earth has nothing I desire besides you" (Ps. 73:25). The Pietist tradition understands this well. But we must be converted *again*, this time back to the breadth of our cultural calling in this present world. Bavinck himself was raised in a Pietist home and went through these "two conversions." Our own similar experiences have led us to be thankful for our Pietist past and its important emphases, as well as our Reformed present with its broader understanding of the gospel. And we are concerned that each of these traditions can neglect the important emphases of the other. It has been our goal in writing this book that the breadth of the gospel would shape it from beginning to end.

Third, the term *worldview*, in spite of all of its philosophical and historical baggage, remains a valuable concept by which to open up the comprehensive scope of the gospel. The term does have its dangers and limitations: it retains some of its early associations with humanistic philosophy, and more recently it has taken on intellectualist overtones within some Christian traditions. But its value as a tool of Christian thought is real, and thus in this book we seek to carry on in the worldview-conscious tradition of James Orr and Abraham Kuyper, whose aim was simply to shine the brightest possible light on the Christian church's mission in the public life of culture.

Fourth, the burgeoning study of mission can immeasurably enrich worldview studies. Those who work in cross-cultural missions have struggled to understand the engagement of gospel and culture at a deep level. Moreover, they have struggled with this issue from the biblical standpoint of how best to embody and announce the gospel—that is, from a missional concern. The literature of missiology, and especially the rich literature on the contextualization of the gospel in other cultures, will inform much of this book.

Fifth, worldview studies must be increasingly ecumenical. Paul says that the breadth and length and height and depth of the love of Christ can be known only "together with all the Lord's people" (Eph. 3:18). "Together" here implies, for us, a dialogue with Christians from other places, from other times, and from other confessional traditions. Both of us have been shaped by the Kuyperian tradition, and surely this tradition has taken the lead in worldview studies. But we are not uncritical participants in this tradition, and we believe firmly that no single tradition is able adequately to grasp or to express the fullness of the gospel. We have much to learn from our brothers and sisters from other parts of the world, from other historical eras, and from other denominations and confessional traditions of the Christian church. Both of us have taught the material of this book in many parts of the world and to people from many different Christian traditions. Those experiences have provided much enrichment and correction, and we hope that this will be evident in this book.

About This Book

Worldview is a concept that emerged in the European philosophical tradition, and it is valuable only insofar as it enables us to understand more faithfully the gospel that stands at the center of the biblical story, and to live more fully in that story. It is for this reason that this study of Christian worldview follows on from our former book, *The Drama of Scripture*. We have found in our teaching that a course on worldview is far more effective when it follows a course on the story of the Bible: worldview follows Scripture so as to deepen our commitment to living in the biblical story.

There is another reason it is important to emphasize that *Living at the Crossroads* follows on from *The Drama of Scripture*. Many traditional evangelical approaches to worldview have seen it in intellectualist terms; that is, they look at worldview as a merely rational system. We believe that worldview should have a narrative- -a *storied*—form, since this is the shape of the Bible itself. We often have occasion to quote N. T. Wright's observation that a story is simply "the best way of talking about *the way the world actually is.*"[8]

This book is meant to be (only) an introduction to worldview. We recognize the danger in simplifying and summarizing large amounts of material on some very complex theological, philosophical, and historical issues. Something that is meant to be simple can all too easily become simplistic, but it does not have to be that way. We believe that this kind of book is needed to get undergraduate students and church members excited about the scope of the gospel and the breadth of their own callings. If you catch a glimpse of the possibilities here, other study can follow later.

When we wrote *The Drama of Scripture*, we constructed a Web site that provides slides, articles, and numerous other resources for studying the Bible as a single, coherent story (http://www.biblicaltheology.ca). The feedback that we have received about that Web site suggests that many of our readers have found it helpful. So we are offering a similar one for *Living at the Crossroads*, at www.christian-worldview.ca. It too will provide slides to be used for teaching, supplementary articles, and much more to help encourage the discussion of Christian worldview generally.

Worldview has to do with the most basic, comprehensive, foundational religious beliefs that we have about the world as they are embodied in a story. This means that Christians will elaborate and understand these beliefs that flow from Scripture. But these beliefs cannot be separated from a cultural context, for the gospel is always expressed and embodied within some human culture. Therefore, in the study of worldview we must also struggle to understand the fundamental beliefs of the surrounding culture within which each Christian community lives. The relationship of the Christian faith to the other cultural "faith" that surrounds it must be explored. This is a very complex and highly dangerous enterprise. As contextualization studies in missiology show, there is always the danger of allowing the gospel to be compromised, accommodated to the idolatry of any given culture. Worldview studies, then, must deal with the Bible's foundational teachings, *and* those of the surrounding culture, *and* the complex interaction of the two belief systems.

This opens up a wide area of inquiry for Christian academics, and many good books on worldview have dealt with various divisions of the topic. However, only Brian Walsh and Richard Middleton's *The Transforming Vision: Shaping a Christian World View* has really shown the potential breadth of worldview studies.[9] That book remains, in our opinion, one of the best texts on worldview studies available, precisely for this reason. Yet it was written over twenty-five years ago, and thus it did not deal with our current complex situation, shaped by globalization, postmodernity, and consumerism. Also, although the way that Walsh and Middleton relate the gospel to culture is, in our opinion, on target, they have not fully explored the dynamic of contextualization. Our book follows Walsh and Middleton's in demonstrating that worldview is a wide-ranging discipline with many smaller fields of inquiry within it. We deal with a biblical worldview, a cultural worldview, and a worldview in action. But between the cultural worldview and a worldview in action we reflect on the way in which the gospel can come alive in a faithful way within a cultural context; that is, we seek to explore the dynamic relationship of gospel and culture.

We begin with the gospel of the kingdom and the call of the church to make known this good news. In chapter 2 we trace the origins of the word *worldview* and how it came to be appropriated by the Christian community, especially by the evangelical church in North America. In chapters 3 and 4 we return to the question of how this concept of worldview might help equip the church for its comprehensive mission today, and to that end we will articulate what we believe to be a faithful biblical worldview: a digest of the most fundamental and comprehensive beliefs about the world that are conveyed by the biblical story. The next three chapters describe the dominant worldview of modern Western culture: chapters 5 and 6 briefly trace the Western story from its origins in Greek culture to the present; chapter 7 asks "What time is it?" in our culture—what are the beliefs and spirits that are shaping our culture? In chapter 8 we turn to consider how the church is to live at the crossroads between these two conflicting and incompatible worldviews. How are we meant to live in two stories and yet remain faithful to the one true story articulated in the biblical narrative? What is involved in a missionary encounter between the gospel and Western culture? And finally, chapter 9 offers snapshots of what such an encounter might look like in six areas of public life: politics, business, art, sports, scholarship, and education.

Acknowledgments

We realize we are deeply indebted to many people, living and dead, who have shaped our understanding of worldview. We mention in particular Al Wolters, Brian Walsh, Richard Middleton, Gideon Strauss, Elaine Botha, Bob Goudzwaard, Jonathan Chaplin, Herman Ridderbos, N. T. Wright, Lesslie Newbigin, Francis Schaeffer, James Sire, David Naugle, and John Newby.

Jim Kinney and his excellent staff at Baker Academic have been helpful in forming this book and bringing it to birth. We are again deeply indebted to Douglas Loney, professor of English and dean of the Foundations Division at Redeemer University College. As with *The Drama of Scripture*, Doug has helped to provide a lively literary style. He has done more than simply edit this book and help to unify two writing styles. Doug has entered into the topics at hand, helped express things more clearly, and provided invaluable help not only on style but also on content.

We are delighted to dedicate this book to Pieter and Fran Vanderpol, and to John and Jenny Hultink. These couples have become our dear friends and have demonstrated their commitment to Christian scholarship in tangible and sacrificial ways, not least in endowing the chairs that we occupy. Without such patrons, this book would not have been possible.

1

Gospel, Story, Worldview, and the Church's Mission

Starting with the Gospel of the Kingdom

As followers of Jesus, our thinking about worldview must begin with the gospel, the good news first announced two thousand years ago by Jesus when he stepped onto the stage of world history: "The kingdom of God has arrived!"[1]

Jesus spoke the language of the Jews of his day, for they well understood the resonance of that word *kingdom*. The Jews had for a long, long time anticipated God's intervention in history. They had waited for God to move again in love and wrath and power, to send his Messiah and restore his reign over the whole world. And at last Jesus does come, claiming the royal title for himself: *he* is God's anointed one, the Messiah. The Spirit of God is on him, he declares, to bring God's purposes for the entire world to their great and terrible climax. The divine King of Creation is returning to reclaim his kingdom!

This proclamation of good news is the climactic moment of a long historical account (told in the Old Testament) of God's redemptive work, stretching back to God's promise to Adam and Eve. God had chosen Israel to be a channel of his redemptive blessing to the nations, but they had failed. Yet, in the midst of their failure, prophets arose promising that God would not let his plan unravel; he would act again in and through a promised king to renew the whole world. Jesus announces that that day has arrived: the power of God to renew the entire creation by his Spirit is now present in Jesus. This liberating power is displayed in Jesus' life and deeds and is explained by his words. But it is at the cross that the triumph of God's kingdom is accomplished. There he battles the power of evil and gains the decisive victory. His resurrection is the dawning of the first day of the new creation. Alive from the dead, he enters as the firstborn into the life to come. Before he ascends to God the Father, he commissions his little group of followers to continue his mission of making the good news of the kingdom known until he returns. He then takes his place at the right hand of God to reign in power over all creation. He pours out his Spirit and by the Spirit makes known his restoring and comprehensive rule in and through his people as they embody and proclaim the good news.

One day Jesus will return, and every knee will bow and every tongue will confess that Jesus is Creator, Redeemer, and Lord. The end of universal history that Jesus announced, revealed, and accomplished will finally arrive in fullness. But until that climactic day, the church is taken up into the Spirit's work of making known, in their lives, deeds, and words, the good news of what God has done for the world in Jesus.

The Bible as the True Story of the World

The proclamation of the gospel of the kingdom is not an announcement about a new religious experience or doctrine. Still less is this an offer of future salvation in another spiritual world. This gospel is an announcement about where God is moving the history of the whole world. Jesus employs a popular Old Testament image to drive this home: the world will one day be the kingdom of God. The good news that Jesus announces and enacts, and that the church is commissioned to embody and make known, is the gospel of the kingdom. We make a grave mistake if we ignore this, the central image of Jesus' proclamation and ministry.

Jesus claims that the establishing of God's kingdom is the ultimate goal of world history. This is not a local tale of interest only to a particular ethnic or religious group. Jesus steps into a long story of God's redemptive work in history that had been unfolding for thousands of years in the Old Testament, into a community that was eagerly anticipating that story's climax. The Jews believed that the God they served was the one and only God, the Creator of all things, the Ruler of history, the Redeemer of all things. After the entrance of sin and evil into the world God had set out to restore his world and his human subjects to live again under his gracious rule. This God was not the God of the Jews only; he was King of the whole earth. The Jewish nation had been chosen to be channels of his redemptive work to the entire world. All Jews believed that this story was leading to the grand culmination when God would act decisively and finally to finish what he had been working toward in their history: the accomplishment of salvation for all nations, for all creation. They disagreed on how this would happen, and when, and by whom. They disagreed on what they themselves should be doing while waiting for God's action. But they all believed that the story of God's redemptive acts was moving toward a climax that would have consequences for all people.

When Jesus came, he announced that he was himself the goal of this redemptive story, the climax of God's dramatic activity. Such a claim was completely astonishing. Jesus was not simply another rabbi offering some new religious or ethical teaching by which to enrich one's own life. He claimed that in his person and work the meaning of history and of the world itself was being made known and accomplished. He warned that *all* people must find their place and meaning within his story, and no other.

When we speak, therefore, of the Bible as a story, we are making a normative claim about the story told in the Bible: it is public truth. It is a claim that this is the way God created the world; the story of the Bible tells us the way the world really is. Thus, the biblical story is not to be understood simply as a local tale about the Jewish people. It begins with the creation of all things and ends with the renewal of all things. In between, it offers an interpretation of the meaning of cosmic history. Christopher Wright puts it this way: "The Old Testament tells its story as the story or, rather, as part of that ultimate and universal story that will ultimately embrace the whole of creation, time, and humanity within its scope. In other words, in reading these texts we are invited to embrace a metanarrative, a grand narrative."[2]

Thus our stories, our reality—indeed, all of human and nonhuman reality—must find their place in *this* story. In *Mimesis*, Erich Auerbach makes this point in a striking contrast between Homer's *Odyssey* and the biblical story: "Far from seeking, like Homer, merely to make us forget our own reality for a few hours, [the Old Testament] seeks to overcome our reality: we are to fit our own life into its world, feel ourselves to be elements in its structure of universal history. . . . Everything else that happens in the world can only be conceived as an element in this sequence; into it everything that is known about the world . . . must be fitted as an ingredient of the divine plan."[3] Normally, when we read myths or novels, or when we watch movies, television, or plays, we are meant at least in part to forget about our own world and to enter and live in the fictional world for a time. When the story ends, we emerge on the other side, return to our own world, and resume our own lives. We have indulged in a kind of escape from reality into fiction, perhaps hoping to be informed, enriched, or at least entertained while we have been "away." Some of us will seek to carry back some nuggets of truth or wisdom or beauty as souvenirs from the world of artifice, giving us perhaps some new (but admittedly limited) insight into an aspect of our lives in the "real" world. But it is not that way with the biblical story. The Bible claims to *be* the real world. This story, among all stories, claims to tell the *whole* truth about the way our own world really is. Here, inside this story, we are meant to find the meaning of our lives. Here we must find a place in which our own experience was meant to fit. Here we are offered insight into the ultimate significance of human life itself.

Thus, the gospel is public truth, universally valid, true for all people and all of human life. It is not merely for the private sphere of "religious" experience. It is not about some otherworldly salvation postponed to an indefinite future. It is God's message about how he is at work to restore his world and all of human life. It tells us about the goal of all history and thus claims to be the true story of the world.

Which Story Will Shape Your Life?

All of human life is shaped by some story. Consider the following illustration offered by N. T. Wright:

> What is the meaning of the following comment? "It is going to rain." On the surface, the statement seems to be quite clear. Yet the meaning and significance of this remark can only be understood when we see the part it plays in a broader narrative. If we are about to go for a picnic that has been planned for some time, then these words would be bad news, with the further implication that perhaps we had better change our plans. If we live in East Africa plagued by drought, where another lengthy dry spell and consequent crop failure appears imminent, the statement would be good news indeed. If I had predicted three days ago that it would rain and you had not believed me, the statement would vindicate my predictive ability as a meteorologist. If we are part of the community of Israel on Mount Carmel listening to the words of Elijah, the statement substantiates the message of Elijah that Yahweh is the true God and that Elijah is his prophet. In each case, the single statement demands to be "heard" within the context of a full implicit plot, a complete implicit narrative.[4]

The meaning of these words ultimately depends on which story shapes it; in fact, each story will give the event a different meaning. It is like that with our lives: "The way we understand human life depends on what conception we have of the human story. What is the real story of which my life story is a part?"[5] What Newbigin is referring to here is not a linguistically constructed narrative world that we fabricate to give meaning to our lives but rather an interpretation of cosmic history that gives meaning to human life. This is the way God has created the world and the way it really is.

Since human beings are created to live in community, some shared story will inevitably shape the whole life of a social group. The gospel invites all who hear it to believe the good news and repent (Mark 1:14–15). All who hear are summoned to believe that this is the true story and to make their home in it, leaving behind whatever other story had been shaping their lives. From these hearers a community is formed of people who have come to believe the gospel and the story of the world that it offers.

The Church's Mission

The church is the community that responds in faith and repentance to the good news of the kingdom. They make their home in the story of the Bible and seek to form their lives by that narrative. But this is a community that also is charged with making this good news known to everyone else. This gospel defines the church's mission and calling in the world. Before Jesus returns to the Father, he gathers his disciples and speaks words that are intended to define the meaning of the rest of their lives: "As the Father has sent me, I am sending you" (John 20:21). These words encapsulate what it means to be a community of Christ's followers. Their mission is to make known the kingdom of God—the end and goal of history—throughout the world as Jesus has made it known in Israel.

Christopher Wright rightly sees mission as "a major key that unlocks the whole grand narrative of the canon of Scripture."[6] He believes that the Bible tells "the story of God's mission through God's people in their engagement with God's world for the sake of God's whole creation."[7] Thus, the mission of the people of God is "our committed participation as God's people, at God's invitation and command, in God's own mission within the history of God's world for the redemption of God's creation."[8] Our identity as God's people comes from that missional role in the biblical story.

Thus, there is a sense in which the church is essential to the gospel. Jesus did not leave behind a book in which the good news of the kingdom was to be bound up. Instead, he formed a community to carry the message: "As you [God the Father] sent me into the world, so I have sent them into the world"

(John 17:18). This community is defined by their mission: to make known the good news of the kingdom.

Since the gospel is about God's rule over all of creation, all nations, and all of human life, the mission of Jesus' followers is as wide as creation itself. They have been commissioned to witness to the gospel in all of public life—business, scholarship, politics, family, criminal justice, art, media—and every other corner of human experience:

> The Spirit thrusts God's people into worldwide mission.
> He impels young and old, men and women,
>   to go next door and far away
>   into science and art, media and marketplace
>   with the good news of God's grace. . . .
>
> Following the apostles, the church is sent—
>   sent with the gospel of the kingdom. . . .
> In a world estranged from God,
>   where millions face confusing choices,
>   this mission is central to our being. . . .
>
> The rule of Jesus Christ covers the whole world.
> To follow this Lord is to serve him everywhere,
>   without fitting in,
>   as light in the darkness, as salt in a spoiling world.[9]

Living at the Crossroads of Two Stories

Jesus says, "I have sent them into the world" (John 17:18). God's people in the Old Testament were unified ethnically (as Jews) and geographically (in Palestine). The story that shaped their cultural and public lives—or should have—was the same story that shaped their religious commitment: the Old Testament. However, in the New Testament all that changes. God's people take a multiethnic and multicultural form as they are sent into all the world to incarnate God's story in the midst of all the various cultures of humankind. This multiplicity of cultures presents an enormous challenge to the church in carrying out its mission to all peoples, in all places, at all times until the Lord's return. Every cultural community shares a story that shapes and organizes its life together, and none of these stories is neutral, either philosophically or religiously. Cultural stories offer widely differing accounts of how the world came into existence, of its meaning, purpose, and destination. Each culture tells and lives out a world-story that is to some degree incompatible with the gospel. This world-story is often held below the level of the individual's conscious understanding, yet it shapes and forms the whole of a culture's communal life.

The story that has shaped Western culture for several centuries is a narrative of progress that says we are moving toward ever-greater freedom and material prosperity, and that we are doing so by human effort alone, especially through science embodied in technology, and in the application of scientific principles to our social life, in economics, in politics, and in education.

Recently there have been two significant complications to the modern story of progress. It has come under severe attack by what has often been called *postmodernity*, because of its failure to deliver that "better world" that it has long promised. At the same time, the story of progress has taken on a new and apparently powerful shape as it spreads around the world in the process called *globalization*. We will have occasion to examine all of this in detail in later chapters. At this stage it is important simply to grasp that this cultural story is a narrative with an understanding of the world and human life that lies at the foundation of Western culture. Even though the members of modern Western culture are often not conscious of this story, it nevertheless functions for them as a lens through which to see and interpret the world, a map to give direction, and a common foundation upon which to build social and cultural life.

Three more things need to be said about this modern Western world-story in order for Christians to understand the cultural context in which they must seek to live out the truth of the biblical story. First, like the biblical story itself, the Western story claims to be the true story of the world. In fact, it often simply assumes this distinction, masking its own grand claim to truth by relegating all other such stories to secondary status, as being merely "religious." Second, like the biblical story, the cultural story is all-embracing, with claims on every aspect of human life. Third, the Western story is radically, although not totally, incompatible with the biblical story.

> In our contemporary culture . . . two quite different stories are told. One is the story of evolution, of the development of the species through the survival of the strong, and the story of the rise of civilization, our type of civilization, and its success in giving humankind mastery of nature. The other story is the one embodied in the Bible, the story of creation and fall, of God's election of a people to be the bearers of his purpose for humankind, and of the coming of the one in whom that purpose is to be fulfilled. *These are two different and incompatible stories.*[10]

Thus the people of God find themselves at a crossroads, at the intersection of two stories, both of which claim to be both true and comprehensive (see figure 1).

Figure 1. Living at the Crossroads

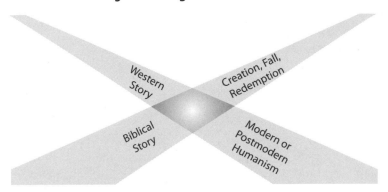

As those who have embraced the gospel, we are members of a community that believes the Bible to be the true story of the world. But as participating and living members of the cultural community, we are also part of the other story that has been shaping Western culture for a very long time. We cannot simply opt out of the surrounding culture: our lives are woven into its institutions, customs, language, relationships, and social patterns. Our embodying of the kingdom of God must take cultural shape in our own particular time and place. So we find ourselves at the crossroads, where we live as part of two communities, in two stories each largely incompatible with the other, but both of which claim to be true—and claim the whole of our lives.

Missionary Encounter or Compromise?

How can the Christian community live at this crossroads? It all depends on which of these stories is held to be basic, nonnegotiable, the true story of our world. The question is whether our faith will find its focus in Jesus and his kingdom as the clue to understanding the whole of the world and its history, or whether we will embrace the cultural story as true, and thus succumb to its pressure to limit our faith to the private realm of mere "religion."

If the church is faithful and committed to demonstrating in its whole life that the gospel is true, there will be a missionary encounter, a clash between the biblical story and the cultural story.[11] Since both stories are comprehensive, and since both claim to be true, such an encounter is inevitable. When this happens, the foundational religious beliefs shared by the surrounding cultural community will be challenged, and the gospel will be held out as a credible alternative way of life. The church, by being faithful to the biblical story, will call people to be converted, to believe the gospel, to come live in the story of the Bible—and also to live it out.

But there is another, darker possibility. If the church, consciously or unconsciously, were to accept the world-story of the surrounding culture as basic, as the true account of the world, then it will be obliged to tailor the gospel to fit somewhere within that cultural story. And if the gospel is adapted to take such a secondary place within another more comprehensive story, the inevitable result for the church is compromise and unfaithfulness, for it will not be offering the gospel to the world on the gospel's own terms, namely, that it alone is the truth about our world and about our lives in it.

Lesslie Newbigin believed that in fact this is what had already happened in the Christian church of the modern Western world. Newbigin had spent forty years as a missionary in India, and when he returned to Europe, he had the gift of "new eyes" to see the incompatibility between the gospel story and that other story that was at work shaping modern Western culture. Newbigin believed that the church had deeply compromised its living out of the gospel, allowing the biblical story to be subsumed within the modern scientific story. He spoke of the Western church as being "an advanced case of syncretism," having accepted the fusing together of two incompatible viewpoints.[12] (In such syncretism, inevitably, the truth claims of one story or both stories are compromised.) When the gospel is merely absorbed into the Western cultural story, it is reduced to the status of a private religious message about a disembodied, future, otherworldly salvation postponed to an indefinite future. Newbigin believed that the church must recover the gospel on its own terms, as the true and comprehensive story of our world and the declaration of the ultimate goal of cosmic history. Only then, he believed, would the gospel story be liberated for its missionary encounter with Western culture.

Liberating the Gospel for a Missionary Encounter: Can Worldview Contribute?

Over a century ago, two Christian thinkers, like Newbigin, came to see that the cultural story of the West was undermining the biblical story as the foundation of life in the Christian community and thus was hindering a genuine missionary encounter between the gospel and Western culture. Although they did not use the language of "missionary encounter," James Orr and Abraham

Kuyper re-called the church to Christ's claim that the gospel alone offers a true and comprehensive view of the world. Both Orr and Kuyper seized the current notion of "worldview" to demonstrate the gospel's claim to offer its own utterly comprehensive view of the world and of human life—a worldview that simply will not be fitted into any other but instead demands to stand on its own. More than a century after Orr and Kuyper, Christians are still faced with their challenge: could this concept of worldview help us to accomplish today what they called the church to do then, to release the gospel from its bondage to modern Western culture? We believe that it can, and to make that case will be our task for the remainder of this book.

2

What Is a Worldview?

Martin Luther once said that the gospel is like a caged lion that does not need to be defended—only released.[1] Indeed the gospel is the power of God for salvation (Rom. 1:16; 1 Cor. 1:18). When it is at work in the words, works, and lives of God's people, it will accomplish its purposes. But the gospel is "caged" when it is accommodated to the story of humanism. Only when the gospel is set free from its captivity to the dominant cultural story will the church be equipped for its comprehensive mission in Western culture. In this book we hope to help set the lion free. And our first question for this chapter is this: Can the concept of "worldview" aid in that task?

A Brief History of the Concept of Worldview

Since ideas and the names that we give to them derive from somewhere and someone, here we take a few moments to consider a brief history of the concept of "worldview" and how worldview came to be appropriated by the evangelical church of the nineteenth and twentieth centuries as a means of regaining the comprehensive scope of the gospel.[2]

The English word *worldview* translates the German term *Weltanschauung*, first used by the Enlightenment philosopher Emmanuel Kant in his *Critique of Judgment* (1790). Kant believed that each human being exercises reason alone in order to arrive at a *Weltanschauung*—an understanding of the meaning of the world and of our place within it. Kant used the term only once, and it did not play a central role in his thought. But Kant's insistence on the autonomy of human reason—that is, reason that is exercised apart from religion and tradition—in the formation of one's *Weltanschauung* was to have a profound and lasting influence on the development of the concept of worldview by those who followed him. As David Naugle notes, "Kant's . . . emphasis on the knowing and willing [human] self as the cognitive and moral center of the universe . . . created the conceptual space in which the notion of worldview could flourish."[3]

And flourish it did. German philosophy, particularly nineteenth-century Idealism and Romanticism, picked up the term from Kant and gave it a significant place in its philosophical system. "By the 1840s, [*Weltanschauung*] had become a standard item in the vocabulary of the educated German, denoting a global outlook on life and the world."[4] By the end of the nineteenth century, the term had achieved "academic celebrity status."[5]

For the Idealist philosopher Friedrich Schelling (1775–1854), the idea of *Weltanschauung* touched on humanity's longing to come to terms with the deepest questions of existence and of the nature of the universe. Schelling's emphasis on worldview as a comprehensive and cohesive understanding of the world was to be highly influential among the philosophers who came after him. In the years to follow, *Weltanschauung* would become "a key word in the thought-world of German Idealism and Romanticism . . . used to denote a set of beliefs that underlie and shape all of human thought and action."[6]

The Danish Christian philosopher Søren Kierkegaard (1813–1855) emphasized a fundamental distinction between the (relatively new) concept of worldview and the ancient discipline of philosophy, arguing that whereas philosophy is an objective system of thought (held, as it were, at arm's length), worldview is a set of beliefs held so closely by an individual that it is appropriate to speak of living within or owning one's worldview.[7] This was particularly important to Kierkegaard in his long effort to distinguish genuine Christian experience from mere nominal Christianity; in his view, one achieved a worldview only through a transforming, existential encounter with the living Christ.

Wilhelm Dilthey (1833–1911) also considered the relationship between worldview and philosophy. Like Schelling, Dilthey emphasized that a worldview is a vision of life that is both comprehensive and cohesive: its aim is to express the deepest meaning of the world, to answer the ultimate questions of life. Thus for Dilthey, a worldview could serve to bring unity and coherence to all the various aspects of human life.[8] H. A. Hodges summarizes Dilthey's concept of worldview thus: it is "a complex of ideas and sentiments, comprising (a) beliefs and convictions about the nature of life and the world, (b) emotional habits and tendencies based on these, and (c) a system of purposes, preferences, and principles governing action and giving life unity and meaning."[9]

For our present purposes, two more aspects of Dilthey's thinking about worldview deserve particular attention. First, for Dilthey, worldview is an underlying set of beliefs about the world that serves to shape all of our subsequent thinking. Thus worldview cannot simply derive from the exercise of reason: "World-views are not products of thought. They do not originate from the mere will to know. The comprehension of reality is an important factor in their formation, but only one. They emerge from our attitude to, and knowledge of, life and from our whole mental structure."[10] A worldview, then, is deeper than either philosophy or science; indeed, philosophy and science stand upon the foundation of one's worldview. As Sander Griffioen puts it, "A worldview's claim to truth can neither be proved nor disproved by philosophy or science. Instead, philosophy itself is dependent on worldview. Dilthey attributed the metaphysical search for ultimate unity to worldviews, which in turn underlie philosophies."[11] Dilthey expressed that understanding of worldview which had by his day become dominant in German philosophy, and it was this same understanding of the concept that Christian thinkers following Dilthey (such as James Orr and Abraham Kuyper) would appropriate: *worldview expresses a set of beliefs that are foundational and formative for human thinking and life.*

Dilthey also emphasized the plurality and relativity of worldviews. Whereas Kant had believed that one worldview could be shared by all people (since all share in the human faculty of reason), Dilthey argued that (since, in his view, human understanding is profoundly conditioned by the individual's particular place and time in history) different worldviews are bound to arise from differing historical circumstances. He believed that all worldviews are but partial expressions of the universe and thus inevitably will clash with each other. Dilthey did not think that the diversity of worldviews would ever be resolved, that any one worldview could emerge as the "winner," because of his conviction that, at the most basic level, worldviews are rooted in faith and are thus both "unprovable and indestructible."[12]

This thumbnail sketch of the concept's history shows that, for Christian thinkers, "worldview" carries with it some associations to be affirmed and others to be wary of. Thus we would agree with Schelling that worldview is a comprehensive and cohesive understanding of the world and of one's place in it. We can also affirm Dilthey's insight that it is one's fundamental beliefs about the world that give shape to thoughts and actions and thus a sense of life's unity and meaning. And surely Kierkegaard was right to insist that a worldview should be held intimately and experientially, and that it should transform one's life.

However, in our search for a genuinely biblical, Christian understanding of worldview, we must not accept Kant's rationalist notion that worldview has its foundation in autonomous human reason. And we should be very wary of Dilthey's relativism and historicism, which imply that worldviews will simply arise from time to time and place to place as a product of historical factors. Although historical circumstances undoubtedly do exert a shaping influence on worldview, we live under the radical claim of the gospel that it is true for all times and all peoples as the testament of the one who is the same "yesterday, today, and forever" (Heb. 13:8).

The Appropriation of Worldview in Christian Thinking

By the start of the twentieth century, worldview as a concept had spread through most academic disciplines. It was chiefly James Orr (1844–1913) and Abraham Kuyper (1837–1920) who appropriated the concept of worldview for Christian thought. Both Orr and Kuyper reached for the concept of worldview in response to the post-Enlightenment culture that was coming to dominate the West. Orr, a theologian, felt strongly that to respond piecemeal to a worldview inimical to Christianity was not good enough. What the time required, he believed, was a demonstration that Christianity was itself a comprehensive and ordered vision of the whole of life:

> The opposition which Christianity has to encounter . . . extends to the whole manner of conceiving the world, and of man's place in it, the manner of conceiving the entire system of things, natural and moral, of which we form a part. . . . It is the Christian view of things in general which is attacked, and it is by an exposition and vindication of the Christian view of things as a whole that the attack can most successfully be met.[13]

According to Orr, a Christian worldview is Christocentric,[14] focused on Christ as the fulfillment of salvation history and embracing (as Christ himself did) the Old Testament view of creation:

> He who with his whole heart believes in Jesus as the Son of God is thereby committed to much else besides. He is committed to a view of God, to a view of man, to a view of sin, to a view of Redemption, to a view of the purpose of God in creation and history, to a view of human destiny found only in Christianity. This forms a "Weltanschauung," or a "Christian view of the world." . . .

> The Christian view of things forms a logical whole which cannot be infringed
> on, or accepted or rejected piecemeal, but stands or falls in its integrity, and can
> only suffer from attempts at amalgamation or compromise with theories which
> rest on totally distinct bases.[15]

Orr was convinced that Christians needed to articulate the whole Christ-centered
worldview implicit in the biblical story, so as to recognize clearly the anti-
supernatural (or anti-Christian) bases of opposing modernist worldviews.

Abraham Kuyper did more than merely put the comprehensive vision of
the Christian worldview into words; he expressed it in his multifaceted life
as journalist, theologian, politician, prime minister of the Netherlands, and
founder of the Free University of Amsterdam. He believed passionately that
Calvinism (the tradition of Protestant thought originating from the sixteenth-
century reformer John Calvin) related to the whole of life. Kuyper used his
Stone Lectures at Princeton University in 1898 to give expression to this as a
worldview.[16] Like Orr, Kuyper saw that modernity had given birth to a worldview deeply antithetical to the Christian tradition: "Two life systems [modern-
ism and Christianity] are wrestling with one another, in mortal combat. . . .
This is the struggle in Europe, this is the struggle in America."[17] In this titanic
struggle, Kuyper believed, only a comprehensive biblical worldview had a
chance of standing up against its opponent: "In Modernism the vast energy
of an all-embracing life system assails us, [thus] we have to take our stand in
a life system of equally comprehensive and far-reaching power."[18]

For Kuyper, the only adequate Christian approach to the challenge of modernism was to be found in Calvinism, and thus his own project was to articulate
the implications of a Calvinistic worldview for religion, politics, science, and
art. For Kuyper, the conflict or antithesis between modernism and Christianity
manifests itself in every element of culture and society but is especially intense
within what the Germans called *Wissenschaft* (often translated as "science,"
but with a broader reference to academic thinking and theorizing in general).
Kuyper argues that there are two distinct types of "science," the one arising
out of those who theorize on the basis of conversion to Christ, and the other
from those who do not: "We speak of two kinds of people. Both are human,
but one is inwardly different from the other, and consequently feels a different
content rising from his consciousness; thus they face the cosmos from different
points of view, and are impelled by different impulses. And the fact that there
are two kinds of people occasions of necessity the fact of two kinds of human
life and consciousness of life, and of two kinds of science."[19]

Perhaps Kuyper oversimplifies this in his stark contrast, but he does make a
crucial contribution to our thinking about worldview in his clear rejection of

the autonomy of human reason. Here he differs from Orr and from other key twentieth-century proponents of a Christian worldview such as Carl Henry[20] and Francis Schaeffer.[21] Although both Henry and Schaeffer did much to promote a thoroughly Christian worldview, both held the view that neutral human reason operating properly will support a Christian perspective of the world. In other words, they concede common epistemological ground with non-Christians. Kuyper's own approach was fundamentally different, since he believed firmly that one's epistemology is itself a development of one's worldview.

Kuyper's type of approach has been taken up by the contemporary Catholic philosopher Alasdair MacIntyre, who argues that rationality is inevitably traditioned; that is, it always functions in the context of a particular tradition or story, or what we call worldview.[22] More recently still, Alvin Plantinga and Nicholas Wolterstorff have developed this element of the Kuyperian tradition by arguing for the legitimacy of a Christian starting point in theorizing.[23]

The tradition that emerged from Kuyper's thought (and that includes other significant thinkers, such as his contemporary, theologian Herman Bavinck) is known as "neo-Calvinism," and its major themes are as follows:

- In and through God's redemption in Christ, grace restores nature. Grace is like medicine that restores health to a sick body. Christ's work of salvation is aimed at the creation as a whole in order to renew it to the goal that God always had in mind for it.
- God is sovereign and orders all of reality by his law and word.
- The cultural mandate given in Genesis 1:26–28 (to exercise royal stewardship over the creation) has ongoing relevance: God calls humankind to develop his creation through history, to his glory.

In recent decades worldview has become widely popular in evangelical circles. Francis Schaeffer played a major role in introducing generations of students to such an approach,[24] and more recently Al Wolters,[25] John Stott, Brian Walsh and Richard Middleton,[26] James Sire,[27] Arthur Holmes,[28] Tom Wright,[29] Charles Colson[30] and Nancy Pearcey[31] (among many others) have contributed to the spread of Christian thinking about worldview. The Lausanne Congress on World Evangelization in 1974 was of particular importance in this respect.

The Lausanne Covenant (which emerged from the Congress) does not use the language of worldview, but it does tackle the same issues, using the language of the relationship between evangelism and sociopolitical activity.[32] The Lausanne Congress marked the significant recovery of a vision for all of life within the evangelical tradition, a vision exemplified in John Stott's books *Christian Mission in the Modern World*[33] and *New Issues Facing Christians Today*,[34] and also in Stott's founding of the London Institute for Contemporary Christianity.[35]

James Sire has been a tireless proponent of a Christian worldview over many years. In his delightful *How to Read Slowly: Reading for Comprehension*[36] he explores how to read fiction, nonfiction, and poetry in part to understand the worldview embodied in them. Sire's best-known book on worldview is *The Universe Next Door.* The title evokes the diversity of worldviews that surround us in a pluralistic culture: our neighbor may see the world in a very different way and thus may live in a "different universe" from ours! For Sire, a worldview is "a set of presuppositions which we hold—consciously or unconsciously—about the world in which we live."[37] Note his important point that one may not be conscious of one's own worldview: it may function like a pair of glasses through which we see our world; only rarely do we look at the glasses themselves. Thus it can be easy for any of us to assume that we are seeing our world in an unmediated, objective, neutral fashion unless we pay deliberate attention to the fact that all experience of the world is mediated through a worldview.

Sire identifies the following worldviews competing for preeminence:

- Christian theism
- Deism (which is what remains of theism when the concept of a personal God is abandoned)
- Naturalism (which abandons God completely but retains its trust in human autonomy)
- Nihilism (which is what results from naturalism once the trust in human reason is eroded)
- Existentialism (which tries to move beyond nihilism by affirming its trust in the power of the individual to will into existence its own conception of the good, the true, and the beautiful)
- Eastern pantheistic monism (in which New Age thought is combined with the existentialists' sense of the self)
- Postmodernism (which denies that we can know reality as it is but asserts that we can get along especially through our use of language; for the postmodernist, "pragmatic knowledge is all one can have and all one needs")[38]

Sire rightly argues that a service Christians can render is to help people become conscious of their worldviews. Sire has developed a series of diagnostic questions that can help discern the contours of a worldview:

- What is prime reality?
- What is the nature of the world around us?
- What does it mean to be human?
- What happens at death?
- Why is it possible to know anything at all?
- How do we tell what is right and wrong?
- What is history about?[39]

Recently Sire has published a small book called *Naming the Elephant*, in which he helpfully reviews current thinking among Christians on worldview and refines his own earlier definition: "A worldview is a commitment, a fundamental orientation of the heart, that can be expressed as a story or in a set of presuppositions (assumptions which may be true, partially true or entirely false) which we hold (consciously or subconsciously, consistently or inconsistently) about the basic constitution of reality, and that provides the foundation on which we live and move and have our being."[40]

There are several significant developments in Sire's revised definition, emphases with which we find ourselves in wholehearted agreement. First, his emphasis on commitment, which need not be conscious, and on the heart relates to his realization that a worldview is not first of all intellectual and propositional but rather a matter of the heart, of spiritual orientation, of religion. Like Herman Dooyeweerd and David Naugle, Sire embraces the view that at the core of our being every one of us is oriented religiously either toward the true God or toward an idol or idols: "Simply by being alive in the world, everyone makes and lives out of a religious commitment."[41] Second, Sire recognizes that a worldview is often expressed as a grand story or master narrative.[42] Worldview is not first of all a rational system of beliefs but rather a story about the world. Third, Sire has introduced an emphasis on the "lived-out" nature of a worldview: it is expressed not merely in words and thoughts but also in the way we live our lives. There is a vital distinction between having and articulating a worldview. Everyone has a worldview, and this is given expression in their lives, but not everyone is able to articulate what that worldview is.

Although Reformed Protestant and evangelical scholars have taken the lead in appropriating the concept of worldview to express the comprehensive vision of the gospel, scholars from other Christian traditions also have made significant contributions, such as the Roman Catholic Romano Guardini[43] and the Eastern Orthodox Alexander Schmemann.[44] In Schmemann's view, humans should relate to the world as priests who bless God in thanksgiving and worship and, by filling the world with this Eucharist, transform life into communion with God. The fall of humankind involved the loss of this sacramental, priestly perspective on life; redemption involves its recovery. In Christ, "the true life that was lost by man was restored, for redemption as new creation means 'that in Christ, life—life in all its totality—was returned to man, given again as sacrament and communion, made Eucharist.' . . . In redemption, the world is restored as God's creation and human beings resume their priestly vocation."[45] Thus Schmemann exhorts Christians to witness to the reality of the world as God's good creation and to be busy with transforming every aspect of life.

Criticisms of a Christian Appropriation of "Worldview"

Despite the widespread acceptance of the concept of worldview to give contemporary expression to the gospel in all areas of life, the worldview approach has not been without its critics. Here we explore some of the major cautions against appropriating worldview in this way.

Objection #1: The worldview approach intellectualizes the gospel.

The tradition labeled "modernity" has overprivileged, even idolized, human intellect and reason. Within modernity, rationality was believed to be the one reliable route to truth about our world. Tradition and story were regarded with suspicion and could be accepted as true only if verified by rational analysis. In order to confront the challenge of modernity, it was essential for Christians to give an adequate (i.e., rational) account of the reason for their hope in Christ. Thus, writing in 1963, in the postscript to his well-known book *The Christian Mind*, Harry Blamires posed this important question:

> Will the Christians of the next fifty years, over against a strengthened secularism, deepen and clarify their Christian commitment in a withdrawn cultivation of personal morality and spirituality . . . [or will they] deepen and clarify their Christian commitment at the intellectual and social levels too, meeting and challenging not only secularism's assault upon personal morality and the life of the soul, but also secularism's truncated and perverted view of the meaning of life and the purpose of the social order?[46]

As Blamires prophetically saw (in line with Orr, Kuyper, Henry, and Schaeffer), Christians were in desperate need of a Christian mind. Demonstrating that the gospel was intellectually credible was the vital task; developing a Christian worldview was an important element of that task. But the danger of opposing modernism on its own terms, in which rationality was all that mattered, was that the gospel or Christian worldview itself might be reduced to a merely intellectual framework. Overemphasis on reason may lead to an inadequate understanding. Worldview is trying to express something much deeper. Worldview is concerned to express our deepest religious beliefs about the world arising from the gospel and the biblical drama. We express our foundational assumptions about the world that flow from a living relationship with Christ. No one warns more clearly of this danger of intellectualism than does the twentieth-century Catholic monk Thomas Merton. In *Contemplative Prayer* he argues,

> It is not enough for meditation to investigate the cosmic order and situate me in this order. Meditation is something more than gaining command of a Weltanschauung (a philosophical view of the cosmos and of life) . . . [for] such a meditation may be out of contact with the deepest truths of Christianity. . . . We should let ourselves be brought naked and defenceless into the center of that dread where we stand alone before God in our nothingness, without explanation, without theories, completely dependent upon his providential care, in dire need of the gift of his grace, his mercy and the light of faith.[47]

"Thinking Christianly" is a vital part of expressing a Christian worldview, but thinking will arise from a worldview. And our worldview is deeply connected to our life in Christ. If thinking Christianly becomes disconnected from the whole experience of life in Christ Jesus, it leads to a distorted, intellectualized Christianity lacking grace and humility. A truly biblical worldview is centered in an existential relationship with Christ; it will be as much about nurturing this relationship as it is about rigorous critical thinking that arises from this relationship.

As part of the present discussion of the danger of intellectualizing the gospel, we must acknowledge Karl Barth's hostility toward appropriating the concept of worldview to articulate the range of the gospel. In his discussion of the doctrine of creation, Barth argues that the Christian theology of creation can never become a worldview. But Barth's opposition rests on his own distinctive definition of the term *worldview* itself. He rightly notes that the Christian doctrine of creation is based on divine revelation, but then he goes on to assert that whereas theology is "concerned only with divine revelation

. . . [worldview], as non-theological thinking, reckons only with such apprehension of the cosmos as is possible to unaided reason. . . . Theology has to recognize and confess creation as benefit because it is the work of God in Jesus Christ, whereas philosophy is intrinsically incapable of doing this."[48] If we grant Barth's assumption that a worldview can apprehend reality only by reason, no doubt he is right that the gospel and a worldview are irreconcilable. But we cannot grant this assumption; indeed, the whole point of a Christian worldview (in the sense in which we have been developing the term) is precisely that it does not rely on reason alone but rather takes as its very starting point God's revelation of himself to us in Christ. Once a Christian worldview is understood to be truly Christian—taking the gospel as its starting point and taking seriously the biblical teaching on creation, which also finds its center in Christ—the sting of Barth's critique is drawn.

Objection #2: The worldview approach relativizes the gospel.

Dilthey's understanding of worldview already put this problem in the foreground. The historicism and relativism of the nineteenth century have only deepened in the late twentieth and early twenty-first centuries in postmodernism. Many postmodern thinkers have abandoned the modern quest for what Schaeffer calls "true truth" about the world, since they have come to believe that such a thing does not exist.[49] Yet rather than despairing over the absence of truth, these postmoderns often seem to celebrate our limitations in a kind of cheerful nihilism. This approach does offer some insight: it recognizes that we are all situated historically, that we all view the world through particular lenses that influence the way we view and interpret the world, and thus, our interpretations of that world will inevitably differ from one another. This plurality of alternative perspectives therefore offers room for a Christian worldview alongside the others, which seems to be a positive thing but comes at the perilous price of reducing the Christian worldview to the status of one among many, legitimate only insofar as it works for you. And here we are in danger of sinking into the swamp of relativism.

In a pluralistic context such as we find in the early twenty-first century in the West, relativism is a real temptation, one that Christians must resist. The New Testament itself was written in a pluralistic context, yet in that context it asserted boldly that Christ is the fullest and final revelation of God and (as Newbigin puts it) is the clue to the whole creation. We must assert the same truth, and it will not often be received kindly. This is not for a moment to deny that other worldviews may offer genuine and profound insights. However, it is our calling to assert unequivocally that Christ is the true light of the world.

At the same time, we must not equate our articulation of worldview with the gospel itself. Indeed, our expression of a Christian worldview must always stand under the critique of the gospel. Nevertheless, we must insist that the biblical story is not just one more story alongside others, but rather that it is the true story of the world. The Bible is normative and comprehensive; it tells the true story of the world, and as such it sets itself up in opposition to alternative stories that try to do the same thing. As Tom Wright asserts, "The whole point of Christianity is that it offers a story which is the story of the whole world. It is public truth."[50]

Objection #3: The worldview approach may become disconnected from Scripture and thus vulnerable to the spirits of the age.

The kind of framework that a worldview yields can be a tool of thought, but any powerful tool used without due care (think of a chainsaw!) can become dangerous to the person who wields it. If our worldview should, by our neglect, lose its roots in Scripture, it becomes vulnerable to being taken over by some story other than that of the biblical drama. It is possible that in the process of developing a conceptual framework from the Bible, the roots in Scripture are loosened, and that framework becomes vulnerable to the various idols of our day. A worldview emerging from the biblical drama must lead us back again and again, and ever more deeply, into that story rather than away from it.

Objection #4: A worldview approach may lead to unhealthy messianic activism.

We have referred already to the danger of a worldview coming to simply mirror that of our culture rather than engaging in dynamic encounter with the culture. The biblical story opens us up to the comprehensive nature of redemption: through Jesus Christ, God is recovering his reign over the whole of creation; when we pray, "Your will be done on earth as it is in heaven," we commit ourselves to participating in the Spirit's redemptive work in the world, in all areas of life. Such a vision is energizing and gets Christians rightly excited about making a difference in the world. But a real danger is that we may start to think that it is we ourselves who will usher in the kingdom. We may become hectically busy trying to transform the world by our own strength. We have quite often mistakenly imbibed the vision of progress (a central tenet of modernity), tending to think that if we just work hard enough, we will usher in the kingdom in our generation. Thus a pernicious workaholism can develop among committed Christians, which mirrors the idolatrous strivings within the surrounding humanistic culture.

Objection #5: A worldview approach may entrench a compromised middle-class Christianity and even neglect the poor and marginalized in the world.

Often an activism that is motivated by reflection on worldview arises from within the mainstream, middle-class dimension of our culture. It is the strength of many Christians who take worldview seriously that they are committed not to escaping from culture but rather to working within culture to transform it. Worldview-conscious Christians insist on working from within to transform the structures and institutions of our cultures, but the danger is always there that we may be contaminated by and accommodated to that culture rather than being agents of its transformation; we may become as useless as salt that has lost its saltiness. The Christian who sets out to transform the unjust structures of business, for example, may eventually be reshaped by the powerful spirits at work in the business world today.

Another danger in attempting to transform cultural and societal structures is that one may neglect those who have been marginalized by those structures. There are many examples in which development of a Christian worldview has led to wonderfully redemptive initiatives. However, it remains true that when we think of truly redemptive initiatives for the poor, what comes to mind are practical movements like L'Arche, initiated by Jean Vanier, in which Christians live in community with mentally and physically handicapped people, and the work of Mother Teresa's sisters and brothers. Worldview-motivated activism among Christians has not often led them quickly to champion the poor and those most in need.

While all these objections must be taken seriously, we do not think that any of them are fatal to the Christian appropriation of "worldview." Indeed, in our opinion the benefits, as will become apparent, far outweigh the dangers.

Our Working Definition of a Worldview

In the literature on Christian worldview, definitions abound. We offer this one:

> Worldview is an articulation of the basic beliefs embedded in a shared grand story that are rooted in a faith commitment and that give shape and direction to the whole of our individual and corporate lives.

Of course, this needs further explanation.

In our opinion, all worldviews originate in a grand story of one sort or another. Thus, much of modern science implicitly frames itself within a

grand story that begins with the "big bang" and proceeds to the evolution
of the cosmos and the appearance of human beings, who seek to master nature and human life, all ultimately on its inexorable way toward the
gradual winding-down of the universe; and all of this transpires without
any reference to the living God. Clearly, this differs fundamentally from the
biblical story, whose basic plot is creation, fall, redemption. As Ecclesiastes
3:11 says, God has put eternity—a sense of beginning and end, a sense of
being part of a larger story—in our hearts, in the very core of our being,
so that we require some larger story within which to situate, to make sense
of, the smaller stories of our lives and cultures.[51] God intended us to find
meaning in our lives through being part of a larger story that gives purpose
and direction to our lives and explains our world. It is important to note,
therefore, that one who rejects the Christian story will not simply live without
a grand story but rather will find an alternative grand story and live by it.
Even the postmodern view, which says that there is no grand story, is itself
a whopper of a grand story!

Because we are communal creatures, these grand stories inevitably are
shared among us. Each of us has been raised in the context of some grand
story that has shaped our culture, even if we are unconscious of this shaping. As Christians, we are aware that we are part of "one holy, catholic, and
apostolic church," part of the people of God down through the ages and on
into the future. With all Christians, we share the basic story of the Bible. We
live as part of a community committed to the truth of that story. Even Western
individualism, with its stress on the freedom of the individual, is an approach
to life that is, ironically, shared by millions in the West today and thus has
become a communal vision that gives expression to much of the public life
of Western nations.

As Ecclesiastes 3:11 signifies, all humans appropriate a grand story of one
form or another because we are creatures and not the Creator. Our heart,
the religious core of our being, is directed either toward the living God or
toward an idol, and the grand story that we indwell is an expression of this
direction of our heart. Grand stories and worldviews are, as a result, always
rooted at their deepest level in religious faith, whether that is in the living God,
in human ability, in some other aspect of God's creation, in an impersonal
spirit pervading the universe, or in any of the multitude of other idols that
humans manufacture.

Embedded in all grand stories are fundamental beliefs about the world,
answers to questions of ultimate significance: What is life all about? Who are
we? What kind of world do we live in? What's wrong with the world? How
can it be fixed?[52] The answers to these great questions are not philosophical

concepts; rather, they are beliefs, often not even articulated, embedded firmly in the particular grand story that we share, and they achieve coherence precisely because they are merely elements of a single, unified vision of the world that arises from that story.

These beliefs give shape and direction to the whole of our lives, both individual and corporate. A worldview not only describes the world for us, but also directs our life in the world. It not only gives us a perspective on how the world is (its descriptive function), but also acts as a guide for how the world ought to be and how we ought to live in the world (its normative function).[53]

In the Christian story, the belief in creation is of foundational importance. Such a belief means that Christians view the world in a way wholly different from the sort of scientific worldview described earlier in this chapter. Within that scientific worldview, the cosmos is a random product of time and chance, whereas from the Christian's point of view, the world is God the Father's good creation, ordered by him and bearing the marks of his workmanship all over it. So too when it comes to working out what is wrong with the world: the Christian story, with its belief in the fall, provides an answer to the problem of evil totally different from any answer that could be derived from the evolutionary perspective. If we believe that God has created us male and female, and that marriage is his provision for companionship, then we will regard marriage as a great gift and as the proper context for sexual expression and the nurturing of children. Apart from such a belief, we might approach sex as simply a means for pleasure to be enjoyed as we do, say, a good meal, whenever and however we like. Not only our ideas, but also our actions, will flow from the worldview that we adopt.

Grand stories, worldviews, shape not only our individual lives but also the lives of nations and all the public dimensions of human life. In South Africa, apartheid—a racist worldview according to which whites are superior to blacks—took root and was deliberately worked out in every area of life. Whites went to different (and much better) schools than did blacks; it was forbidden by law for a white to marry a black; by law, whites and blacks lived in separate areas; the best jobs were reserved for whites; and so on. In retrospect, it is hard to believe that such a worldview could be held by so many for so long, but the example of apartheid illustrates clearly the way in which a worldview is comprehensive and will shape not only our individual lives but also those of our communities and nations.

Our fundamental beliefs about the world and human life that underlie and shape all of our lives often remain below the level of consciousness, unarticulated and assumed. They function like tectonic plates that lie beneath the surface, unseen and yet powerful in their effect. As Roy Clouser puts it,

The enormous influence of religious beliefs remains, however, largely hidden from casual view; its relation to the rest of life is like that of the great geological plates of earth's surface to the continents and oceans. The movement of these plates is not apparent to a casual inspection of any particular landscape and can only be detected with great difficulty. Nevertheless, so vast are these plates, so stupendous their power, that their visible effects—mountain ranges, earthquakes, and volcanic eruptions—are but tiny surface blemishes compared with the force of the mighty plates themselves.[54]

These beliefs powerfully shape our lives, as they are embedded in the story of the world that we have adopted. Yet we can become increasingly conscious of those foundational beliefs and their impact by doing three things: (1) giving summary expression to the grand story; (2) lifting out the fundamental beliefs of that story; (3) articulating and explicating those beliefs. This is what worldview reflection is concerned to do.

This task assumes that it is important to make a clear distinction between having a worldview and articulating a worldview. We all have a worldview in the sense that we all hold fundamental beliefs about the world as part of a bigger story that gives shape to our whole lives. However, it is another thing to be able to articulate that story and those beliefs. We are highlighting the importance of becoming conscious of those beliefs by identifying and formulating them.

So worldview reflects on the story and the foundational beliefs that are central to our grand stories. This enables us to see more clearly their fundamental coherence and to understand their implications more fully. Thus, a Christian worldview is about abstracting and expressing the most comprehensive beliefs embedded in the biblical drama, through which we understand God, humanity, and the world. Yet Christian worldview must also deepen our consciousness of the story and fundamental beliefs that shape our culture. So it is essential to articulate the Western story and formulate its fundamental beliefs.

The Relationship between Scripture and Worldview

Down through the centuries, Christians have found it necessary, in their engagement with their own cultures, to find ways to express the unity of Scripture. One such way is biblical theology, which seeks to articulate the unity of Scripture according to Scripture's own categories, such as covenant and kingdom. The aim of biblical theology is not to impose systematic categories from without but rather to excavate the underlying categories that are found within the Bible itself. In this sense, our book *The Drama of Scripture* is an exercise in biblical theology. Scripture itself has a narrative shape, and we sought to follow this in our retelling of the story of the Bible. Another way to articulate the unity of Scripture is to analyze the framework of the Bible's most fundamental and comprehensive beliefs, those that are embedded or embodied in the biblical drama. Thus, a Christian worldview sets out the main elements or beliefs that constitute the biblical story and shows how they fit together in a coherent framework. These beliefs can, of course, be analyzed further according to theological and philosophical categories. The point of a Christian worldview, however, is that the biblical story embodies and implies a framework of basic beliefs that can be set out to equip Christians in their lives. The framework of basic beliefs inherent to the biblical story is not for scholars alone but rather is for all the people of God. The different levels can be set out as follows:

- Scripture
- Biblical theology (our narrative telling of the biblical story)
- Christian worldview (setting out of the comprehensive framework of a Christian's basic beliefs about things as embedded in the drama of Scripture in interaction with our culture's basic beliefs)
- Systematic theology and Christian philosophy (which reflect on Christian beliefs at a more theoretical level)

Of course, these categories are not watertight. It would be foolish, for example, to imagine or pretend that one's worldview was informed only by Scripture and biblical theology. As Dilthey rightly notes, worldviews emerge out of life and experience. All of us work out of worldviews, and these have been formed in part by our reading of Scripture and biblical theology, as well as by Christian tradition. But our worldviews have also been formed in part by those ideas that we have absorbed, often unconsciously, from the surrounding culture. Acknowledging this, we nevertheless strongly assert that the primary sources of a Christian worldview should be Scripture and biblical theology. This is why *Living at the Crossroads* follows *The Drama of Scripture*, in order to abstract a framework from Scripture one needs a strong sense of the geography of Scripture and of its narrative unity. We need to be as conscious as possible of the ecology in which we work, including the dimensions of the cultures in which we live. But we must make Scripture and the biblical drama our constant and normative reference points as we map out the contours of a Christian worldview. As we do so, it is important to remember that even at this level a worldview is an abstraction from Scripture and can never replace Scripture.

It will be truly Christian insofar as it emerges clearly from the biblical drama, and as it leads us back deeply into Scripture again and again.[55]

Why and How Should We Move "beyond" Scripture? A Missional Imperative

Of course, there is a fundamental sense in which we never can and never should move "beyond" Scripture. We use the term *beyond* merely to refer to the task of abstracting from Scripture and articulating the comprehensive framework of basic beliefs embodied in the Christian story. Why is it important to abstract and articulate these basic beliefs?

We have seen already how Orr and Kuyper were driven to articulate the gospel as a worldview in response to the powerful challenges of opposing world-views in their cultural contexts. In other words, their impulse was missional: in order to engage their culture with the gospel and to bear a credible witness to Christ, they needed to demonstrate that the gospel embodied a worldview that provided a real and vital alternative to the powerful worldviews of their day. And it has always been so throughout the history of the church. Not that the early church fathers made use of the concept of "worldview" explicitly, but it soon became apparent to them that if they were to witness to Christ in their Greco-Roman context, they would need to articulate the basic Christian beliefs and show how they cohere as a credible system. As S. MacDonald notes of Augustine of Hippo, "He was not the first to defend Christianity as the true wisdom sought by philosophy. But he was the thinker who, above all, and at a critical historical moment, demonstrated that Christianity could be mined for philosophical insight, made to answer philosophical questions in philo-sophically sophisticated ways, and presented as a philosophically satisfying worldview rivalling pagan philosophical systems."[56] And, following Augustine, Thomas Aquinas would make use of Aristotle's philosophy to expound the gospel in ways credible to his contemporaries.

The point is that Christians have always found it to be a missional imperative to explain the coherence of the biblical message and to relate it in a rational and coherent way to the cultures of their day. Proof-texting is simply woefully inadequate in this regard; what is needed is a sense of how the major beliefs of the drama of Scripture hold together and how one can build on them to develop a Christian understanding and critique of the culture of the day. This is not to say that Christians have always done this well. As we have seen with the concept of worldview itself, ideas, concepts, and languages them-selves carry philosophical baggage, and if one is not careful, one can end up importing alien philosophies into Christianity rather than allowing the gospel to transform the culture.

Apologetics—the business of engaging the worldviews of the day intelligently and thus bearing witness to Christ with credibility—and cultural engagement in general require an explanation of the logic of the gospel that moves beyond the drama of Scripture. If, for example, one wanted to develop a business along Christian lines, one would need more than a list of biblical texts relating to work. One would want a sense at least of how work fits in the plan of God for humankind: what it was intended to be when God designed it, how it has been twisted by sin, and how Christ's work in us might redeem our experience of work and direct us in the work that we choose to do. We will explore this type of engagement in more detail in the final chapter of this book. But for now, we simply observe that a starting point for such reflection is to achieve a good understanding of the comprehensive framework of basic beliefs embedded in the drama of Scripture. Such a framework provides the conceptual scaffolding upon which to build a Christian perspective on the subject of business and work today.

A good example of the application of a Christian perspective to an academic discipline is Oliver O'Donovan's sterling work on political theory and politics today.[57] As O'Donovan rightly insists, we need to take seriously the authority of Scripture because it is God's Word for the whole of life. However, to do political reflection in the light of Scripture, the drama of Scripture by itself is not enough. Political theory requires concepts, and O'Donovan insists that these concepts need to be developed from Scripture; indeed, in *The Desire of the Nations*, O'Donovan's development of concepts for political theory leads him back to Scripture again and again.[58] Thus at both the academic and practical levels, serious Christian engagement with life and culture—that is, Christian mission—requires the development of a Christian worldview. Since we live and think out of our worldviews, it is not a question of whether we have one worldview or not. The question, instead, is this: Out of which worldview will we think, live, and work? If we refuse to develop and indwell a Christian worldview, we will merely leave ourselves vulnerable to the influence of the worldviews present in the culture that surrounds us. But if we are serious about bearing witness to the Lord Christ with the integrity and depth that such witness requires in our modern day, the development and appropriation of a Christian worldview rooted in the drama of Scripture will become a priority. Our mission demands it.

Practical and theoretical engagement with our culture requires the development of a worldview. But how, exactly, should we make this move beyond Scripture? In our opinion, the way forward is to lift out from the drama of

Scripture its central beliefs—in particular, the pattern of creation, fall, and redemption—and to explore how these beliefs hold together, so as to ensure that at this pretheoretical level we stay as close to Scripture as possible. A Christian worldview articulates and develops the most basic, the most fundamental, the most comprehensive beliefs of the biblical story in a way that enables those beliefs to become both a lens through which we may see the world and a map that will give us direction in the world; it is the grid into which we place all else. The development of a Christian worldview is one way we can mediate the most basic categories of the gospel to all of life, thereby equipping the church for its missional task. A Christian worldview can establish a solid foundation for vigorous cultural engagement by providing specific insight and conceptual tools to carry out our tasks in the world—in the home and the church and the public square. The following exposition of a biblical worldview will make each of these benefits concrete.

3

A Biblical Worldview

Creation and Sin

If we truly believe that the Bible is God's Word to us, the true story of the world, it seems clear that our worldview must be rooted and grounded there. In the next two chapters we will articulate a biblical worldview.

Jesus Christ, the Biblical Story, and Worldview

We begin with the person of Jesus Christ and with the simple yet profound biblical confession of the early church, "Jesus is Lord" (Rom. 10:9; 1 Cor. 12:3). This confession was made in defiance of the public confession that bound the Roman Empire together: "Caesar is Lord." In the Roman Empire "lord" was the title of one with absolute authority. When the early church said, "Jesus is Lord," what they had in mind was more than mere political authority. The Greek word *kyrios* ("lord") was used to translate the Hebrew "Yahweh" in the Greek translation of the Old Testament. "Yahweh" was the primary name for God throughout the Old Testament. Thus, to confess "Jesus is Lord" is to identify Jesus with the God of the Old Testament story: Jesus is Creator and Sustainer of the world, Ruler of history, and Redeemer and Judge of all things.[1]

This confession opens up into a trinitarian understanding of God. Jesus says that he has been sent by God the Father to make him known and to complete the redemptive work that he has been doing throughout the Old Testament story. In his person and work, Jesus is the full presence of the living God in human flesh: "Anyone who has seen me has seen the Father. . . . It is the Father, living in me, who is doing his work. Believe me when I say that I am in the Father and the Father is in me" (John 14:9–11). When Jesus returns to the Father, he promises not to leave his followers as orphans but rather to come and live again among them with the fullness of his presence in the Holy Spirit (John 14:16–18). A faithful biblical worldview begins with this trinitarian confession—there is one God in three persons—centered in Jesus Christ.

To confess that Jesus is Lord is to say that Jesus, together with the Father and Spirit, has created all things; he sustains and upholds all things, he rules history and guides it to its goal, he restores and renews all things, and at the end he will judge all things. If we confess only "Jesus is my personal Savior" and neglect "Jesus is Creator, Ruler, Redeemer, and Judge," then we have an emaciated worldview. A biblical worldview is about getting right who Jesus is.

But a biblical worldview is also about getting the gospel right. Jesus announced the good news that the kingdom of God had arrived, and this announcement stands at the climactic moment of a long story. God is acting in love and power to restore a fallen (but essentially good) creation, to live again under his good and gracious rule. God is becoming king again. In the announcement of the arrival of the kingdom we have the great plot of the drama of Scripture: (1) God (in Christ and by the Spirit) creates the world; (2) sin cripples, twists, and thwarts that creation; (3) God acts to heal, straighten, and restore; (4) God finally reconciles the entire cosmos to himself. While the major focus of the biblical story is about God's saving work, which includes both the whole of the Old Testament after the fall in Genesis 3 and the whole of the New Testament, that story of rescue and salvation assumes and is set against the backdrop of the first two acts of the drama: the creation of the world and its fall into sin. Salvation has meaning only when we point to what is being saved and why it needs to be saved. The Bible's main plot is the story of how God restores a creation that had been disfigured by sin: first comes the creation followed by the fall, and then comes the restoration.

In this chapter we deal with the backdrop of the biblical story of God's saving work: creation (what is being saved) and sin (why it needs to be saved).

Creation: The World as God Meant It to Be

Often we use the word *creation* simply to refer to God's act of making the world in the beginning—"When it comes to origins, I believe in creation, not evolution." Or we may use the word to refer to the nonhuman parts of our material world—"We went for a walk today in the woods and enjoyed God's creation." These are not mistaken uses of the word, but they are far too limited, too narrow. For the biblical story is chiefly about the restoration of creation: God is restoring his good creation to live again under his gracious rule. To understand "creation" as what it is that God is restoring is essential to a healthy Christian view of the world.

The Creator God

The biblical story begins with God: "In the beginning, God. . . ." And what a God this is! Perhaps it is hard for us, so many thousands of years after these words were written, to feel the impact that this opening phrase would have had on the original hearers who were being bombarded by a pagan view of "the gods." Genesis 1 was written, in part, to counter the pagan notions dominant in their day. This startling beginning tells us that there was a time when only God existed; he reveals more about who he is as the creation account unfolds. He is one God (not many gods), he is sovereign over the whole creation (not a petty tribal deity), and he is incomparable and utterly unique, good and kind, righteous, and wise (unlike the capricious and often wicked gods of the rival accounts). Here we are introduced to the God who will be the main actor in the biblical drama.

A biblical worldview must therefore begin with this God, the God glimpsed first in the creation account and then revealed much more fully throughout the biblical drama. And while worldview is concerned to elaborate how to view this world (as the word *worldview* implies), one cannot properly view this world without understanding its proper relation to the living God, for this world is created by him, upheld by him, ruled by him, and permeated with his presence, glory, and revelation. The doctrine of creation includes an understanding of the basic relationship between the awesome God and everything else, since everything else exists only because he has called it into existence.

Biblical authors maintain that God did not create the world and then remove himself from it. This concept of an absent God is the perilous idea at the heart of deism, in which view God has created the world as a watchmaker creates a watch. All that the mechanism needed for the watch to be self-operating is built right in, so that (once the watch is finished) the watchmaker himself is no longer required. A deistic view of God sees God as building "natural laws" right into the creation in such a way that his presence and power are no longer needed for the creation to continue to exist.

But this is decidedly not the biblical view of God. The biblical story speaks of a God who is intimately connected with what he has made at every moment of its history—a living, present king, not an absentee land-lord. God's presence fills the universe. This is expressed succinctly by Paul when he speaks to pagan Greeks in Athens: God created the whole world and everything in it, gives all human beings life and breath and everything else that they have, guides and rules history, and governs all nations. His activity is such that all people should seek him, reach out to him, and find him, for he is close to all of us: "For in him we live and move and have our being" (Acts 17:28). This is one of the foundation stones of a genuine biblical worldview: the world is saturated with the presence of God. John Henry Newman rightly says that God "has so implicated Himself with [the creation], and taken it into His very bosom, by His presence in it, His providence over it, His impressions upon it, and His influences through it, that we cannot truly or fully contemplate it without in some aspects contemplating Him."[2]

If God is present in the universe in this way, then the world is full of his glory and majesty:

> "There is not an atom of the universe in which you cannot see some brilliant sparks at least of his glory." God is immanent in all creation. The pure of heart see God everywhere. Everything is full of God. "I confess that the expression, 'Nature is God' may be used in a pious sense by a pious mind!"[3]

In "God's Grandeur" Gerard Manley Hopkins puts it this way:

> The world is charged with the grandeur of God.
> It will flame out, like shining from shook foil;
> It gathers to a greatness, like the ooze of oil
> Crushed.

For Hopkins, God's grandeur is intimately connected with the creation and declares itself as emphatically as the reflected light that dazzles the eyes like lightning when a sheet of gold foil is shaken in the sun. God's grandeur is like an electric current (and this idea was front-page science news when Hopkins wrote his sonnet in the middle of the nineteenth century) latent in the battery or the generator but ready to be revealed in a blinding electric arc when the switch is thrown. God's splendor is like the oil that permeates the olive berries on their twigs but is revealed in its golden fullness only when they are picked and brought under the crushing force of the olive press—and here Hopkins is hinting that God's grandeur has been revealed to us most fully in Jesus Christ, who also was "crushed." The world is charged—packed and tingling—with God's glorious presence.

God's presence in the world means also that he is involved in all aspects and events of the creation. It seems as if Newman has Paul's speech in Acts 17 in mind when he writes,

> He is One who is sovereign over, operative amidst, independent of, the appointments which He has made; One in whose hands are all things, who has a purpose in every event, and a standard for every deed, and thus has relations of His own towards the subject-matter of each particular science which the book of knowledge unfolds; who has with an adorable, never-ceasing energy implicated Himself in all the history of creation, the constitution of nature, the course of the world, the origin of society, the fortunes of the nations, the action of the human mind.[4]

In the whole of human life one comes face to face with the living God. All of human life is lived *coram Deo*, "before the face of God" or "in the presence of God." This Latin phrase is found about fifty times in the Vulgate (Jerome's Latin translation of the Bible).[5] The biblical phrase harks back to an image in the ancient Eastern court, the throne room of the monarch, where the king's servants stood before him waiting, alert, always aware of his presence, ready, prepared to respond to the king's bidding. To live *coram Deo* is to live in and to be aware of God's presence, responsive to his word, ready to serve him. Thus a Christian *world*view must begin with the fact of God's presence and involvement in the world. To live in the world pictured in the Bible is "to live and move and have our being" here, in God himself.

Although God's presence and activity permeate the universe, God must not be identified with the creation. According to Genesis 1, there is one God, and everything else is the work of his hands. God freely calls forth the whole creation *ex nihilo*, "out of nothing." A basic distinction between Creator and creation, between God and everything else, is a fundamental orientation point for a Christian worldview. Newman is right to stress that although God is present and at work within the creation, he is also "sovereign over" and "independent of" it.

Our worldview journey begins with God, with both his presence and activity in the world and his independence from and sovereignty over it.

The World as God's Good and Ordered Creation

The first chapter of Genesis is rich in teaching not only about the Creator God but also about what it is that he creates, and this creation is described as ordered, good, and historical. We will treat each of these qualities in turn.

AN ORDERED CREATION

Genesis shows us a movement from a dark, unformed, and empty creation to a beautifully ordered cosmos, and this is accomplished by God's word.[6] Eight times we read that God speaks something new into being, with the simple phrase "Let there be. . . ." The end result is a many-splendored creation. "By the word of the LORD the heavens were made, their starry host by the breath of his mouth," sings the psalmist (Ps. 33:6, 9; cf. Heb. 11:3). But the divine word that speaks all things into being in the first chapters of Genesis does not simply fall silent afterwards: God constantly and continually speaks to uphold and rule the creation. Peter tells us that the world continues today "by the same word" by which God made it (2 Pet. 3:5–7). The psalmist says, "He sends his command to the earth; his word runs swiftly" to accomplish the falling of snow and hail, the coming of a warm wind, and the thawing of ice when the storm has passed (Ps. 147:15–18). The Bible pictures the creation as continually and constantly responding to God's word, his originating, preserving, and ruling decree. Bruce Milne expresses this well:

> God has called the universe into being out of nothing, and hence at every mo-
> ment it "hangs" suspended, as it were, over the abyss of non-existence. If God
> were to withdraw his upholding Word, then all being . . . would instantly tumble
> back into nothing and cease to exist. The continuation of the universe from
> one moment to the next is therefore as great a miracle and as fully the work of
> God as is its coming into being at the beginning. In this profound sense we all
> live "every instant only by the grace of God."[7]

God's ordering words are comprehensive in scope: both the nonhuman creation and the whole of human life exist and are ordered in response to God's
Word. This is not hard for us to see in regard to the nonhuman creation. We
can readily acknowledge the regular patterns and lawfulness that we discover
in physics, chemistry, and biology. The more difficult thing is to understand
that all of human life too is ordered by God, that (as Abraham Kuyper argued)
the scope of God's Word is as broad as creation itself:

> All created life necessarily bears in itself a law for its existence, instituted by
> God himself. . . . Consequently there are ordinances of God for our bodies,

for the blood that courses through our arteries and veins, and for our lungs as the organs of respiration. And even so are there ordinances of God in logic, to regulate our thoughts; ordinances of God for our imagination, in the domain of aesthetics; and so also, strict ordinances of God for the whole of human life in the domain of morals.[8]

It was this understanding that led Kuyper to argue that all of life must be lived in response to God: "Everything that has been created was, in its creation, furnished by God with an unchangeable law of its existence. And because God has fully ordained such laws and ordinances for all life, therefore . . . all life [must] be consecrated to His service, in strict obedience."[9]

All of creation, human and nonhuman, responds to God's ordering words, but there is a fundamental difference between the way nonhuman creation responds and the way human beings respond. The response of the nonhuman creation is "necessary": the stormy wind does his bidding without having decided to do so; when the sun's rays strengthen in the spring, the ice melts because it must do so (Ps. 148:8; 147:18). But men and women have been created by God with the power of choice; this is an important aspect of his image in us, but it also means that we may, and often do, choose not to obey his laws for our lives. The response of human creatures is free, responsible, and creative, which also means that God's rules for human life "can be violated in any number of ways, and they also leave a good deal to the resourcefulness and responsible imagination of the human being who is called to implement them."[10]

Human beings embody and implement God's order in particular historical and cultural situations. There is a good deal of freedom and room for creative responses. While certain emotional responses are appropriate to given situations (e.g., joy is the appropriate response to the experience of God's blessings), there is a wide range of ways in which joy may be expressed by different peoples (a South American or African public expression of joy most likely will be more exuberant and demonstrative than a European or North American one), but each of these expressions may be appropriate in its own time and place to reflect faithfully God's order for human life.

This opens up the very difficult question of how we can know what God's will is for emotional life, for the state, for marriage, for our imagination. How do we know if homosexual unions conform to or are contrary to God's order for marriage? How do we know if democracy is a faithful political order? How can we discern the degree to which capitalism conforms to God's law for healthy economic life? How much are the structures of our schools in keeping with God's law for faithful education? Is there art that is contrary to God's will for aesthetic life?

Discerning God's order will always be difficult, but there are guidelines. The beginning of such discernment is to recognize that it is the work of God's Spirit, not simply a matter of our rational calculation. The Spirit of creation uses means by which to communicate God's will to us. The first is Scripture itself: what does the Bible have to say about the matter? In some areas there may be much direct guidance, but in others, little. For example, God gives Israel the law in the Old Testament, a concrete expression of God's order for human life at a particular time and place in history. Similarly, in the New Testament Paul's letters are full of exhortation to the young churches that he has planted; they too offer a visible implementation of God's creation order for the life of those churches at a certain point in history. Although there are dangers in asking the Bible to answer questions that it was never meant to answer, and in transporting norms from another time to ours, Scripture offers a divinely authorized understanding of God's will for his people at various points in history. Since God's creation order for human life is stable and constant, those particular historical manifestations will have much to offer.

There are other principles that may help us to understand Scripture and discern God's will in the creation. For instance, we are often blinded to God's abiding order for our lives by our own local cultural and theological preju- dices, but listening carefully to Christians who come from other confessional traditions, other cultural contexts, and other historical periods can alert us to our blindness. Moreover, when we see a stable or constant pattern across time and culture, it may warn us of a distortion that departs from this regularity. Further, God's covenant with the creation means that a response of obedi- ence will often bring blessing, and disobedience will bring judgment (Deut. 30:15–20). Discerning life and death, blessing and curse, in our activity may help us to see God's path. Finally, God has created in each of us a sense of his order in our conscience, which Albert Wolters defines as "intuitive attunement to creational normativity."[11] All of these may guide us, but there is nothing automatic or certain here. Each of these may be abused to justify evil. This, no doubt, is why Paul so often prays that the church might grow together in wisdom, discernment, and insight (Eph. 1:15–23; Phil. 1:9–11; Col. 1:9–12).

Another way of describing how we are to discern God's creational order for human life—the pattern and design by which we may acknowledge his kingship over us, and so enjoy his blessing—is to use the biblical language of wisdom, which Gerhard von Rad defines as "practical knowledge of the laws of life and of the world, based on experience."[12] Wisdom is the discovery of the order of creation found in both nature and society, and it implies a willingness to live in conformity with that order as it is discovered. God's wisdom is manifested in the order that he has established in the creation; true human wisdom is manifested in recognizing and conforming to that order. Gordon Spykman observes, "Our calling is to bring the order *of* our life in God's world, whether in the pulpit or in politics, in our halls of learning or in our marketplaces, into conformity with God's good order *for* our life in his world."[13]

Isaiah 28:23–29 (NIV) provides us with this link between creation and wisdom:

> Listen and hear my voice; pay attention and hear what I say.
> When a farmer plows for planting, does he plow continually?
>   Does he keep on breaking up and harrowing the soil?
> When he has leveled the surface, does he not sow caraway and scatter
>   cummin?
>   Does he not plant wheat in its place, barley in its plot, and spelt in
>   its field?
> His God instructs him and teaches him the right way.
> Caraway is not threshed with a sledge, nor is a cartwheel rolled over
>   cummin;
> caraway is beaten out with a rod, and cummin with a stick.
> Grain must be ground to make bread; so one does not go on threshing
>   it forever.
> Though he drives the wheels of his threshing cart over it, his horses do
>   not grind it.
> All this also comes from the Lord Almighty, wonderful in counsel and
>   magnificent in wisdom.

This farmer knows the creaturely nature of the seeds and the land that he deals with, and knows also the best methods of sowing those seeds, of harvesting, and of threshing. But the farmer knows all this by virtue of his experience with God's orderly creation. God instructs the farmer, says Isaiah, but he does not use Scripture to do so directly; instead, wisdom—God's instruction—comes as the farmer discerns and conforms to the order that he observes in God's creation.

Creation and wisdom refer to all of human and nonhuman creation. Von Rad notes, "Israel did not differentiate between a 'life wisdom' that pertained to the social orders and a 'natural wisdom' that conformed to so-called natural laws."[14] In other words, "creation" had a much broader scope of meaning for Old Testament Israel than it often does for us today. Creation includes the cultural and social endeavors of human beings and thus covers the whole of human life—personal, social, cultural. Social institutions are not merely subjectively shaped; cultural formation always works within the boundaries of God's order, which makes these institutions possible. Thus, for example, Scripture teaches clearly that marriage, a cultural and societal development, has been created by God to be received with thanksgiving (1 Tim. 4:3–4); political authority is similarly described as having been created or ordained by God (1 Pet. 2:13).[15] Thus we must honor the way God has created marriage and political authority. Wisdom extends to the whole of human and cultural life.

A VERY GOOD CREATION

Throughout the creation account we hear repeatedly, "God saw that it was good." And at the climax of the story, "God saw all that he had made, and it was very good" (Gen. 1:31). What comes afterward is not all good, of course, but Genesis insists that the goodness of creation as it comes from the hand of God had no taint of evil in it. In vivid contrast, pagan creation stories tell of a world composed of good and evil, order and disorder. In the pagan view, good and evil are part of the very fabric of the world. In the biblical view, evil is like a stain on the pure fabric of creation: it comes later, it is not essential to the nature of the world, and it may be removed without changing the essential nature of that which it has disfigured.

In the New Testament, the apostle Paul argues against the (heretical) belief that physical matter is evil, that food and sex (so clearly belonging to our "material" existence) are therefore also intrinsically evil. The apostle levels a powerful counterblast against such a view: to teach such things, Paul avers, is to abandon the faith, to follow deceiving spirits, and to embrace doctrines taught by demons. The truth of the matter, Paul insists, is quite different: marriage and food were created by God "to be received with thanksgiving by those who believe and who know the truth. For everything God created is good, and nothing is to be rejected if it is received with thanksgiving" (1 Tim. 4:1–5).

In Genesis 1 God declares of each individual creature that "it is good"; when the creation is complete, God says of the whole that "it is very good." We may observe from this that each part of creation is good, but the harmony of the whole is very good, more than the sum of its parts:

> The creation is a symphony where we find a variety of creatures each singing the praises of the Maker in accordance with its unique character, different from creatures of another "make." The lion is to serve the Lord like a lion, the dandelion like a dandelion. The difference in service depends on the difference in the Word addressed to them. The response of the creation to the one all-embracing Word—serve Me!—is thus a symphony of voices in which each type of creature performs its unique function in the indispensable setting of the whole.[16]

This harmony should be true also of the range of cultural, social, and personal expressions of the life of humankind. Technology and art, schools and businesses, imagination and emotion—all these make their contributing sounds in the symphony of God's creation. Each is good as it conforms to God's creational design, and all are very good as together they serve him in harmony. Idolatry, discord, and cacophony arise when we begin to take one aspect of creation and exalt it to a position beyond its God-ordained creational place. Goodness in creation is a matter of conforming to God's order in its diversity (God's words) and its harmony (God's Word).

A HISTORICAL CREATION

Finally, the first chapter of Genesis describes a creation that is not static but rather moves and develops historically toward a goal. A stable order and historical development do not contradict one another.

God blessed Adam and Eve with the task of subduing the earth and ruling over it (Gen. 1:28). This is fundamental to the way God meant the world to be. From the beginning, God intended that the historical development of creation should continue in the human cultivation of the rich potentials of God's creation through the responsible cultural activity of human beings. All of culture and society, all of human civilization, is in response to this one divine mandate. In the beginning, the creation was like a healthy newborn child. It was "very good" in the sense that there was nothing wrong with it as a newborn; it was complete and healthy in all its parts. But a healthy newborn child must continue to grow and to develop. So it is with the creation: God's intention from the beginning was that the creation should unfold and develop and move toward a goal.

Human rebellion enters the story of how humankind begins to develop the latent potentials of the creation very early on, yet rebellion does not destroy the historical structure of the world. Nor does it change the meaning of history. Rather, when God sets out on the long historical road of redemption, he does so precisely to reaffirm and reestablish the original goal and meaning of history. The Bible tells the story of creation's historical development as moving from a garden to a city, from Eden to the new Jerusalem, into which all the cultural treasures of history will be brought (Rev. 21:24–26).[17] This great city, the goal of history, is the work of God's redemption, his restoring of the whole creation, including its history, to reach its appointed goal.

Thus the constancy of creation order and the dynamic unfolding of that creation are essential to a biblical worldview. Indeed, the historical development is possible only because God has ordered his creation and remains faithful to his word.

The Role of Human Beings in God's Creation

HUMANITY AS GOD'S IMAGE

The creation story progresses beautifully with repetition and rhythm. "And God said, 'Let there be . . .' and there was. . . . God saw that it was good. . . . And there was evening, and there was morning—the first day . . . the second day . . . the third day. . . .'" One settles into the gentle pattern and cadence of the story, until one is jolted to new attention when the rhythm is broken: "Then God said, 'Let us make human beings in our image'" (Gen. 1:26). Something new is taking place here. God, king over all, announces to his royal court that he is about to create a creature in his own image to mediate his own rule. We have reached a climactic point in the story, and this too is important for a Christian worldview. What does it mean to be human? What is the role of human beings in the biblical story? Who are we?

Surely, the characterization of humankind and its role in the world set forth in Genesis 1 would have shocked the first hearers of this story. They were immersed in a pagan worldview whose myths set out a very different picture of what it means to be human: human beings were described in their stories as mere savages, slaves of the gods, created only to serve. This was true for all mortals except the king (and sometimes the nobility), who alone was the image of God. To say that human beings—all human beings, not just kings—were created in God's image would have been a shocking assertion.[18]

For the author of Genesis to speak of humanity as being created in God's image would mean, first, a life of creaturely dependence. Henri Blocher notes that an "image is only an image. It exists only by derivation. It is not the original, nor is it anything without the original. Mankind's being as image stresses the radical nature of his dependence."[19] Indeed, the command not to eat from the tree of the knowledge of good and evil was a constant reminder of humankind's creaturely dependence (Gen. 2:16–17).

Second, to be God's image is to live in relationship to God. According to Genesis, it is not only the king who has access to the gods: all of humanity has a relationship with the one creator God. And if God constantly orders all things by his word, then human life is meant to be a life of constant response to him. Responding to God, living in communion with him, and enjoying him are essential elements of what it means to be human.

Third, to be God's image is to reflect God, to be like him, to mirror his character. Men and women do not share in the divine nature, but they are finite, creaturely reflections of the infinite Creator. Like God, human beings can, for example, see, hear, think, love, pursue justice, get angry, and show mercy. Yet it is not just in possessing these capabilities that we image God; it is also a matter of the way we use them. It matters what we think, what we love, how we use our eyes and ears, what makes us angry. Moreover, we reflect God not just individually but also communally. Some image him as fathers, as they show compassion, as they listen to others patterning their actions toward one another after his actions toward us.[20]

This "God-likeness" enables us to know, love, worship, and enjoy God because we can in some way understand who he is and what he is doing. Being fathers or having fathers helps us to understand what it means for God to be our Father; showing compassion helps us understand God's compassion. The close connection between reflecting God and knowing God is seen in Blocher's comment that we are the "image of the divine Glory . . . that Glory which mankind both reflects and beholds."[21] Since humanity reflects God's glory, we are able also to behold God's glory.

Fourth, to image God is to represent God in the creation as his vice-regents and stewards. The biblical picture of a steward is instructive. Such a person was responsible to rule on behalf of the master, not for self-serving pleasure but rather for the good of the household and in accordance with the master's wishes. At the end of the period of stewardship the steward was accountable for the way he had ruled on behalf of the master. Humankind was called to just this sort of stewardship over the rest of God's creation, though not in God's absence but rather in constant communion with him.

What is clear in all these elements of the image of God is that the very core of human existence is religious. Human life is dependent on and oriented toward God. Human beings have been created to respond to God by worshiping, knowing, loving, enjoying, thanking, and obeying him. As his image, we are inextricably bound to him. The choices available to us are either to seek to live out our true nature in intimate relationship and communion with him or to seek to thwart the relationship that he intends. There is no such thing as human life apart from God; all human life is in response to him—that is, either in communion with him or in rebellion against him.

Human life is not only religious; it is also communal. Among the repetitive and positive affirmations of the goodness of the creation we hear the startling words "It is not good for the man to be alone. I will make a helper suitable for him" (Gen. 2:18). Human beings were not made to live solitary lives: "From the very beginning, the human being is . . . a being-with; human life attains its full realization only in community."[22] Already in Genesis 1 there is a hint of this communal dimension when the writer says, "God created human beings in his own image, in the image of God he created them; male and female he created them" (Gen. 1:27). The truly human life is lived in relationship not only with God but also with other human beings.

The Task of Humankind: The Creation Mandate

After creating humankind in his own image, God blesses them and says, "Be fruitful and increase in number; fill the earth and subdue it. Rule . . ." (Gen. 1:28). Here we are given our human calling with God's word of blessing: rule and subdue the creation.[23] With these words, history begins.

The narrative of Genesis 1 unfolds in three stages. The first stage takes place in the first two verses. Here God calls the creation into being and we learn three things about it: it is dark, formless, and empty. The second stage completes this work: the darkness yields to light (day one), the formlessness is structured into sky, land, and seas (days two and three), and the emptiness gives way to a fullness of living creatures (days four through six). When at last, and as the climax of his creative action, God creates humankind and calls them to rule and subdue the creation, he explicitly bids them to carry on his own work of developing the creation. Men and women will now continue to form and fill the world that God has made, in obedience to his call, taking up the tasks of developing society and culture. We may refer to this period during which humankind participates in God's work as the third stage of creation.

In stage two God had stamped his glory on the creation by his own creative work of forming and filling. Now, in stage three, God creates a creature like himself to continue that work. God makes a finite and creaturely "stamp" of himself, as it were, to continue to imprint more of his glory on the creation as it is developed. The whole cultural and social task of humankind is to reveal the glory of God latent in the potentials of the creation.

Some have seen the call to rule and subdue the earth as a license for tyranny and have blamed precisely this text for the ecological disaster that we now face in the world.[24] But Genesis 1 gives us instead a picture of stewardly care, a loving rule that has at its heart the motive of service: "The LORD God took the man and put him in the Garden of Eden to work it and take care of it" (Gen. 2:15). These two words, "work" and "care," summarize the delightful calling that human beings have been given. We are to work, to discover and develop the potential of the creation, to form relationships and human institutions, to make tools and buildings and all that goes into human civilization. But since we now (in the twenty-first century) live in a world in which development has proceeded in such a way that it endangers the whole nonhuman creation, we must emphasize strongly the second word of God's charge to us: care. As we develop the creation, we are to protect and care for it. Jonathan Chaplin puts it this way: "We may press the grapes into wine, but not pollute the vineyard. We may develop sophisticated technology, but not at the expense of rewarding human work. We are free to eat of every tree in the garden, but not to spray them with destructive chemicals for short-term gain."[25]

God is a loving Father who fills the creation with good gifts waiting to be enjoyed and discovered. Ours is a delightful task that opens the way to a rich and abundant life. God's creation is "evidence of the caring hand of the Creator reaching out to secure the well-being of his creatures, of a Father extending a universe full of blessings to his children."[26] Our response in receiving this creation as a gift should be one of love, thankfulness, and joy.

The Original Shalom

The Hebrew prophets used a word to describe the anticipated renewal of the creation that can rightfully be employed here to describe the original creation: *shalom*. This word is often translated simply as "peace," but it means much more than simply the absence of hostility. *Shalom* describes the creation as it was meant to be, a life of flourishing and prospering in which our relationships with God, with each other, and with the nonhuman creation are luxuriant and thriving.[27] A world of *shalom* is characterized by justice, love, thankfulness, and joy:

> The webbing together of God, humans, and all creation in justice, fulfillment, and delight is what the Hebrew prophets call *shalom*. . . . In the Bible, shalom means *universal flourishing, wholeness, and delight*—a rich state of affairs in which the natural needs are satisfied and natural gifts fruitfully employed, a state of affairs that inspires joyful wonder as its Creator and Savior opens doors and welcomes the creatures in whom he delights. Shalom, in other words, is the way things ought to be. . . . In a shalomic state each entity would have its own integrity or structured wholeness, and each would also possess many edifying relations to other entities.[28]

Shalom is God's creational intention. As a loving Father, he wants this, and only this, for his creation.

Sin: The Corruption of the Good Creation

Treason in the Garden and Its Aftermath

The opening act of the drama of Scripture shows us a very good creation. Everything is as it should be. But the second act tells the tragic story of human rebellion, in which the *shalom* of God is vandalized.[29] After sin enters the world, everything is suddenly not the way it is supposed to be.

In Genesis 2 God sets Adam and Eve in a garden where all that they could want is freely offered them, but the "tree of the knowledge of good and evil" is forbidden. Why does God issue this command? The tree is there to remind them of their creaturely status. Adam and Eve would continue to enjoy the fullness of God's creation only if they continued to submit themselves to God, to trust his word and obey him. The command focuses attention on God's absolute lordship; Adam and Eve must learn to obey for no other reason than because God says so. Their continual obedience is to help them understand their place as obedient children, as submissive creatures, as God's image—uniquely privileged among God's creatures, and yet creatures still.

God allows Satan to offer Adam and Eve another word to live by. Satan engenders doubt in God's goodness ("Did God really say . . . ?"), stirs unbelief ("You will not surely die . . ."), and fires the imagination with an alternative and illusory vision ("Your eyes will be opened and you will be like God . . ."). Choosing Satan's words to live by, and rejecting God's, Adam and Eve commit an act of treachery and disobedience against their creator. In this decision, "Man has taken leave of the relation of dependence. He has refused to obey and has willed to make himself independent. No longer is obedience the guiding principle of his life, but his autonomous knowledge and will. Thereby he ceases, in effect, to understand himself as a creature."[30]

All of human life is affected. Already in these first few chapters of the biblical story sin rises in "ominous crescendo," echoing in every part of human life.[31] According to Genesis, Adam and Eve are alienated from God (3:8, 23–24). Their relationship to one another becomes one of self-serving mastery rather than selfless love (3:16).[32] Work is burdened by sin's effects (3:17). Fratricide makes its ugly entrance, shattering a family (4:8). Polygamy twists what was intended in marriage (4:19). Metalworking begins (4:22), but before long it is used in the service of war. The distortion of literature and poetry is evident when Lamech creates a beautiful poem but uses it to celebrate murder and revenge (4:23). Human wickedness becomes so great that God regrets making human beings and vows to wash the earth clean of them (6:5–7). But the flood does not wash away the foul odor of sin; every inclination of the human heart remains evil (8:21, cf. 6:5). The whole sorry mess climaxes at the tower of Babel, where we see how sin has twisted communication, architecture, urbanization, and religion. Genesis 3–11 is designed in part to show how dark the world soon became as a result of Adam and Eve's sin.

Against You, You Only, Have I Sinned

We have a tendency to minimize the gravity, scope, and power of sin, often reducing it to a matter of merely individual disobedience. But sin is more than that; it is "a very vicious and mortal enemy, an irascible and persistent power, which must certainly be *known* in order to be *overcome*."[33] When we recognize how creation is infused with God's presence, we immediately realize that sin is first and foremost against God. David confesses this succinctly: "Against you, you only, have I sinned and done what is evil in your sight" (Ps. 51:4). Humanity has been created in such a way that the whole of our creaturely existence is to be centered in and oriented toward God. When men and women are alienated from God, they do not stop being religious; rather, they place their religious allegiance somewhere else, in some aspect of creation. As Paul puts it, "They exchanged the truth of God for a lie, and worshiped and served created things rather than the Creator" (Rom. 1:25 NIV). Chaplin adds, "If human beings are inescapably religious, driven always to seek an object of worship, then the fall cannot be characterised solely as revolt *against* the rightful Lord: It must be described further as *exchange of religious allegiance*."[34] If they reject God, human beings will find something else as their lives' center, and this new center is what the Bible calls an idol.

The close connection between idolatry and adultery in Scripture helps us to see the religious and relational nature of sin. A husband has the right to the exclusive loyalty of his wife, and the wife to that of her husband. Marriage is an exclusive relationship that admits no third party. Sin is portrayed in Scripture as religious adultery: a third party (some idol) has insinuated itself into that exclusive relationship and adulterated it.[35] Sin is religious and relational: it is against God.

Put another way, sin is the rebellion of children against a loving Father who has created the world for them to enjoy and delight in. Out of the depths of his kindness and generosity God created his children with an exalted place in the creation, with the delightful calling to walk in warm fellowship with himself, exploring, caring for, delighting in, and developing the creation. Sin is the ungrateful refusal to acknowledge the love and goodness of God. It is an arrogant assertion that we know what is best for us. It is treason—not against a rightful yet distant authority but rather against a loving, generous, ever-present Father. It is life turned away from God's loving intention.

And You Shall Earn the Penalty for Your Idolatry

Although sin is first and foremost an offense against God, it is an offense also against the creation, against human life, *shalom*, health, prosperity, wholeness, and human flourishing. Jeremiah records the Lord's words about idolatrous Israel: "Am I the one they are provoking? declares the Lord. Are they not rather harming themselves, to their own shame?" (Jer. 7:19). Brian Walsh and Richard Middleton comment that "disobedience goes against the very grain of creation itself. Sin is rebellion against both the structure and the Structurer of reality. Such rebellion is inevitably self-defeating and self-destroying."[36]

The notion of the covenant, so central to the biblical story, helps us understand how sin can cause lives and relationships to disintegrate. Moses articulates this covenantal structure just as Israel is about to enter the promised land:

> See, I set before you today life and prosperity, death and destruction. For I command you today to love the Lord your God, to walk in his ways, and to keep his commands, decrees and laws; then you will live and increase, and the Lord your God will bless you in the land you are entering to possess. But if your heart turns away and you are not obedient, and if you are drawn away to bow down to other gods and worship them, I declare to you this day that you will certainly be destroyed. . . . I have set before you life and death, blessings and curses. (Deut. 30:15–19 NIV)

As the diagram makes clear (see figure 2), God gives his word to us. If we respond to him in trust and obedience, we will experience life, prosperity, and blessing. If, on the other hand, we respond in unbelief and disobedience, we will face death, destruction, and God's curse.

Figure 2. Covenant Structure

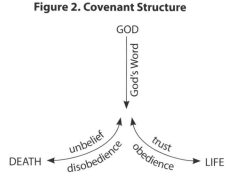

Sin is a power, "seductive . . . damning, an active, dynamic and destructive force."[37] Paul's depiction of sin in Romans 7 is remarkable: it is a personal power at work in human life, one that seizes opportunities, springs to life, deceives, wages war, enslaves, and produces death. It redirects our allegiance from God to some idol, it aims at our destruction, it conceals its appalling nature from us as it lures us to our death, and it corrupts and distorts God's good creation.[38] "Sin is a power that seeks to rule and ruin everyone and everything."[39]

The Relation of Sin to Creation

How, then, are we to understand the relation of sin to creation? We begin by considering sin's relationship to God's good creation as being akin to that of a parasite to its host.[40] A parasite is an organism that lives off the life blood of another, an "uninvited guest that keeps tapping its host for sustenance."[41] Sin lives by feeding off of God's good creation. It attaches itself to the creation, twisting, distorting, disrupting, and perverting it. It uses the very structure and movement of the creation for its own malevolent purposes. As C. S. Lewis puts it, "Goodness is, so to speak, itself: badness is only spoiled goodness. And there must be something good first before it can be spoiled."[42] Herman Bavinck says that sin "is nothing and can do nothing apart from the creatures and the powers which God has created; yet it organizes all these in open rebellion against him. Sin does not destroy the creation: the world of human culture remains . . . part of God's good creation, but sin corrupts and pollutes."[43] Wolters speaks of sin as a power that misdirects every part of God's good creation.[44] Thus, for example, sin does not destroy the economic dimension of creation; it perverts it from being stewardly to being selfish and greedy. Sin does not destroy the power of media to communicate; it uses it to communicate a false view of the world. Sin does not destroy sexuality; it misdirects sexual desire in wrong directions. Thus in each case we must distinguish the good creational design in every created thing from what it has become by the twisting and corrupting force of sin.

The Scope of Sin

Sin defiles and disfigures every inch of the creation. It sullies human beings in their personal lives, in their emotions, reasoning, and speech; much of the Bible inveighs against individual immorality—lying, stealing, adultery, complaining, lust, greed, and so on. Yet sin is not simply personal; it also expresses itself communally. Since human beings live in community, they may give their corporate allegiance to idols. Since humankind's fall, the center of each culture is found in some form of communal idolatry that shapes all aspects of social and cultural life and organizes them in rebellion against God.

In *Aid for the Overdeveloped West*, Bob Goudzwaard refers to "three basic biblical rules": (1) "every man is serving god(s) in his life"; (2) "every man is transformed into an image of his god"; (3) together, "mankind creates and forms a structure of society in its own image."[45] He goes on to elaborate this idea: "In the development of human civilization, man forms, creates and changes the structure of his society, and in doing so he portrays in his work the intention of his own heart. He gives to the structure of that society *something of his own image and likeness*. In it he betrays something of his own lifestyle, of his own *god*."[46]

Finally, sin touches and distorts not only human life but also the nonhuman creation. The apostle Paul explains it this way: "The creation was subjected to frustration, not by its own choice, but by the will of the one who subjected it. . . . The whole creation has been groaning as in the pains of childbirth right up to the present time" (Rom. 8:20, 22). It is not only the life of humanity that is nasty, brutish, and short; the whole nonhuman creation shares in it. Our environmental crisis brings this home in a poignant way. An enormous amount of data on environmental issues has been published that points to destruction of the ozone layer, global warming, acid rain, loss of biological diversity, contamination of air, water, and soil by toxic chemical waste, deforestation, and more. Truly, God's good creation groans under the burden of our sin.

Sounding Three Hopeful Notes

Before we leave the subject of sin and end this chapter, there are three hopeful observations to be made. The first is that sin does not belong to God's creation; it is accidental. Sin certainly has stained the fabric of the creation, but that stain can be removed, and God himself has made it his purpose to remove it. The second hopeful observation is that even before his final restoration of the creation is accomplished, God does not allow sin to run its full destructive course. He remains faithful and continues to restrain the devastating effects of sin. Spouses still love one another, parents still nurture their children in love, political authority still seeks justice to some degree, art still reflects something of the *shalom* of God's good creation. Honesty, friendship, love, and joy are still to be found in God's world. These evidences of God's restraining influence on sin are called by some theologians "common grace."[47] God does not abandon the work of his hands; something of its original goodness can still be seen.

And our third and last observation is that the power of sin, as great and deadly as it is, is overwhelmed by a greater power: the life-giving power of the gospel. The "good news" is not just a theological message to be understood, but it is "the power of God that brings salvation" to be believed and experienced (Rom. 1:16; 1 Cor. 1:18; 2:4–5). Ultimately, sin stands no chance against God. For God's broken world, that is good news indeed!

4

A Biblical Worldview

Restoration

What was God's response to the sinful rebellion of Adam and Eve? God was angry—justly angry! His good creation was now bent on destruction by the foolish and rebellious insurgence of those whom he had lovingly created to enjoy life with him. We trivialize both sin and God's love for the creation if we dismiss his wrath from the biblical story. But wrath is not the last word. God does not turn his back on his mutinous world; he embraces it in love. Steadfast covenant love moves God to act in a selfless, sacrificial, and self-giving way. Out of this love God promises to crush all the evil powers that Adam and Eve have unleashed. And as the story continues, God so loves the world that at last he gives his own Son for it.

Salvation as the Story of a Comprehensive Restoration of Creation

A biblical worldview must observe three characteristics of God's saving work. First, salvation is progressive: God's redemptive work commences near the dawn of human history, and we have not reached sunset yet. Second, salvation is restorative: God's saving work is about reclaiming his lost creation, putting it back to the way it was meant to be. Third, salvation is comprehensive: all of human life and all of the nonhuman creation are the object of God's restorative work. He intends to reclaim nothing less than the whole world as his kingdom. Simply put, salvation is the restoration of the whole of God's good creation.

Redemption Is Progressive

God could have snapped his fingers and healed the creation immediately, but he did not. Instead, he set out on a long journey of redemption, a journey that continues until the present day. In our book *The Drama of Scripture* we traced the redemptive journey in this story in four acts: Israel, Jesus, the church, and the new creation.[1]

The progressive unfolding of the biblical narrative is a story of redemption against the backdrop of creation and sin. This story might be described in terms of mission—God's mission, Israel's mission, Jesus' mission, and the church's mission. Christopher Wright has expressed this succinctly: "The Bible renders to us the story of God's mission through God's people in their engagement with God's world for the sake of the whole of God's creation."[2] God's mission is his long-term purpose or goal to restore the peoples from all nations, the whole of human social and cultural life, and the whole nonhuman creation from the mess that sin has created. It unfolds progressively through his work in the life of Israel and in the person and work of Jesus, and it continues today in the mission of the church.

Redemption Is Restorative

The biblical story of redemption is about the restoration and healing of God's good creation. In order to understand this biblical concept well, it is instructive to compare it with that of the Greek philosopher Plato, whose beliefs, though based on a completely pagan worldview, have often been adopted by Christians. (We will explore the long history of Plato's powerful influence on Christian thought more fully in the next chapter.) In Plato's thought, salvation is:

- vertical (our destiny is upward in heaven)
- otherworldly (our souls are saved into another spiritual world)
- an escape (we are saved not as part of this world but rather from this world)

But a genuinely Christian worldview contradicts the Platonic view at each of these points, since biblically, the goal of salvation is:

- horizontal (we look forward in history to the renewal of creation)
- of this world (the creation is to be renewed)
- integral to God's ultimate plan for this world (no escape necessary)

The argument that salvation is the restoration of creation can be summarized as follows:[3]

- The creation is very good, the way God intended it. As Albert Wolters has put it, "God does not make junk, and he does not junk what he has made."[4]
- Human beings are created to live in the context of the creation. We are made to live not as spirits in some ethereal world but rather as embodied people in this world.
- The materiality of creation is not what is wrong with it; the problem is sin. God's redemptive work is to remove the sin that has infected the creation.
- In the Old Testament (and especially in the prophetic promises) the future kingdom is described as restored life within a new creation.
- Jesus proclaims the gospel of the kingdom. No Jew immersed in the Old Testament (as Jesus himself was) would have ever conceived of the kingdom as something "heavenly" or "spiritual"; it was God acting in power and love to defeat sin, death, and Satan and to restore his creation.
- Jesus' resurrection is a preview of what we can expect for ourselves. Jesus goes to be with the Father after his death (cf. Luke 23:43) but returns in resurrection as the firstfruits of what is coming. We too are with the Lord at death but will be resurrected in our bodies in the final day.
- The biblical images of redemption, restoration, and renewal all point to the good creation coming back to what it was meant to be.
- Satan's goal from the beginning had been to ruin and destroy God's world. A final destruction of the creation would signify a powerful victory for Satan—a victory that God has no intention of allowing.
- Salvation is about continuity between the original creation and a restored creation.

But there are two further points to be aware of. First, restoration does not mean a return to the undeveloped state of creation as it was in Eden. Wolters speaks of restoration and not "repristination," which "would entail the *cultural* return to the garden of Eden, a return that would turn back the historical clock. Such a move would be historically reactionary or regressive."[5] Rather, restoration involves the renewal of the whole creation, including the historical and cultural development that has taken place since the beginning of history. Second, although continuity is the fundamental theme of salvation, an element of discontinuity does exist between the original creation and its restoration. Richard Middleton comments, "We may think of Paul's contrast in 1 Corinthians 15 between the present mortal body and the resurrection body, a contrast analogous to the difference between a seed and fully-grown plant. Likewise, the resurrected Jesus is portrayed in the Gospels as being able to walk through walls and perhaps materialize at will. Nevertheless, the resurrected Jesus is still recognizably the same person and even eats a meal of fish with his disciples on the beach—which suggests fundamental continuity between creation and redemption."[6]

Redemption Is Comprehensive

Scripture is clear in its affirmation that redemption does not concern only solitary individuals, or even just their souls. Peter interprets the message of the prophets in terms of a comprehensive renewal: "Heaven must receive [Jesus] until the time comes for God to restore everything, as he promised long ago through his holy prophets" (Acts 3:21). God himself announces at the end of the biblical story: "I am making everything new" (Rev. 21:5). Paul is clear on this point as well:

> And he made known to us the mystery of his will . . . to bring all things in heaven and on earth together under one head, even Christ. (Eph. 1:9–10 NIV)

> For God was pleased to have all his fullness dwell in [Christ], and through him to reconcile to himself all things, whether things on earth or things in heaven, by making peace through his blood, shed on the cross. (Col. 1:19–20)

God's renewal is across the whole range of human life but also extends to the nonhuman creation. Paul pictures the nonhuman creation as groaning in anticipation of renewal, yearning for the time when the final liberation of God's people will take place, for then it too will be liberated from the bondage of sin. Nature will no longer be "red in tooth and claw," but instead lions will lie down with lambs. In the delightful words of the Christmas carol "Joy to the World," salvation will extend as "far as the curse is found."[7]

The Progressive Unfolding of God's Comprehensive Restoration

The Mission of Old Testament Israel Was to Embody a Comprehensive Restoration

Israel was chosen by God to be a light to the nations, to be a people whose communal life of *shalom* would point to the original intention of God for all people. Thus God sought to order the whole of their lives in their particular historical and cultural setting according to his creational design. We see this in at least three places: (1) the Torah, (2) wisdom literature, and (3) prophecy.

The law or Torah ("instruction") of the Old Testament covers the whole range of human life, from worship to human relationships to the treatment of animals. This pattern of life expressed in the early books of the Old Testament is a cultural and historical contextualization of God's constant creation order.[8] In it we get a concrete historical look at the way God's people should live according to God's will in a certain time and place.

In the wisdom literature of the Old Testament, proverbs point the way to a rich life in God's world in every dimension of human experience, including friendship, sexuality, money, and communication. But this counsel reaches beyond private life: in Proverbs 8, Woman Wisdom cries out in the public square for Israel to listen and to bring its social, judicial, and political life in line with what is true and right in God's world.[9] Thus Israel's public life too is to be conformed to God's creational pattern, so that as a nation it will manifest God's justice and righteousness before the nations that surround it.

And, finally, the full breadth of what creational life restored in Israel will be is heard in the thundering judgments of the prophets against a people whose social, political, and economic lives have failed to embody God's intentions for them (e.g., Amos 5:7–15). All these—the law, wisdom, the prophets— were God's gifts to Israel, his means of instructing them in how they were to embody his creational design.

A Comprehensive Restoration Is Inaugurated in Jesus' Disclosure of the Kingdom of God

The central theme in Jesus' mission is his announcement of the good news and the inauguration of the kingdom of God. The good news is that God is acting to defeat all opposition to his *shalom* so that he might reassert his rightful rule over the whole of the creation. This is clear in the life, deeds, and words of Jesus, as they make known the coming kingdom. He launches an all-out attack on evil in all its forms—pain, sickness, death, demon-possession, immorality, loveless self-righteousness, special class privilege, broken human relationships, hunger, poverty, and death.[10] Jesus' mighty acts demonstrate that in the kingdom that he inaugurates, evil will be eradicated and God's good creation will be completely restored and reclaimed.

Most of Jesus' words and actions pertain to human life, which God is restoring in all of its dimensions to its original *shalom*. Salvation is the restoration of all aspects of human life—religious, political, economic, social, and physical.[11] And so his mighty works or miracles address the range of human life. But Jesus' works also point to the restoration of the nonhuman creation. Colin Gunton notes that the so-called nature miracles—for example, the calming of the storm (Mark 4:35–41)—though at first glance "appear to have no point to them," are in fact signs of God's restoring his loving rule over the whole nonhuman creation, "a militant reestablishment of the rule of God over a creation in thrall to evil."[12]

A Comprehensive Restoration Is Accomplished in Jesus' Death and Inaugurated in His Resurrection

The death of Jesus signals the defeat of every enemy of God's rule and also the restoration of the whole creation to live again under that rule. There are many images in Scripture that describe what the death of Christ accomplishes. One helpful image is what John Driver calls the "conflict-victory-liberation" image,[13] drawn from military life. The victory is the culmination of a fierce conflict that rages between God and powers of evil for the creation. The cross is where the climactic battle takes place and triumph is gained, paradoxically, through shame and humiliation. This victory liberates the entire creation and the whole life of humankind from the evil powers that enslave it (John 12:31–33; Col. 2:15; Rev. 7:7–12).

There is a tendency in North American evangelicalism to view the cross of Christ in a very individualistic and personalistic way: "Jesus died for me." In the words of Lesslie Newbigin, we "privatize this mighty work of grace and talk as if the whole cosmic drama of salvation culminates in the words 'For me; for me.'"[14] But we must not lose sight of the fact that in the crucifixion God defeats the powers that enslave cultural and social as well as individual life. It certainly is true that Jesus' death is for us, but this is too narrow a version of the truth. In the biblical drama Jesus dies for the whole world, for every part of human life, for the whole nonhuman creation. The cross is an event whereby the course of cosmic history is settled.

The resurrection of Jesus is the dawning of the age to come in which God will transform the entire cosmos. "Resurrection" meant, for first-century Jews, a large-scale event that would occur at the end of history in which God would restore the whole creation, including the bodily life of humankind. But no first-century Jew expected one man to rise in the middle of history. New Testament writers who reflect on the significance of Jesus' resurrection in this Jewish context conclude that in Jesus the end-time life of the kingdom has begun. He is the beginning, the firstborn from the dead, the firstfruits of the final restoration. In him, God's rule over all creation has begun.

A Comprehensive Restoration Is Given by the Exalted Christ in the Spirit

The risen Jesus takes his ordained place of authority over the whole creation as its rightful Lord, the embodiment of the living God, who (in contrast to the Caesar of Rome) truly has all authority over the entire creation (Phil. 2:9–11). The rule of God begins, and Jesus is now at work giving comprehensive renewal by his Spirit.

Pentecost is the sending of the Spirit. Since the prophets had declared that the Spirit would be poured out (in the last days) to bring about God's cosmic renewal (Ezek. 36:24–38; Isa. 42:1; Joel 2:28–32), Peter interprets the events of Pentecost as signaling the beginning of that era (Acts 2:14–21). The Spirit is a gift of future salvation given in the present.[15] By the Spirit, the future flows into the present; the comprehensive salvation of the end-time kingdom begins now by the Spirit.

With the coming of the Spirit, the kingdom of God is already here, but it has not yet arrived in fullness. The New Testament uses two images to describe this "already–not yet" tension. The first describes the Spirit as a "deposit" (2 Cor. 1:22; 5:5; Eph. 1:14). Money is paid in advance to a shopkeeper as a pledge to pay the whole amount at a future date. It is not a promissory note or an I.O.U. but rather real cash, a guarantee of good faith and a promise that there is a much larger amount to come. The Spirit is like that: he is not only a promise of the future kingdom but also a real gift here and now. The salvation of God's kingdom is really experienced in the Spirit's present work—its joy, *shalom*, righteousness, and knowledge of God—and he also carries the pledge of God that the fullness of God's gracious reign is yet to come.

The second New Testament image of the Spirit carries the same significance: the Spirit is referred to as the "firstfruits" of kingdom salvation (Rom. 8:23). The first part of the crop is real grain or fruit or corn. But it is more: it points to the rest of the coming harvest. Both of these pictures point to the fact that we have the future salvation now but also hope for its fullness in the future.

We have been given the gift of the Spirit so that we might embody this all-encompassing salvation for the sake of the world. We have been given a foretaste of salvation so that we might be a preview of what is coming in the future.

The Mission of the Church Is to Make Known a Comprehensive Restoration

COMMISSIONED BY JESUS

Before the Spirit is given, Jesus commissions his community of disciples to take up his own mission: make known God's rule over all of creation. After the resurrection occurs, the mandate to continue Jesus' mission is explicit: "As the Father has sent me, I am sending you" (John 20:21). Jesus breathes the Spirit on the disciples to empower them for their mission, to follow in the way that he has demonstrated for them.[16] Their whole lives are to be lived under God's rule. Like Jesus, they are to erect signs of God's future kingdom in knowing God, in living together in love, and in challenging forces that oppose God's caring rule over all of life.

The climax of Matthew's story of Jesus is his concluding commission to the disciples: "All authority in heaven and on earth has been given to me. Therefore go and make disciples of all nations, baptizing them in the name of the Father and of the Son and of the Holy Spirit, and teaching them to obey everything I have commanded you. And surely I am with you always, to the very end of the age" (Matt. 28:18–20). This has often been misinterpreted as a commission only to evangelize or travel to other lands to make known the gospel. Of course, evangelism and missions are important, but much more is at stake here. The disciples are themselves to make other disciples, to help form followers of Jesus in the same way that Jesus has formed them, disciples who will in turn obey everything Jesus has commanded.

In continuing the mission of Jesus, his disciples also take up the mission of Israel. The same missionary identity that formed Israel, a people who embody God's creational intention (Exod. 19:3–6), now becomes the identity of the New Testament church (1 Pet. 2:5–9). But the social circumstances of Old Testament Israel and of the New Testament church are radically different, and to understand this is important to establishing a biblical worldview. The church, unlike Israel, is launched into every nation and culture of humankind. God's people no longer take the shape of an independent and separate nation living under their own sociopolitical law and on their own land. They are now a community that must live in the midst of various nations and various other dominant cultures. The urgent question is how the church can live faithfully under the comprehensive authority of God's Word, embodying his all-encompassing renewal, and at the same time live within cultures in which other all-embracing worldviews and powers hold sway.

Kingdom and Church

Jesus announced the coming of a kingdom, but what actually emerges in history is the church. How are we to understand the relationship between these two?

Jesus announced the good news that the kingdom of God had arrived, that people could now repent, accept God's offer of redemption, and begin to experience the blessings of his reign. The church is made up of those who have responded in faith and repentance to Jesus' message and now taste the gifts and power of the kingdom. They have been taken up into God's kingdom purposes and placed on the side of Christ in the great cosmic battle for the creation.[17] Of the two, church and kingdom, the greater entity is the kingdom, for the church both functions within it and receives its identity and definition from it.

There are three major ways we can picture the relationship between the church and the kingdom of God: as (1) firstfruits, (2) instrument, and (3) sign. First, the church is the firstfruits of the kingdom (James 1:18), the place where God's reign has become visible in the present, where Christ's lordship is acknowledged and God's Spirit is already visibly at work. Second, the church is an instrument of the kingdom. In the mission of Jesus we see that the coming of the kingdom involves a battle against the spiritual forces that oppose God's reign. As the church takes up the mission of Jesus, it becomes an instrument of God to make his kingdom known, to preach the good news, and to challenge opposition to God's gracious rule. Third, the church is a sign of the kingdom. By embodying God's rule in their lives and in their work in the present, the members of the church together point toward the future coming of the kingdom in its fullness.

MISSION AS THE MEANING OF THE "ALREADY–NOT YET" ERA OF THE KINGDOM

The kingdom has not yet come. We live in that gap between the time when Jesus inaugurated the new creation (in his death and resurrection) and the time when he will return to finish what he has begun. The kingdom of God is already here by the work of the Spirit, but has not yet been completed. But why does this "already–not yet" gap exist?

> The meaning of this "overlap of the ages" in which we live, the time between the coming of Christ and his coming again, is that it is the time given for the witness of the apostolic Church to the ends of the earth. The end of all things, which has been revealed in Christ, is—so to say—held back until the witness has been borne to the whole world concerning the judgment and salvation revealed in Christ. The implication of a true eschatological perspective will be missionary obedience, and the eschatology which does not issue in such obedience is a false eschatology.[18]

Missionary obedience is what this "time between the times" is all about. The question is this: how are we to bear witness obediently to the coming of God's kingdom?

In the early twentieth century Dwight L. Moody saw the church's primary mission as one of rescuing souls from a shipwrecked creation: "I look at this world as a wrecked vessel. God has given me a lifeboat, and said to me, 'Moody, save all you can. God will come in judgement and burn up this world. . . . The world is getting darker and darker; its ruin is coming nearer and nearer. If you have any friends on this wreck unsaved, you had better lose no time in getting them off.'"[19] Moody's concern for evangelism and his sense of urgency are admirable. However, his understanding of mission "between the times" has been drastically diminished, even disfigured, by an unbiblical view in which salvation is individualistic and concerned with escape from this creation.

The church is, indeed, defined by an urgent call to mission: "'As the Father has sent me, so I send you' defines the very being of the Church as mission. In this sense everything that the Church is and does can be and should be part of mission."[20] Yet this mission is not narrowly "spiritual" or individualistic; it is all-embracing. Following Jesus, we are called to make known God's rule over all of human life, embodying it in our lives, demonstrating it in our actions, and announcing it with our words.

Because mission takes place during this period in the biblical story, which we have described as "already–not yet," it must involve an antithetical encounter with the powers of evil that continue to oppose the coming kingdom of God. At times, mission has been portrayed falsely as a victorious march ever onward to recover more and more territory (either geographical or cultural) in God's creation. Yet Jesus shows us that our kingdom mission will face formidable opposition: the parable of the weeds shows that opposition to God's kingdom does not diminish but rather intensifies as the "harvest" approaches (Matt. 13:24–30, 36–43). Like Jesus, the church is called to make known the all-embracing rule of God. We too will face opposition and rejection that may well mean suffering (John 15:18–25). Yet we can face this opposition with the calm assurance and joy that the victory of God's kingdom has been won on the cross and that victory will come. Ours is a witness to the victory of the kingdom that is coming.

The Bible does not give us a sense of how fully or how widely his reign will be known in the present age. There is no indication of how deeply the renewing power of the good news will penetrate society, culture, or the nonhuman creation before Christ returns. The church should never believe that it can build or usher in God's kingdom. But we can make something of God's kingdom visible in our lives, actions, and words. As David Bosch puts it, "We know that our mission will not usher in God's reign. Neither did Jesus' [mission]. He inaugurated it but did not bring it to its consummation. Like him, we are called to erect signs of God's ultimate reign—not more, but certainly not less either. . . . As we pray 'your kingdom come!' we also commit ourselves to initiate, here and now, approximations and anticipations of God's reign."[21] As God's people, we are a "good news" community that erects signs of God's present-and-yet-coming kingdom in our communal life, in our callings in the public life of culture, across the whole spectrum of our family and individual lives.

THE NEED FOR HEALTHY COMMUNITY AND VIBRANT SPIRITUALITY

The more one realizes the wide scope of the church's mission and the equally comprehensive scope and power of idolatry in the surrounding culture to oppose that mission, the more one must ask how the church can carry out this task responsibly. We believe that only if it is rooted in the gospel will the church be true to its mission. And this rootedness can happen only in healthy community and with a vibrant spirituality. We see both of these elements in Acts 2:42–47 in the church in Jerusalem, in which the believers are deeply committed to one another (as members of a community) and also to the Scriptures, prayer, fellowship, and the Lord's Supper. As persecution and difficulty assaulted the church, by these steadfast commitments they continued to support and nurture their mission (e.g., Acts 4:32–35).

A vibrant spirituality is essential to the church's mission. In the midst of Jesus' final preparation of his disciples for their mission in the world (John 14–17), he spoke to them of the absolute necessity of abiding in him if they were to bear fruit. Like branches of the vine, we receive the life-giving sap of Christ's life "through a million tiny channels hidden behind the hard bark of the trunk and branches."[22] By such means as adoring God, giving thanks to him, committing ourselves to following him, interceding on behalf of others, and reading and meditating on Scripture, we are equipped and sustained for our mission in the world. And all these means of receiving God's grace are meant to be experienced in communion with one another.

The Relationships among Creation, Sin, and Restoration

We have examined the major story line of the Bible—creation, sin, and restoration—and begun to see the relationships among these three: sin corrupts God's good creation, and God's salvation restores it. But not all in the church embrace this understanding.

NATURE AND GRACE

One way of unpacking the different understandings of creation, sin, and restoration among Christians is to look at how various traditions of the church have related "nature" (the human creation as it has been perverted by sin, discussed in our first chapter on biblical worldview) and "grace" (God's saving work, discussed in our second chapter). There are at least four ways in which orthodox Christians have understood the relationship of salvation to the fallen creation.[23]

(1) The first view is "grace against nature." Here, grace and nature are opposed to each other; the Christian withdraws from the evil world and seeks a salvation that is separate from it. (This view has been associated, often unfairly, with anabaptism, monasticism, and some strains in the early church.)

(2) The second view is "grace above nature." Here, grace is not hostile to nature but rather fulfills or completes it: grace is *super*-natural, above nature; nature is incomplete without it. Salvation offers completion by adding something to nature. (This view has been associated with Thomas Aquinas and some who follow him in the Roman Catholic tradition. It is prominent in Protestantism as well.)

(3) The third view is "grace alongside nature," in which nature has its own integrity and the Christian life simply exists side by side with life in God's creation. (This view is often held within some Lutheran and some North American evangelical traditions. Luther's "two kingdoms" is an example.)

(4) The final view is "grace infuses nature." Here, grace is seen as a healing power that infuses creation and heals and restores all of it from the sin that corrupts it. (This view often is associated with the Reformed tradition, but it has many adherents among evangelicals, Anabaptists, Roman Catholics, and others.)

These differing understandings of the relationship between nature and grace will lead to differing approaches to our kingdom mission in the midst of surrounding cultures. The first of these options (grace against nature) sees clearly the impact of sin's power but does not rightly see the continuing goodness of creation; nor does it see salvation as the restoration of all of God's good creation. This view may lead the church to withdraw as much as possible from culture. The second and third options (grace above or alongside nature) do not sufficiently recognize the twisting power of sin on the creation. Those who hold these views may not see the cultural mission of the church as a life-and-death battle. They may feel that the Christian is free to participate in scholarship, politics, economic life, and so forth in precisely the same way as his or her unbelieving neighbors do. There is little sense of tension or antithetical encounter between the Christian worldview and other worldviews.

The fourth view, in which grace is seen to infuse nature, is the one that we believe to be most closely aligned with the gospel. It is the view that we have elaborated in this chapter. In the next section we offer three illustrations of it.

CREATION, SIN, AND RESTORATION:
THREE LENSES OF A BIBLICAL WORLDVIEW

To look at the world through Scripture is, in fact, to look at the world through three lenses at the same time: as something created by God, twisted by sin, and being redeemed by the work of Christ. Remove any one of these lenses and the biblical worldview is distorted. This is like an LCD projector that requires three glass panels—red, yellow, green—through which the video signal passes. All are needed to give proper color. Remove one of those lenses, and the image is untrue. Remove any of the lenses of creation, sin, or restoration, and our view of the world is distorted. The following illustrations may serve to make this clearer.

(1) The good creation is like an earthly kingdom. It was ruled by God (its proper ruler) until a usurper (Satan, bringing sin) insinuated himself into this kingdom and was able to impose his own cruel regime there, corrupting it all and enslaving its inhabitants. But the original ruler began a long campaign to defeat the usurper and reclaim his kingdom. He waged war, and in a critical battle (climaxing at the cross) he won the war. Yet although the victory is sure, it is not yet complete. The usurper continues his fierce struggle. As kingdom citizens, we remain part of that battle, awaiting the certain completion.

(2) The good creation is like a healthy newborn child.[24] She is complete, in the sense that she is as she should be, but she also has potential, in that she is intended to become more than she was at the moment of her birth: she will grow, develop, and change. But then the child contracts a disease that does not destroy her outright but rather begins to corrupt and warp her development so that two different processes are at work in her at the same time. Her body is attempting to grow and develop naturally, but the disease within is also growing and developing. (This is a picture of how sin affects the creation: not killing outright or at once but rather corrupting, polluting, and distorting the creation as time goes on.) Now suppose a doctor were to find a cure and begin to treat that child. The doctor's remedy is meant not to destroy the child or make her something different than she had been but rather to destroy the disease so that she might again be healthy. That is the way God's healing work takes place. He does not destroy the creation, nor does he turn it into something different; the whole work of salvation is meant to remove the sin that has sickened the creation and to restore it (and us) to health.

(3) Finally, the distinction between "structure" and "direction" made by Wolters is quite helpful. The structure of creation is the original design of it as God made it. Sin, a spiritual power, misdirects every aspect of the creation away from its rightful Lord, its healthy functioning, and its intended goal.

God's work of renewal is, by his own spiritual power, to redirect that whole creation back to himself, to its healthy functioning, to its intended goal, and to its place in the creation order. Thus we can speak of the way that God designed language, sex, economic life, political authority, scholarship, sports, and so forth to function. All these have been adversely affected by the power of sin. All have been misdirected; none functions the way God intended. Yet God's reconciling work is aimed at countering this distorting power with a loving power: to redirect and renew all these things so that they may function as he had always intended for them.

THE DANGER OF DUALISM

Looking at the world through the lenses of creation, fall, and restoration in this way will keep us from a dualism, prominent in Western evangelical Christianity, whereby life is divided into "sacred" and "secular" realms (see figure 3). In such a dualistic view, prayer and worship, for example, might be considered sacred activities, while entertainment and sex would be seen as merely secular. A minister or missionary would be seen as "doing the Lord's work" (in the sacred realm), but a journalist or politician would be in a secular occupation. The church (and perhaps the family) would be sacred; the university and the business world would be secular. In a dualistic worldview, social institutions, work, and activities within the "sacred" realm are usually thought to be superior to those in the "secular" realm; thus, prayer is better than entertainment, a minister is better than a journalist, the church is better than the university.

Figure 3. Sacred/Secular Dichotomy

Sacred	Secular
Activities	
Prayer	Entertainment
Worship	Sex
Professions	
Minister	Journalist
Missionary	Politician
Social Spheres	
Church	University
Family	Business

But there are many problems with such a dualistic view of life. First of all, those activities, professions, and social spheres in the "secular" realm belong to God just as much as those in the "sacred" realm. Entertainment, sex, journalism, politics, scholarship, and business are all part of the "very good" of creation. God has ordered those dimensions of life just as he has the "sacred" ones. We are to serve God in all those areas of life, for the whole world and all of human activity belong to him.

Moreover, all the activities, professions, and social contacts in the "sacred" realm have also been twisted and distorted by sin. They cannot be considered good simply because they are "sacred." There is shoddy worship and selfish prayer, just as there are unfaithful ministers, lazy missionaries, and dysfunctional churches, and all need God's healing, redirecting, and redeeming touch.

God has created all things to find their proper place in his very good world. Whether "sacred" or "secular," every created thing has been soiled by sin, and each can be—and will be—purified and restored to conform to God's will.

Consummation: Restoration Complete

A Christian worldview must take account of the goal to which the biblical story is moving: is it toward a spiritual existence in heaven, or is it toward a restored bodily life on a new earth? The more common view among Western evangelicals, at least in the past, has been that the goal of redemptive history is for individual Christians to live in heaven forever. But we believe that the Bible shows the goal of God's redemptive work to be a renewed creation. This distinction has very important implications for a biblical worldview in general, and for the church's cultural mission in particular.[25]

The Kingdom of God as Restoration of Creation

David Lawrence rightly states, "The whole Bible leads us to expect a glorious renewal of life on earth, so that the age to come will be an endlessly thrilling adventure of living with God on the new earth. With his presence pervading every act, we shall be more fully human than we have ever been, liberated from sin, death, and all that hurts or harms."[26]

The kingdom of God will be restorative and comprehensive: all of human life and all of creation will be restored to serve the Lord as they were meant to do. This is the goal of the biblical story. Why is this so important for a biblical worldview? Again, Lawrence answers: "Seeing God's ultimate plan for us as being 'heavenly' and 'spiritual' has led us to imagine that spiritual things are God's chief concern. If a spiritual heaven is God's greatest good for us, then the earth and our physical existence on it must be somehow 'second best.'"[27] But, as we have seen, God loves his good creation and has never wavered from his plan to reclaim it for himself. It is not "second best," and to act as if it were would be not only to dishonor the Creator but also to distort our mission as his people in the in-between time.

We have seen that mission is the meaning of this time period between the first coming of Jesus and his return, and that mission is to be, to speak, and to do the good news. If redemption is, as the Bible teaches, the restoration of the whole of creation, then our mission is to embody this good news: every part of creational life, including the public life of our culture, is being restored. The good news will be evident in our care for the environment, in our approach to international relations, economic justice, business, media, scholarship, family, journalism, industry, and law. But if redemption were merely about an otherworldly salvation (as, for example, Moody believed), then our mission would be reduced to the sort of evangelism that tries to get people into heaven. Most of life would then fall outside the mission of the church. We would be forced to surrender most of God's creation to the evil powers that claim it for their own, and we would fail in our calling to proclaim that Christ is Creator and Lord of all.

Embodying Good News in Western Culture

Our place in the biblical story is to embody the good news that God is restoring the creation. This incarnational witness will always be contextual; it will take shape and form in a specific cultural context according to both the time and the place in which God puts us. And, since each cultural context will pose its own peculiar opportunities and dangers, our faithfulness requires that we know our own cultural context. In what particular cultural milieu are we called to make known that Jesus is Lord? Some answers to that question will occupy us in the next chapter.

5

The Western Story

The Roots of Modernity

At the center of the Christian faith is the confession that "the Word became flesh" (John 1:14). Jesus Christ, the fullest revelation of God and of his purposes for the creation, made known the good news of the kingdom in a particular historical and cultural context. Likewise, Jesus' followers are called to embody the good news in their own particular cultures, and those cultural contexts will always give a particular shape to Christian witness. Thus it is necessary for us to reflect on the story and worldview of that singular culture and time in which we find ourselves.

Since every human culture since Eden has been shaped at least in part by a vision of life that is incompatible with the Christian faith, it is important that we understand well our own Western cultural setting and the beliefs that have shaped it, as Lesslie Newbigin urges: "Incomparably the most urgent missionary task for the next few decades is the mission to 'modernity.' . . . It calls for the use of sharp intellectual tools, to probe behind the unquestioned assumptions of modernity and uncover the *hidden credo* which supports them."[1] The next three chapters are intended to help uncover the "hidden credo"—the worldview—undergirding Western culture.

We divide the story of Western culture into three phases. In this chapter we treat the roots of modernity in the classical period, in the gospel, and in the medieval blending of classical humanism and the gospel. In the next chapter we narrate the development of the modern worldview from its "rebirth" in the Renaissance through the twentieth century. And, finally, we ask this question: What are the currents shaping the West today?

A Humanist Credo: "Must We Ourselves Not Become Gods?"

The term *humanism* has a wide variety of meanings, and in its best sense it merely acknowledges the dignity of human beings and the necessity of working to improve the human condition. However, here we speak of *confessional humanism* as the spiritual center of Western culture: a belief system in which human beings have replaced God as Creator, Ruler, and Savior.

Over a century ago the German philosopher Friedrich Nietzsche (1844–1900) told a chilling parable of a madman who makes the startling accusation that we have killed God: "*We have killed him*—you and I. All of us are his murderers.*" (Nietzsche was alluding to the eighteenth-century Enlightenment, which we will examine in the next chapter, when Western culture excluded God from public life.) "How shall we comfort ourselves, the murderers of all murderers?" the madman asks. "Must *we ourselves not become gods* simply to appear worthy of it?"[2]

The madman speaks rightly here, for if there is no God, then there is no Creator to give the meaning of human life, to order the creation and give universal standards of right and wrong. If God is indeed dead, then it is up to human beings to take up the role of the Creator: they must define life's purposes; they must construct order; they must decide what is right, true, and good. In addition, if there is no God, there is no sovereign Ruler to guide history toward its goal, to give it meaning. Humanity, it seems, must take up this task as well. And finally, if there is no God, and thus no Savior to liberate our world from evil, then it is humanity's task to save itself. As *Humanist Manifesto I* puts it, "Man . . . alone is responsible for the realization of the world of his dreams, [and] has within himself the power for its achievement."[3] Corliss Lamont confirms this when he says that humanism "assigns to us nothing less than the task of being our own savior and redeemer."[4]

We might refer to the confessional humanism that shapes our Western culture as *secular*, from the Latin *saeculum*, which simply refers to this time-and-space world. The word *secular* can, however, be used to imply the belief that this world has been severed from God. In such a view, whether or not God exists, he has no continuing relationship with this world. Humanism may also be described as *naturalistic*, espousing the belief that this world is all there is.[5] And finally, confessional humanism may be described as *rationalistic*, or committed to the belief that human reason will enable humankind to fulfill the daunting role of playing god. The rationalist believes that human reason (particularly when it is guided by the scientific method) is capable of understanding the laws of both the nonhuman creation and human society, giving humans the power to control creation and subdue it for their own purposes. And, since the scientific method plays such an important role here, we might also describe confessional humanism as *scientific*—founded on the beliefs that (with the help of the natural sciences and technology) reason can conquer the nonhuman creation, and that (with the help of the social sciences) reason can manage and organize all of human culture, including economics, politics, education, and law. The humanist believes that if we faithfully follow this path, trusting in our reason and in science, we may be assured of progress toward a world of happiness, freedom, material prosperity, truth, and justice.[6]

Confessional humanism—secular, naturalistic, rationalistic, scientific—has also been called by other names, including "the Enlightenment worldview," "the modern worldview," or simply "modernity." To speak of this worldview as "modern" is to distinguish it from older worldviews that are supposedly "religious" or "mythical" or "superstitious." This, of course, implies the value judgment that human beings have in our own day at last become mature, leaving behind their outmoded and childish "religious" views of the world. The term *Enlightenment* simply refers to the historical period (the eighteenth century) in which this form of humanism came to maturity and became the dominant worldview within secular Western culture.

Such a worldview entails a very real faith commitment, and it has been a formative power in Western culture for several centuries. It developed over a long history in Europe, was transported to European colonies such as those in North America, and continues to be spread around the world today in the process of globalization. It is also under attack at many points from the new humanist spirit labeled *postmodernism*. The Enlightenment vision of life stands in many ways against the worldview of Christians who seek to bear witness to Christ's all-embracing authority. It may even be "a much deadlier foe than any previous counter-religious forces in human history."[7] Therefore it is important that the Christian community understand it well.

The Christian Story and the Historical Development of Modernity

Modernity, or confessional humanism, has, ironically, been shaped in large part by the Christian story. Michael Polanyi has said that the explosion of modernity in Western culture in the last two centuries is the result of the ignition of the flame of classical humanism in the oxygen of the gospel.[8] Cultural historian Christopher Dawson observes that it was "the accumulated resources of the Christian past" that gave spiritual impetus and form to humanism.[9]

The development of modernity is a long history of interaction between the Christian and the classical humanist worldviews. Classical humanism had its roots in pagan Greek culture, and Jesus himself was born into a world saturated with this vision of life. He offered in the gospel an alternative comprehensive view of the world. But, since the gospel always tends to take on cultural form, the early church embodied and expressed the Christian faith in the cultural idioms and forms of classical humanism. Thus began the long relationship and interaction of two all-embracing, and often opposing, visions of life: Christianity and classical humanism.

Each of these worldviews was forced to make concessions to the other in order to form a relatively stable synthesis throughout the so-called Middle Ages (up to the thirteenth century). In this synthesis, though the gospel was compromised to some degree, it also saturated and shaped the humanist worldview that began to emerge in the Renaissance (fourteenth and fifteenth centuries). The Reformation (sixteenth century) gave new impetus to this shaping process as it served to rediscover some aspects of the gospel that had been neglected. But paradoxically, the Reformation also served at various points to reinforce the humanist vision of life. The Scientific Revolution (sixteenth and seventeenth centuries) developed under intertwined Christian and humanist worldviews. Yet as that period drew to a close, the humanist strand was becoming dominant, and this gave birth to the Enlightenment (eighteenth century). From this point on, the humanist worldview increasingly distanced itself from the Christian worldview until, as Nietzsche said, it seemed that Western humanity had "killed" God. The confessional humanist worldview, still profiting from its long contact with the gospel, was given social and cultural embodiment in the industrial, social, and political revolutions of the nineteenth and twentieth centuries. Today, although confessional humanism (or "modernity") is under attack in "postmodernity," it remains a formidable force that continues to shape our global world.

How Do We Tell the Story?

An African proverb says, "Until lions have their own historians, the hunter will always be the hero of the story." The way the history of the West has normally been told is not neutral, for its "hero" is the basic beliefs of confessional humanism. Consider the following common historical labels for four periods of Western history: *classical* (sixth century BC through fifth century AD), *medieval* (fifth through fifteenth centuries), *modern* (fifteenth century to present), and *postmodern* (late twentieth and early twenty-first centuries). These labels are not neutral: they make value judgments, assessing the merit of each historical period. The word *classical* is a positive one, referring to something that has recognized worth or which represents an exemplary standard (think of, e.g., "classical music" or "Coke Classic"). The word *modern* also is a positive one, describing what is up-to-date, not old-fashioned, obsolete, or antiquated (after all, no one wants to be obsolete!). The word *medieval* is much more ambiguous: the first definition given by the *Oxford English Dictionary* indicates a time period, "related to the Middle Ages," but its second definition is "very old-fashioned or outdated." How is it that a time period over two thousand years ago (the classical period) has recognized value, but an era that ended less than six hundred years ago (the medieval period) is, though much nearer to us in time, thought to be outdated? Surely it is the emergence of humanism among the (classical) Greeks that has led scholars to think of their (pre-Christian) historical period as somehow exemplary for our own day. And it is the suppression of this humanism by the churched culture of the Middle Ages that has given the word *medieval* its negative connotations.

As we consider the historical development of the two great competing worldviews in the West—Christianity and confessional humanism—we want to offer a different set of labels for history, labels inspired by the work of Dirk Vollenhoven, a Christian historian of philosophy.[10] Vollenhoven's designations quite deliberately cast the gospel in the role of "the hero of the story." Thus we will refer to the Greco-Roman (classical) period as *pagan*, not to imply that theirs was a backward culture but rather simply to remind ourselves that it developed apart from the light of the gospel. The medieval period we will identify as the period of *synthesis*, since it was characterized by a compromise, fusion, or amalgamation of the two comprehensive worldviews. The modern period we will describe as *antithetical* in order to highlight the growing hostility between the humanistic and Christian worldviews after the Middle Ages. What many refer to as the "postmodern" period could be labeled *neo-pagan*.[11] Whereas *pagan* refers to a culture that never had the light of the gospel, *neo-pagan* designates a culture born of rejection of the gospel.

Modernity, the dominant worldview of our Western culture, did not one day simply drop out of the sky; it is the product of a long history. We will now attempt to briefly trace the historical developments that gave form to the fundamental beliefs at the foundation of Western culture, to try to tell the story that Western people live by.[12]

The Roots of Western Worldview I: Greco-Roman Paganism
(Sixth Century BC through Fifth Century AD)

The origins of modernity, or confessional humanism, perhaps may be traced back to the views of three Greeks—Thales, Anaximander, and Anaximenes—who lived in the early sixth century BC in the Ionian city of Miletus. These men believed that the world could best be understood not through myth or religion (as had been the rule among the Greeks and all ancient peoples) but rather by discerning and then explaining a rational order in the world through close observation and reason alone. For example, Thales (636–546 BC) suggested that earthquakes were not caused by Poseidon (the god of the sea) but rather came about when the earth experienced the turbulence of the water on which it floated. Anaximenes (585–525 BC) proposed that rainbows were not manifestations of the goddess Iris but rather were the consequence of the sun's rays falling on dense air.

Others followed, attempting to explain the order of the world without recourse to myth or divine authority. The earlier mythical worldview was displaced by a "growing reliance on independent reason. . . . Rationalism permeated the whole social and cultural development" of Greece, as architecture, art, politics, medicine, history, astronomy, ethics, and scholarship increasingly came to be ordered by this growing confidence in unaided human reason.[13]

The pagan Greek worldview finds its most comprehensive and systematic philosophical expression in Plato (427–348 BC) and his student Aristotle (384–322 BC). The driving concern of both of these men was to find unchanging order and truth that would transcend the changes in human culture. Their pursuit was not just theoretical speculation. They believed that finding universal truth was essential to provide order for the flourishing of individual and social human life. For example, Plato's work *The Republic* attempts to discern justice and how it might shape Athens' way of life; Aristotle's concern in *Politics* is to shape the Greek city-state. Since neither man had access to the Scriptures, they did not understand that God had given a good created order that could be discerned by the fear of God. So they sought truth in an unchanging rational order that could be discerned by reason. However, they differed on the nature of this cosmic order and on how reason could discern its truth—differences that would have a profound effect on the later Western worldview. The basic difference is illustrated in Raphael's painting *The School of Athens* (1510–1511) (see figure 4).

On the left is the entire painting; on the right is a detail of Plato and Aristotle from the center of the painting. Note the older Plato on the left: his

Plato and Aristotle

Figure 4. Raphael's *School of Athens*

hand points skyward, indicating that truth is to be found in a transcendent world of ideas. In contrast, Aristotle holds his right hand over the ground, signifying that truth lies in the observation of an unchanging order within this material world.

For Plato, the world was comprised of two realms, the visible (or material) and the invisible (or spiritual). In the visible, material world we find individual, particular things, such as chairs, marriages, and acts of justice. In the invisible, spiritual world (toward which Plato gestures in the painting) we find universal ideals or ideas of a chair, marriage, or justice. The individual particulars may participate in these universal ideas, but it is the ideals themselves that give us the unchanging order for the world. By the exercise of reason, humankind can gain access to these unchanging ideals in order to shape knowledge and ethical and social life. Along with this dualistic view of the world, Plato held a correspondingly dualistic view of the human person. He distinguished between a material body and a rational soul: at death, the body would expire, but the soul would eventually return to the invisible world, to the higher realm of universal ideas and the source of order. Thus Plato's orientation was always upward, toward the spiritual realm, and the only way to be in touch with the spiritual realm that provided unchanging order was through reason. For Plato, both the material world and the body were evil impediments to true spiritual and rational life.

In Raphael's painting, Aristotle gestures toward the ground on which he stands; for Aristotle, reason discovers truth by observing unchanging ideas in the world. One examines individual, particular things (again, such as chairs, marriages, and acts of justice) in order to determine what is universal in all of them. To do this, Aristotle forged a whole workshop full of analytical tools that remain important in Western thought to the present day.[14] It was in Aristotle's philosophy that the Greek worldview, with its profound "confidence in the power of human thought to comprehend the world rationally," achieved its "fullest expression and climax."[15]

The pagan worldview would continue to evolve through the periods of the Greek and then the Roman Empires. About five hundred years after Aristotle, Plotinus (AD 205–270) revived Plato's ideas and developed their religious form in neo-Platonism. The Roman Empire was by this time in decline, exhibiting internal unrest and serious social and economic weakness. Citizens of the declining empire sought security and salvation and an escape from the world; many mystery religions arose to meet these needs. Plotinus developed and strengthened four tenets of Plato's thought:

- there is a basic division between a good spiritual world and an evil material world;
- human beings are made up of an inferior material body and a superior rational soul;
- bodily life in this material world is inferior to spiritual life;
- human life has an otherworldly, spiritual orientation.

For Plotinus, salvation was the soul's release from its bodily prison, allowing it to ascend to a superior, invisible, spiritual realm. These emphases in Plotinus's thought came to influence medieval culture deeply as the Christian worldview assimilated his neo-Platonism.

The Roots of Western Worldview II: The Gospel

Into the Roman Empire of the first century, shaped as it was by the humanism, rationalism, secularism, and naturalism of the pagan Greek worldview, stepped Jesus of Nazareth. His message was rooted in the Hebrew Scriptures, which told the story of history that would climax in the coming of God's kingdom. Jesus announced that the kingdom of God had arrived—a message of staggering significance and proportions, and most certainly not one that could be accommodated neatly to the prevailing worldview. Jesus declared that the whole meaning and purpose of human history and life, indeed the purpose of the whole cosmos, were being revealed in his own person and work. Thus the gospel offered a comprehensive view of the world, and of the place of human beings in it, that conflicted radically with the dominant cultural worldview of classical humanism.

The gospel gave rise to a community that believed it to be true and therefore followed Jesus. The early Christians refused to be known as adherents of a merely private religion, one that offered spiritual, individual, future, and otherworldly salvation. Instead, the church declared itself to be a public community that offered truth to everyone: the true meaning of the world, of history, and of human life.

Since both the gospel and the classical humanism of Rome were comprehensive worldviews, a clash was inevitable. The early Christian community could have denied the comprehensive scope of the gospel and accommodated it to the dominant cultural worldview. But they refused to do so: they would not relegate the Christian faith to some private realm of spirituality with no bearing on the public life of the Roman Empire. By confessing that Jesus, not Caesar, was Lord, and by making it clear that they were a public assembly and not a private cult, they challenged the pagan way of viewing the world, offering their own, alternate vision. And for this boldness in witness, the church earned Rome's anger and suffered persecution.

The gospel is a comprehensive vision of life, but it is also adaptable or translatable into all cultures. It does not stand simply as a self-contained alternative to the prevailing cultural worldview. The very nature of the gospel is incarnational: this allows, indeed requires, that the gospel take on various cultural forms but without surrendering its comprehensive demands. It was not meant to remain merely Jewish; it was to find a home in each culture into which it moved. The gospel affirms the genuine insights of any culture, including those of the pagan classical culture into which it was first introduced.

Yet there is always a danger that when the gospel takes cultural form, it will be contaminated by the idolatry of the surrounding culture. In fact, while we wait for the revelation of God's final kingdom, our struggle with cultural idolatry will always be only more or less successful. We might call those attempts at embodying the gospel faithfully and rejecting idolatry "faithful contextualizations" of the gospel, as opposed to "unfaithful compromises" between the gospel and the idolatry of the prevailing culture. But it is important to acknowledge that all contextualizations of the gospel will fall somewhere between these poles. Thus, in the early years of the church there is evidence of both unfaithful compromise and faithful contextualization as the gospel penetrated a world committed to pagan humanism. And in the historical development that followed in the Middle Ages there is evidence both of the powerful influence of Christianity on European culture[16] and of unfaithful accommodation of the Christian faith to the humanistic worldview inherited from Greece and Rome. We turn now to the synthesis of these two visions of life as it developed in that period.

Early Medieval Synthesis: The Gospel and Neo-Platonism (Fifth through Tenth Centuries)

For the first three hundred years of the church's life, the cultural milieu of the Roman Empire was hostile to the Christian faith. When the emperor Constantine became a Christian and legalized Christianity (AD 311), and then as emperor Theodosius made Christianity the only religion of the empire (AD 380), the church moved from the margins to the center. This would have the positive effect of enabling the church to bring the gospel to bear on public life, but it would also have the negative effect of causing the church to surrender much of its antithetical stance. Thus the church became increasingly vulnerable to the idolatry of the empire.

The man whose thought would provide the framework for medieval culture was Augustine of Hippo (AD 354–430), whose book *The City of God* was to shape the thinking of generations over the next millennium. Augustine struggled to contextualize the gospel faithfully as it became clothed with ideas inherited from Greek culture. But even within Augustine himself, there was evidence of a tension between conflicting worldviews: prior to his conversion he had been a neo-Platonic philosopher, and he was converted under the influence of the neo-Platonic bishop Ambrose.[17] Thus there is disagreement among scholars concerning how faithful to a biblical worldview Augustine actually managed to be in his contextualizing of the gospel. Certainly Augustine challenged the paganism of neo-Platonism at many points: he affirmed the goodness of creation (over against the neo-Platonist's rejection of it as evil); he understood sin as religious rebellion (and not as ingrained in the materiality of creation); he understood, at least to some degree, that redemption must involve the restoration of human life (as opposed to being merely a flight to a spiritual world).

However, something of the neo-Platonic spirit lives on in Augustine's synthesis, and this was to have negative consequences for the development of Western culture. *The City of God*, for example, appears to combine elements of Scripture and neo-Platonism. While much of his discussion sounds as if the goal of history is a restored creation, other parts betray his neo-Platonism, by which the goal of the people of God is to ascend from the earthly realm to the heavenly. Richard Tarnas perhaps overstates the case as far as Augustine's own beliefs are concerned, but he does illustrate how Augustine's ideas were understood and lived out by many who followed him in medieval Europe: "Escape from this world to the next, from self to God, from flesh to spirit, constituted the deepest purpose and direction of human life. . . . In Augustine's vision . . . the transcendent spiritual realm was the only realm that genuinely mattered."[18] This vertical orientation would impress itself deeply on the medieval imagination: human life increasingly was directed toward the "spiritual" realm.

Perhaps the medieval cathedral best expresses this orientation. Upon entering, one's eyes are inevitably drawn heavenward; this might be understood as an encouragement to respond faithfully to God, a reminder that cultural life is God-ordained and ought always to be directed toward God's glory. And sometimes this is what it did mean, especially to many monks. But this is not always how the meaning of a cathedral was perceived. Too often it was felt to be teaching that life in this world is not a worthy focus of human effort, that it has no significance in and of itself, and that one must look upward to find meaning and value. Thus life in this world tended to be depreciated, since cultural and social life needed to be lifted heavenward in order to be sanctified. This was accomplished as the church (the institution that most clearly belonged to the "spiritual" realm) mediated grace to consecrate various cultural endeavors. In this way the church took a unifying and integrating role in medieval culture, directing many cultural tasks in education, science, art, business, and even politics.

There is no doubt that some good things did come out of the churched culture of the Middle Ages. The light of Scripture certainly was brought into focus on public life. European culture was infused with the gospel, and this brought benefits that have continued right up to the present. But the price of the church's cultural dominance was an unbiblical and unwholesome depreciation of life in this world. The medieval orientation toward heaven thus has both Christian and pagan elements. The pagan neo-Platonic element produced an otherworldly and vertical orientation that undermined authentic Christian living, yet Christian influence in the medieval period shaped that culture in ways that would impart many benefits to succeeding generations.

Late Medieval Synthesis: Platonized Christianity and Aristotle (Eleventh through Thirteenth Centuries)

From the eleventh century to the thirteenth century, cultural activity increased in Europe, social life developed along vertical lines, and technology advanced markedly. The vertical and world-denying element in the worldview of the early Middle Ages was challenged by a growing interest in this world. This challenge heightened when in the twelfth century a number of Aristotle's writings were rediscovered and translated into Latin and made their way into the mainstream of European culture through the newly formed universities. This precipitated a crisis in European society. The otherworldly orientation of Platonized Christianity, which supposedly had been divinely sanctioned by Scripture and expressed in the theological and political shape of medieval society, was now threatened by the this-worldly emphasis of Aristotle.[19] Initially a council of bishops in Paris banned Aristotle's writings under the threat of excommunication, but the genie was already out of the bottle—the more secular and naturalistic spirit of Aristotle quickly gained momentum in medieval society.[20] It is in this context that we must understand the Herculean attempt by Thomas Aquinas (1225–1274) to forge a finely tuned synthesis that would both honor the vertical orientation of the Christian life as it had been shaped in the Middle Ages and give due emphasis to life and empirical reason in this world.

Aquinas was committed to the authority of the Bible while also seeking a place for Aristotle within his faith. His motivation was thoroughly Christian. He believed that the creation was good, beautiful, and orderly, that cultural life had a God-given place, and that empirical reason was an element of God's image enabling humanity to examine the lawfulness of creation. These aspects of the biblical testimony had been suppressed for centuries, and now, as they emerged in the late Middle Ages, Aquinas attempted, along Aristotelian lines, to justify them. This was not necessarily bad; as we have insisted, the gospel must always take cultural shape. But the danger was that the idolatry of Aristotle would be ingested along with his insight. Thomas synthesized biblical faith, Platonized Christianity, and Aristotle in a system of thought that continues to exercise remarkable influence to the present day.

The synthesis by Thomas Aquinas is complex, but the main lines can be described as follows. The dualistic world structure of the early Middle Ages was maintained, with its lower storey of nature and its upper (supernatural) storey of grace. Thomas maintained the concept of the superiority of the upper world, holding that human life should be oriented upward, toward God. However, Thomas affirmed the goodness of our present world, of the body, of social and cultural life, and of empirical reason as they had rarely been affirmed in preceding centuries. Nevertheless, he subordinated them to the soul, the church, faith, revealed truth, the uniqueness of the Christian life, and theology (see figure 5). Cultural life is, in Aquinas's philosophical system, not yet free to develop as God intended.

Figure 5. Two Storeys of Thomas Aquinas

Spiritual realm	Eternal	GRACE	Supernatural	Superior
Soul Church	Christian life	Faith	Revelation	Theology
Material realm	Temporal	NATURE	Natural	Inferior
Body Society	Cultural life	Empirical reason	Natural law	Science

Aquinas finds a place for Aristotelian reason in the lower storey. In his view, philosophical or scientific knowledge of the realm of nature is possible as empirical reason examines the natural laws of creation. There is an important movement of thought here that was to have far-reaching significance in the modern world. Before Aquinas, reason had been firmly subordinated to faith; in the post-Augustinian world reason was understood as formally correct thinking used in service of the defense and explication of the Christian faith. In other words, reason became primarily an instrument for theology.

With Aquinas, reason remains subordinated to faith, but a new definition of reason is introduced: for Aquinas, reason is empirical, oriented to the examination and observation of natural and social laws in this world. This new definition would lead to a growing interest in the natural world and to increased confidence in the power of reason to understand it. The seeds of modern science are found here.

The difficulty in building a two-storey structure is in keeping it together, and, as Hans Küng observes, "the Christian mediaeval synthesis presented by Thomas is one of extreme tension, and in the dynamic of historical development had effects which were to prove self-destructive: there was to be an unprecedented and all-embracing *movement of secularization and emancipation* 'at the lower level.'"[21] Aquinas did not give autonomy to the lower realm of "nature"—he was too committed to the biblical worldview for that. Indeed, for Thomas, grace permeated and perfected nature; furthermore, God upheld and ruled the creation. But the separation of the two storeys would take place in the centuries that followed: the theologians John Duns Scotus (1266–1308) and, to an even greater extent, William of Ockham (1285–1349) separated the upper storey from the lower, unable to maintain the biblical emphases and finely tuned synthesis of Aquinas.

In the ensuing centuries the lower storey of the natural world, cultural life, and reason would increasingly be disengaged from the upper. In effect, most of human life would be severed from the authority of God and the power of the gospel. Reason was divorced from faith, a self-sufficient nature was divorced from the upholding Word of God, and human society was divorced from God's normative ordering word. Each and all of these disastrous separations would have appalled the deeply Christian Aquinas. In these divisions lay the seeds of the secularism that was soon to blossom in the history of the West. Brian Walsh and Richard Middleton note how this process gained momentum during the Renaissance: "While scholastic theologians [had] granted a limited degree of autonomy to the realm of our natural life (and natural reason), the Renaissance humanists so greatly expanded the autonomy of nature that there was no longer any need for the realm of grace. If God and Christianity were already basically irrelevant to most of life, why not make their irrelevance complete?"[22] And indeed, over the course of the next five centuries God and the gospel were increasingly excluded from the natural and cultural life of the West. The secularism that we know today finds its source in the ideas of the scholastic theologians of the late Middle Ages.

We have been critical here of the way Christianity was compromised by its fusion with Greek humanism, and so we should also note the positive impact of the gospel on the West that began in this historical era. Newbigin describes the medieval period as "the first great attempt to translate the universal claim of Christ into political terms."[23] While recognizing the damage done by the settlement between Christianity and pagan culture, Newbigin also believes that, as a result of that one-thousand-year synthesis, "the Gospel was wrought into the very stuff of [Western Europe's] social and personal life."[24] Newbigin's missionary experience in a culture dominated by Hinduism enabled him to see that Western culture has been positively shaped by the gospel and "that we still live largely on the spiritual capital which it generated."[25]

However, the synthesis between the gospel and classical humanism was about to gradually come apart and a more antithetical relationship between them to emerge. To this we turn in the next stage of our story.

6

The Western Story

The Growth of Modernity

Two words that have become commonplace in our telling of the Western story give us a clue to what takes place over the next five or six centuries. The word *Renaissance* indicates that we believe something has been "born again." The word *Enlightenment* implies that the "light of the world" has arrived. Indeed, these words are profoundly religious.[1] In themselves, they tell a story: the humanism of classical-pagan culture was reborn and grew until it became the world's true light. In this chapter we trace that story.

The Renaissance: Humanism Is "Born Again" (Fifteenth and Sixteenth Centuries)

Whereas medieval historians thought of history as divided into two eras—before Christ and after Christ—in the Renaissance a new, threefold structure began to emerge in which history was divided into ancient, medieval, and modern periods.[2] This is evidence that a revolution of consciousness was gripping the minds of these writers, causing them to see their time as a radically new "modern" era, deserving of its own title to differentiate it from what had gone before. Yet it is clear that most of Europe was still very much rooted in the Middle Ages. Indeed, it was not until the late nineteenth century that the

Renaissance began to be distinguished as a historical period distinct from the Middle Ages.[3] But it is clear that, somewhere between the fourteenth and seventeenth centuries, the religious foundations of Europe shifted.

During the medieval period the dominant worldview of Platonized Christianity had narrowed the field of academic disciplines to metaphysics, law, theology, and logic. The otherworldly orientation inherited from neo-Platonism had placed limits on scientific and technological development and had restricted the scope of most art to religious themes. The totalitarian authority of the church curtailed human freedom, and a static and hierarchical social structure hindered development. But beginning in the fourteenth and fifteenth centuries there was a rebirth of classical scholarship and a renewed interest in the humanities—literature, poetry, history, and languages. There was a revived interest in the present world, as evidenced by scientific examination, technological inventions, and a turn toward natural themes in the arts. The worth of the individual and of knowledge of this world was reaffirmed, in part perhaps in rebellion against the overweening authority of the medieval church and its otherworldly neo-Platonism.

Much of this development the Christian can affirm, in that it moved culture away from some of the pagan elements that had been retained in the medieval synthesis. Yet in northern Italy a radical and anti-Christian form of humanism arose among people such as Pico della Mirandola, Ficino, and Bocaccio. We might describe this as the beginnings of secular humanism—a humanism that ultimately rejects the authority of God over human and natural life. This is not to say that these men rejected the Christian faith; their writings remain suffused with Christian language and themes. Nevertheless, the orientation of their thought was increasingly opposed to a biblical worldview.

We can note four dimensions of Renaissance secular humanism:

(1) There was a renewed interest in the present world. John Dewey speaks of a shift in focus "from another world to this, from the supernaturalism characteristic of the Middle Ages to delight in natural science, natural activity, and natural intercourse."[4] Thomas Aquinas's two storeys were coming apart: the natural world—the *saeculum*—was becoming separated from the realm of grace, and it was also becoming the principal focus of scholarly interest. In itself, this renewed delight in God's good creation was undoubtedly a healthy development, but increasingly it would come at the cost of diminishing or even denying God's involvement and authority in this world.

(2) This renewed emphasis on the secular realm encouraged in many people a sense that humankind is autonomous.[5] In the biblical story human beings find their nature prescribed for them in the way God created them, and their whole lives are lived under the authority of God's word. Secular humanism

defined human life apart from God, bearing "the law of its existence within itself."[6] Human freedom was conceived of as freedom from God's authority. Here, for example, is an excerpt from Pico della Mirandola's *Oration on the Dignity of Man* (1486), in which God is imagined as speaking to humanity at the creation:

> The nature of other creatures, which has been determined, is confined within the bounds prescribed by Us. You, who are confined by no limits, shall determine for yourself your own nature, in accordance with your own free will, in whose hand I have placed you. I have set you at the center of the world, so that from there you may more easily survey whatever is in the world. We have made you neither heavenly nor earthly, neither mortal nor immortal, so that, more freely and more honourably the molder and maker of yourself, you may fashion yourself in whatever form you prefer.[7]

Although Pico is a Christian, his language clearly betrays an unbiblical sense of human autonomy.

(3) According to the secular humanist view, the nonhuman world has its own autonomy from God. Not only humankind, but the whole of Aquinas's lower storey, once it is considered to be separated from the upper, loses its intimate connection with the Creator. "The world lost its character of 'creation' and became 'nature.'. . . In seeing the world as nature, [the humanist] takes it out of God's hand and makes it independent."[8] Nature, separated from God's ordering word, is now conceived of as being ordered by built-in laws. The regularity observable in the natural world is no longer seen as its ordinate response to God's Word (cf. Ps. 147:15) but rather as the necessary condition of its own mechanical structure. The cosmos increasingly is considered to be only an elaborate and intricate machine operating automatically, independently, without need of any further involvement of its designer and maker.

(4) As a corollary of the first three points, it was inevitable that humanity would set itself the task of becoming the master over nature. Of the three fundamental human relationships—with God, with each other, and with the nonhuman creation—the relationship with God had dominated during the medieval period, while humanity's relationships with one another and especially with the nonhuman creation had been undervalued. But in the Renaissance, increasingly, human

> destiny is realized primarily in his relation to the natural things of this world. . . . The centrality of the relationship of man with nature . . . is one of the most characteristic features of western culture since the Renaissance. . . . We distinguish ourselves as human beings primarily by the shape we give to this world

through human thought and creative activity rather than by the meaning of our lives to other persons.[9]

A culture is shaped by the collective religious understanding that a people have of the purpose and meaning of their lives. A desire to control and to dominate the nonhuman creation for human social purposes was to evolve from this seed, beginning in the Renaissance. Guardini explains, "Man himself who before this had been the adorer and servant, now became the 'creator.' All this is expressed in the word 'culture.' In this word also there lies the claim to autonomy. Man grasps existence in order to shape it according to his own will."[10]

The budding secular humanism of the Renaissance does not arrive brand new on the stage of human history. A secular spirit did not simply replace a religious spirit; the demand for human freedom did not suddenly supplant acceptance of church authority; an orientation toward this world did not suddenly displace an orientation toward God. The seeds of a modernist worldview appeared first among a few thinkers in northern Italy, and both the thinkers and their thoughts remained for a long while still in Christian clothing. It is because those seeds began to grow and to shed their Christian expression that (looking back on this period of history) we speak of the Renaissance at all. Ronald Wells is correct: "In another context, shorn of its religious casing, a new pattern of human assertiveness *will* (necessarily) issue in a secular worldview. But in the Renaissance we do not have that final break. Though the potential for it is definitely there, and will come in time, it does not happen in the fourteenth to sixteenth centuries."[11] Thus the humanism "born again" in the fourteenth century was not to claim the status of "the light of the world" until the eighteenth century.

The Reformation: "Salting" and Secularizing (Sixteenth Century)

"Once upon a time a pair of fair-haired twins named Renaissance and Reformation, persecuted and abused, turned against their wicked doddering stepmother, the Catholic Church of the Middle Ages." So begins Crane Brinton's tongue-in-cheek fairy tale, caricaturing the version of the Western story that simply subsumes the Reformation into the overarching tale of the rise of secular humanism. The Reformation and the Renaissance were spiritual "twins" in that both sought to be freed from the restraints laid upon them by the church in the Middle Ages.[12] Although this popular telling of the story is simplistic and one-sided, Brinton notes that it is not wholly mistaken, for there is a sense in which authority can be equated with the spirit of the Middle Ages, and liberty with that of the Reformation and the Renaissance. But there is another way of telling the same story, in which the two spiritual forces—Christian and humanist—that struggle for dominance in Western culture find their local roots in the Reformation and the Renaissance respectively.

Although there is some truth in both of these stories, either one by itself can be misleading. The Renaissance was not simply humanist, for much of its framework remained Christian. And the Reformation too shows a mixture of elements. It did serve to recover much of the Christian worldview, and perhaps this is its primary spirit. But at the same time, the Reformation also accelerated the secularizing trend in modernity.

To deal with the positive elements of the Reformation first, we must acknowledge it to have been a thoroughly Christian renewal, recovering many dimensions of the gospel that had become obscured. The Reformers reaffirmed the goodness of creation. Reacting against the dualism that had placed monks and priests on a higher, "sacred" plane, the Reformers Martin Luther (1483–1546) and John Calvin (1509–1564) insisted that in all cultural callings we serve God by serving our neighbors. Thus, Luther imagines that Mary, immediately after her visit by the angel Gabriel (Luke 1:26–38), simply returns to her household duties—milking, cooking, washing, and sweeping. In other words, even after the annunciation, Mary returns to her God-given calling as a maidservant. For Luther, every human responsibility is a sacred vocation—and equally sacred, whether one is called to bear the Christ child or to put supper on the table. The Reformers also insisted on the scope and depth of sin, a concept that they believed had been neglected in the euphoric reemergence of humanism. Furthermore, the Reformers taught (though not always consistently) that salvation was the renewal of human creational life. These and many other significant elements of the gospel were rediscovered and diffused through Western culture as a result of the Reformation. Richard Tarnas notes that although secularism triumphed in the nineteenth century, numerous benefits of the Christian worldview continued to shape Western culture, including Christian ethical values, a high estimation of reason, and a sense of the intelligibility of the world, of the human calling to exercise dominion, of humanity's intrinsic dignity and inalienable rights, of the moral responsibility of the individual, and of the imperative to care for the helpless and less fortunate, in addition to an orientation toward the future and belief in historical progress, and more.[13]

There is, nevertheless, another side to the Reformation: it also served to accelerate the secularizing process at work in Western culture. Sometimes this came about because the Reformers were not sufficiently critical of the humanism of their day. But quite often the secularizing influence was unintentional;

indeed, sometimes it was directly contrary to the Reformers' concerns. The powerful stream of humanism in the West would take up the Reformation, often against its own original impulse, into its development.[14]

In the last section we noted that two of the fundamental tenets of Renaissance humanism were a zeal for human freedom and autonomy, and a life-orientation toward the nonhuman creation. The Reformation often fed these tendencies even though, theoretically, it opposed them. Thus when Luther was pressed to recant his "heretical" views, he responded with these words: "Unless I am convicted by Scripture and plain reason—I do not accept the authority of popes and councils, for they have contradicted each other—my conscience is captive to the Word of God. I cannot and I will not recant anything, for to go against conscience is neither right nor safe. God help me. Amen."[15] This could be read as a declaration of Luther's submission to divine authority in Scripture. However, it could also be read as an assertion of autonomous freedom from institutional authority on the basis of individual conscience, and if his words are read this way, then Luther seems to be committing an unprecedented act of rebellion. Likewise, the Reformers' quest for the freedom of cultural life from the authority of the institutional church, in itself a good and proper development, could be turned to the task of liberating culture from all divine authority. Similarly, the Reformers reaffirmed the goodness of creation and the worthiness of scientific endeavors. But the science that flourished in this atmosphere could itself be turned to serve confessional humanism. Thus in these and many other ways the Reformation not only reinfused the Western worldview with Christian faith but also accelerated its movement toward secularism.

The Scientific Revolution: Science and the Development of Modernity (Sixteenth and Seventeenth Centuries)

Two Visions for Science: Christian and Humanist

Science has played such a central role in the development of the Western worldview that Newbigin refers to modernity as the "modern scientific world-view."[16] Science (both as a body of knowledge and as a methodology by which to gain that knowledge) is a powerful instrument, a good gift from God that can be directed according to either a Christian or a humanist vision of life. In fact, both visions were evident during what came to be known as the Scientific Revolution. Nicolaus Copernicus (1473–1543), Johannes Kepler (1571–1630), Isaac Newton (1642–1727), and most of the other major figures in this "revolution" were, in fact, Christians. Nevertheless, by the eighteenth century it was the humanist vision that would dominate the sciences in Western culture.

During the medieval period the development of science had been impeded by an otherworldly perspective that lacked a positive appreciation both of this world as a proper field of investigation and of the human calling to develop and explore the creation. Both the Christian worldview and its humanist offspring in the Renaissance contributed views that would serve to remove medieval obstacles to the advancement of science. In biblical perspective, human beings are creatures uniquely called by God to explore and care for the good creation, and science can provide the means to do both well. In the humanist vision, the concept of stewardship can become skewed so that it seems the right of autonomous humankind to dominate and exploit the creation for its own social purposes. Science in the Western world of the Renaissance (and after) offered both the tools and the tradition by which humanity could come to understand the laws of nature. With such knowledge would come remarkable power, as nature itself could be harnessed to do the bidding of humankind. Thus the new science had the potential to advance either Christian stewardship or the confessional humanist domination of nature.

Of course, these two spiritual orientations were not neatly distinguished at this time. A mingling of Christian and humanist worldviews is evident in the works of both Francis Bacon (1561–1626) and René Descartes (1596–1650). Bacon believed that "knowledge is power"; he thought that scientific knowledge of nature's laws would enable human beings to predict how the nonhuman creation would behave, and technology would enable them to harness nature's powers for social purposes.[17] Bacon writes, "The empire of man over things is founded on the arts [technology] and sciences alone, for nature is only to be commanded by obeying her."[18] Bacon believed that as a result of the fall, human beings had lost both their relationship to God and their dominion over nature. The first, he thought, would be repaired by religion and faith; the second would be restored by science and technology (in the messianic role to which Bacon assigned them). But if science were to lead humankind to a new civilization, it would first be necessary to establish a new understanding of knowledge. One needed a rigorous method to cleanse the mind of all the subjective distortions and mistaken views of the medieval scholastics. Bacon's method was empirical: from now on, knowledge was to be based solidly on experimental examination of the world and inductive reasoning from the observed particulars.

Descartes accomplished on the European continent what Bacon did for England. Descartes has been called the "father of modernity" because of his commitment to autonomous scientific reason as the final arbiter of truth.[19] Like

Bacon, Descartes believed that by science humankind could capture the laws of nature, and by technology could apply those laws, to become the "masters and possessors of nature"[20] and the authors of progress itself. To realize this vision, he too offered a method to render knowledge more rigorously objective and to purify the mind from all subjective prejudices—those of the senses, imagination, emotions, tradition, authority, and opinion. Descartes' solution was expressed in an architectural metaphor: methodological doubt was the solid foundation on which to build a structure of knowledge; therefore, begin by doubting everything you think you know. Upon such a foundation, you may build a solid edifice of knowledge by following a rational method, subjecting every truth claim to judgment by reason alone, and embracing as true only that which can be analyzed and measured in quantitative terms. Thus, to complement Bacon's empirical and experimental method, Descartes offered a rationalist and mathematical method.

It remained to Isaac Newton to fuse these two approaches into a scientific method that gave due place to both experimental observation and mathematical rationality (see figure 6). From the time of Newton, science was to take a central place in the Western worldview; humanism itself increasingly took scientific form. It seemed to many that science now offered both revelation and salvation, revealing the true nature of the world and saving humankind from the consequences of sin. Science, in other words, was poised to become the dominant idol of the West, as Alexander Pope (1688–1744) suggests in his impish paraphrase of Genesis 1:3 and John 1:4–9: "Nature and nature's laws lay hid in night. God said 'Let Newton be!' and all was light."[21]

Figure 6. Development of Method

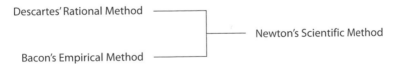

Descartes' Rational Method

Bacon's Empirical Method

Newton's Scientific Method

The Triumph of Humanism—Why?

It could have been different. Science could have equipped humankind for their proper role of caring for and developing the creation in a stewardly way. How, then, did science become so thoroughly co-opted by confessional humanism? Here the church must take some blame, for it made two mistakes that would increasingly marginalize the Christian worldview.

The first great mistake of the church was to react so negatively to the rise of the new science. For fifteen hundred years the church had understood the world in terms of the pagan Greek astronomer Ptolemy (366–282 BC), for whom the earth was the stationary center of the universe. And this seemed to support a Christian worldview: because God had sent his Son to earth, surely it must be the center of his creation. Thus when Copernicus, Kepler, Galileo, and Newton, building on one another's work, presented scientific evidence that the earth was not the center of the universe but was in fact rotating on its axis and revolving around the sun, the church responded with bitter antagonism.

The first opposition to these new discoveries in astronomy came from the Protestants. Because of their *sola Scriptura* belief, they mistakenly interpreted the Bible as offering a scientific view of the world in texts such as "He set the earth on its foundations; it can never be moved" (Ps. 104:5) and "The earth remains forever. The sun rises and the sun sets, and hurries back to where it rises" (Eccles. 1:4–5). These texts, among many others, seemed to say that a stationary earth was at the center of the cosmos. Thus, many in the Protestant church believed that to argue for a heliocentric view of the universe was to contradict Scripture. So it was that Luther (with Josh. 10:11–13 in mind) mildly ridiculed Copernicus: "So it goes now. Whoever wants to be clever must agree with nothing that others esteem. He must do something of his own. This is what that fellow does who wishes to turn the whole of astronomy upside down. . . . I believe the Holy Scriptures, for Joshua commanded the sun to stand still and not the earth."[22] At first the Roman Catholic Church responded with tolerance to the new science, but it changed that posture during the time of Galileo and attempted to suppress the new discoveries.

The Christian church could have responded differently. It could have asked if its traditional interpretations were correct; it could have rearticulated the Christian faith for a new time. The Roman Catholic theologian Max Wildiers comments, "Instead of accepting the challenge and reflecting on faith in a new perspective, the Church opted for an easy conservatism, keeping the enemy at bay by means of its anathemas. . . . This failure to accept the challenge of a new world picture was a great loss to the Church and to Christianity."[23] Increasingly, the church would be seen as obscurantist and a barrier to free inquiry into the truth. Tarnas comments, "The ultimate cultural meaning of the Galilean conflict was that of Church versus science, and, by implication, religious versus science. And in Galileo's forced recantation [of his work in astronomy] lay the Church's own defeat and science's victory."[24] But it did not have to be this way; religion and science are not in irreconcilable conflict.

There is another way in which the church contributed to the victory of humanism. The Reformation led to the shattering of Christendom—both the splintering of the church itself into various confessional groups and the fragmenting of Europe into various political units. As each state vied for complete control over the continent, Europe became soaked with Christian blood. And at the very same time that Christians were killing each other, the Newtonian paradigm of science was advancing knowledge on many fronts. Thus two parallel processes were at work in Europe: religious wars threatened to tear it apart, and Newtonian science (whose discoveries were often achieved by international cooperation among scientists) seemed to hold out the promise of peace and unity (see figure 7).

Figure 7. Conversion of Europe

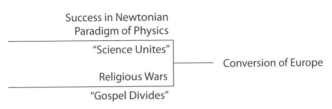

This would lead an increasing number of Europeans to see scientific reason itself as the new center around which a stable European society might be built (see figure 8).

Figure 8. Paradigm Shift in European Society

The Enlightenment: The Conversion of the West to a New Faith (Eighteenth Century)

The scientific humanism that rose in the seventeenth century would become widespread in Europe in the Enlightenment of the eighteenth century, becoming the dominant religious vision and culturally formative worldview. In this century Europe converted to a new faith: scientific humanism seemed to replace the gospel as "the light of the world," and its core beliefs may be summarized under these headings: (1) faith in progress, (2) faith in reason, (3) faith in technology, and (4) faith in a rationally ordered social world. In the next few pages we will deal with each of these articles of the Enlightenment credo.

Faith in Progress

Augustine had believed that God would steer history to a climactic conclusion in the city of God. The Enlightenment writers "demolished the Heavenly City of Augustine, only to rebuild it with up-to-date materials."[25] The myth of progress was the new form given to the concept of providence or universal history. Immanuel Kant (1724–1804), perhaps the most important and best-known of the Enlightenment figures, says this: "The destination of the human species as a whole is toward continued progress. We accomplish it by fixing our eyes on the goal, which, though a pure ideal, is of the highest value in practice, for it gives a direction to our efforts, conformable to the intentions of Providence."[26]

Images of a future paradise crowd the writing of this time: Henri de Saint-Simon (1760–1825) states that the golden age lies not behind us in history but rather ahead of us in the future. Joseph Priestly (1733–1804) writes, "Whatever was the beginning of this world, the end will be glorious and paradisiacal, beyond what our imaginations can now conceive."[27] William Goodwin's vision sounds like the new Jerusalem of Revelation 21: "There will be no war, no crimes, no administration of justice, as it is called, and no government. Besides this, there will be neither disease, anguish, melancholy, nor resentment. Every man will seek, with ineffable ardour, the good of all."[28]

Carl Becker notes that for Enlightenment thinkers, "the end of life is life itself, the good life on earth instead of the beatific life after death."[29] This good life on earth is especially defined in terms of economic growth and material prosperity. In 1767 the French Enlightenment philosopher Mercier de la Rivière wrote, "Humanly speaking, the greatest happiness possible for us consists in the greatest possible abundance of objects suitable for our enjoyment and in the greatest liberty to profit by them."[30] Likewise, Adam Smith believed that happiness depended on material bounty. Lawrence Osborn notes that for Enlightenment thinkers, "progress is identified with economic growth"[31] and, therefore, "the economy [is] the chief instrument in modernity's pursuit of happiness."[32] We should pause here to note that this obsession with the prospect of material abundance is understandable in a world bound by poverty and natural disaster, and such was the world known by the Enlightenment economists. But this commitment to material prosperity, accompanied by the leisure time and freedom to enjoy it, was to become a propelling force in our own consumer society of the West in the twentieth and twenty-first centuries, where the same poverty does not abound.

Ronald Wright speaks of "our practical faith in progress" as a "secular religion . . . [a] 'myth' in the anthropological sense" of a story of universal history that gives shape to a culture.[33] And let us be clear: faith in progress *is* a religion, a genuine faith. There is nothing to prove that Western culture is moving in the direction of "progress," of increasing material prosperity for all. In fact, much evidence today points in the opposite direction.

Faith in Reason

It was believed that progress toward a better world would be propelled by reason and science. The Enlightenment era has been dubbed the "Age of Reason" because of its supreme confidence in human rational ability, its conviction that "man is capable, guided solely by the light of reason and experience, of perfecting the good life on earth."[34] Tarnas adds, "For the robust civilization of the West at the high noon of modernity, it was science and reason, not religion and belief, which propelled that progress. Man's will, not God's, was the acknowledged source of the world's betterment and humanity's advancing liberation."[35]

In the Enlightenment view, scientific reason was to be *autonomous*, liberated from a (Christian) faith increasingly dismissed as obscurantist, ignorant, and superstitious. Moreover, scientific reason was to be *instrumental*, employed to control, predict, and shape the world. Finally, scientific reason was to be *universal*, to transcend human culture and history, to discern such laws as are true for all people at all times.

Faith in Technology

According to the Enlightenment creed, progress would come as scientific reason became translated into technology, to exploit natural laws for humanity's benefit. Knowledge of the laws of nature would give humanity control over the nonhuman creation through technology, and over human society through rational organization. In the seventeenth century Francis Bacon had foretold the union of science and technology, though this would not really take place until the nineteenth century. But the vision for technological control to further progress and prosperity certainly was evident in the Enlightenment of the eighteenth century. One example of this confidence in science and technology is from a book written in 1770 by Sébastien Mercier, entitled *L'An 2440* (*The Year 2440*): "Where can the perfectibility of man stop, armed with geometry and the mechanical arts and chemistry?"[36] Similarly, in his *Sketch for a Historical Picture of the Progress of the Human Mind*, the Marquis of Condorcet

(1743–1794) outlines his vision of progress toward material abundance, led by science and technology.

Faith in a Rationally Ordered Social World

In Enlightenment thought, scientific reason, if applied to human society, could organize it in a rational way and so achieve progress in the social sphere. Since Newton's physics had succeeded on the basis of his discoveries of immutable order in the nonhuman world, perhaps a similar order could be discerned in the social, political, economic, and educational world as well. Enlightenment philosophers began to believe that they could establish the heavenly city by discovering such order by reason alone and organizing human society and culture accordingly. The free exercise of scientific reason was to be the key to this bold initiative in social organization. Many Enlightenment thinkers believed that the oppressive political and social structures that had dominated Europe were the fruit of the Christian faith. They saw themselves as soldiers armed with scientific reason, engaged in battle against these repressive and outdated institutions, holdovers from the Middle Ages.

Since material prosperity was to be a central feature of the new "heavenly city," it is not surprising to see the prominence given to the rational organization of economic life. Adam Smith (1723–1790) published his immensely influential *The Wealth of Nations* in 1776, the Enlightenment vision for a rational economics. Smith believed that if we let the market be free, the economic decisions of self-interested individuals would guide us to a better future for all.[37]

Scientific reason was applied to political theory by John Locke (1632–1704) in *Two Treatises of Government* (1689), in which he challenged the divine right of kings and advocated a more rational politics in which the right to govern would be derived from the consent of the people. Others pressed for a more rational education system. In fact, "more treatises were written on education during the eighteenth century than in all the previous centuries combined."[38] Still others developed theories for a more rational legal system based on the work of Hugo Grotius (1583–1645) from a century before. Throughout the breadth of society Enlightenment thinkers offered blueprints for a rational society based on scientific reason.

This widespread desire for a rational society was deeply indebted to Newton, whose scientific method inspired the way Enlightenment social, political, and economic philosophers developed their own theories. In Newtonian physics one starts with the smallest particle to discern the laws that govern it and harmonize its relations with others like it. Paul Tillich refers to this as "technical reason" that "analyzes reality into its smallest elements, and then construes out of them other things, larger things."[39] This method came to be applied to social organization as, for example, economic and political philosophers began with the smallest unit of society, the individual, and looked for laws by which each of those individual human beings might relate to the others. George Soros has observed that Enlightenment economic theory (and, we might add, political, social, and educational theory) "is based on a false analogy with physics."[40] Newbigin notes how this false analogy works in economics: "It became the science of the working of the market as a self-operating mechanism modelled on the Newtonian universe. The difference was that the fundamental law governing its movements, corresponding to the law of gravitation in Newton, is the law of covetousness assumed as the basic drive of human nature."[41]

This "theory of universal laws" has its roots (oddly enough) in the long Christian tradition of "natural law" theory, newly adapted (in the eighteenth century) to the Enlightenment worldview. In the Middle Ages Aquinas had given definitive expression to the Christian concept of natural law, saying that the laws by which the universe is ordered had been built into it by the Creator and therefore reflected God's own purposes for his creation. Natural law was thus for Aquinas an evidence of God's presence. This concept held sway more or less until the Enlightenment, when some philosophers began to speak of natural law as an immanent order built in to the creation apart from God. Paul Hazard comments that the "object of this movement was to divorce law from religion."[42] Hugo Grotius is often considered the originator of this rationalist, secular view of natural law, arguing that these laws are valid in and of themselves, independent of whether or not God willed them. Grotius's Enlightenment successors followed his line of reasoning until the "natural law which they elaborated was entirely secular."[43] Newbigin comments on this "new understanding of 'Law'": "There is no longer a divine law-giver whose commands are to be obeyed because they are God's. Laws are necessary relationships which spring from the nature of things (Montesquieu). As such they are available for discovery by human reason."[44]

Thus, the Enlightenment notion of natural law—an idea that would revolutionize society—is, ironically, rooted in the Christian notion of creation order; Enlightenment social theory lives off the capital of the Christian worldview. Although, in our view, Thomas Aquinas had already granted too much autonomy to natural law, he had rightly maintained his belief that the order of creation displayed the purposes and will of the Creator. When the Enlightenment figures disposed of God, they could not so easily dispense with God's order, which remained a necessary concept for their theorizing upon the ordering of society. If one is setting out to form a social institution, it certainly

would help to recognize some kind of normative order for that institution! In
the Enlightenment, the way had been cleared for these assumptions: (1) this
normative order had been established by nature itself; (2) human reason can
discover these immutable, universal, and impersonal laws built into nature;
and (3) revealed law and a divine lawgiver are no longer necessary concepts.

The Enlightenment worldview, in its understanding of both the human and
nonhuman creation, thus enshrined deism. Deism is a transitional faith between
Christianity and a more radically secular worldview, retaining a mere vestige
of the Christian doctrine of creation to serve as a basis for human society.
"According to the Deistic philosophy, God's role has already been played in
creating the natural order, and . . . he can be safely left out of account as a
factor in the present."[45] Deism is the "last compromise with religion";[46] it is
a rationalism with a "heart-hunger for religion."[47]

The Clash between the Enlightenment Faith and the Gospel

As the Enlightenment worldview matured, it co-opted only certain elements of the Christian worldview, tailoring them to fit within its own story
and thus implicitly denying the comprehensiveness of the Christian worldview. As Europe warmed to this new faith, a clash with Christianity became
inevitable. With the Enlightenment view dominating the hearts and minds of
Europeans, it seemed that the gospel must either be eliminated or be made
to fit and serve the new order of things.[48] Tragically, it was often Christians
themselves who surrendered the gospel's claims to universal validity, so as to
accommodate it to its new status within the Enlightenment faith. They thus
abandoned the comprehensive worldview implicit in the gospel, allowing it
to take on "a new and far less encompassing intellectual role" and to become
"focused exclusively on inward spiritual concerns."[49]

Newbigin, in many of his writings, has noted this reduction in the scope
claimed by Christians for the gospel, by describing the "fact-value dichotomy" that lies at the foundation of modern Western culture. When humanism
triumphed in the Enlightenment, scientific reason was accepted as the sole
arbiter of truth: any truth claim that could be proven by scientific rationality
occupied the high ground as public fact, to be accepted as truth by everyone
in society. Truth claims that could not be verified scientifically were relegated
to the lesser sphere of private values (or tastes, or preferences), with no role
in the public life of culture. The gospel thus becomes a merely personal taste.
(One may prefer chocolate ice cream to vanilla, but to say that chocolate ice
cream is the truth is to confuse one's categories.) In this view, for any person
to say that the gospel is good for himself or herself is acceptable, but to claim

that it is true and that it has authority in cultural life would be to cling to the religious remnants of a bygone age.

We may illustrate this with the following diagram (see figure 9). The sieve of scientific reason filters and separates truth claims. Those that can meet the criteria of scientific reason—such as $1 + 1 = 2$ (math) or a description of the right of private property (politics)—achieve the status of facts to be publicly embraced. (A teacher in a public school who asks a class what the sum of $1 + 1$ is does not celebrate plurality when different students answer "3" or "4"!) However, those truth claims that cannot meet this scientific standard are relegated to the realm of mere values, preferences, tastes, and opinions: they may be privately held, but they must not be proclaimed as public truth.

Figure 9. Fact-Value Dichotomy

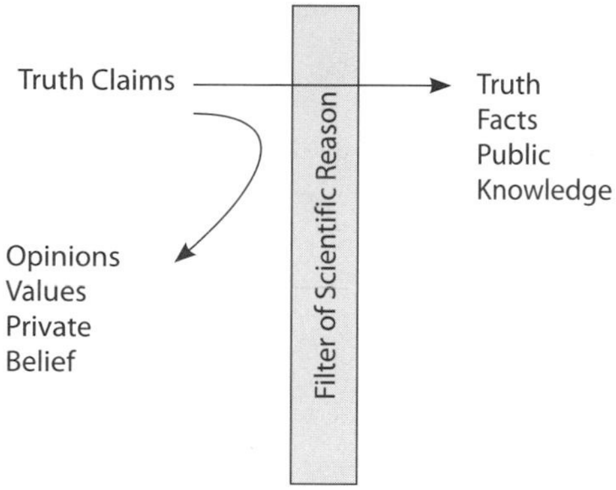

Truth Claims → Truth / Facts / Public / Knowledge

Filter of Scientific Reason

Opinions / Values / Private / Belief

When the dogma of scientific humanism operates, the gospel is considered to be a matter of merely private taste, which has no role in public life. Our shared life in culture (we are told) must proceed on the basis of a universal rationality from which all our subjectivities, including the Christian faith, have been filtered out by the scientific method. Science, politics, economics, and so forth are part of the public and factual domain of life; the gospel is banished to the private realm of values. It is thus considered by those who hold the Enlightenment worldview that to speak of the light of revelation or the authority of Scripture in the arena of public life is to confuse one's categories.

This is, of course, a devastating obstacle to Christian involvement in the public square. Within the Enlightenment view, the gospel is excluded, and it can no longer function as a directing power in social and cultural life. When we allow the gospel to be domesticated by scientific humanism, we have in fact abandoned the gospel revealed in Scripture.

The Age of Revolution: Bringing Society into Conformity with Enlightenment Faith (Nineteenth and Twentieth Centuries)

"The West had 'lost its faith [in God]'—and found a new one, in science and in man."[50] But no real faith commitment can remain forever only in the heart or mind, on paper or in words; it will always take on social, political, and economic flesh. For those who hold the Enlightenment vision to be true, "the establishment of *new* social institutions is not a tedious, incidental task, but a dire necessity and a high ethical imperative. In that case, the narrow way to the lost paradise can only be the way of *social revolution*."[51] Thus the Enlightenment worldview was embodied in Western culture in a series of revolutions—national, industrial, social, and political—in the eighteenth, nineteenth, and early twentieth centuries. Here we take a brief look at some significant features of the Industrial and French Revolutions that are important for an understanding of how the Western worldview developed.[52]

Before the Industrial Revolution the fundamental economic unit had been the family. The home was both workshop and place of business. Labor was manual and not specialized or divided up to any great extent. Most people lived in the countryside. All this was to change during the Industrial Revolution, as manual tasks were taken over by machines, labor became divided and specialized, and moved from home to factory, from countryside to industrial city. The factory provides a shining example of the rational organization and technological control of society that emerged in response to the dominance of the Enlightenment worldview.

In the Industrial Revolution science and technology became truly united: "Despite Francis Bacon's announcement of the marriage of science and the mechanical arts at the beginning of the 17th century, it was almost three centuries before the marriage was consummated. In practice, both continued to be essentially separate enterprises. . . . By the 19th century the search had begun for a more direct path between science and technology. The intense interaction that occurred resulted in a scientific technology."[53] Lynn White, looking back on these events from a twentieth-century vantage point, says that the "marriage between science and technology . . . may mark the greatest event in human history. . . . Somewhat over a century ago science and technology—hitherto quite separate activities—joined to give mankind powers which, to judge by many of the ecologic effects, are out of control."[54]

This technology was channeled primarily toward economic activities. The steam engine, the water frame, and the spinning jenny were all put to work in the cotton textile trade. Machines increased human labor capacity tremendously—the steam engine gave one person the power of an entire workforce.

Added to this technological control was a more efficient organization of human labor in which jobs were specialized and ordered in the factory for maximum production. And together, the combination of specialization and mechanization produced remarkable productivity.

In the period from 1840 to 1900, while Britain industrialized, its gross national product per capita (GNP) tripled from just over $300 to around $900; during the same period, the GNP of Portugal (which had not industrialized) increased only slightly, from about $250 to $260.[55] This seemed firm evidence that the Enlightenment vision of progress toward a prosperous society—progress produced by scientific control and technological development—was being realized. It reinforced Europe's newfound faith that "science [had] the answers to the world's problems," because "from the perspective of the age of steam, of the nineteenth century, progress seemed the stuff of the universe, and science was the key that could unlock the secrets of utopian bliss."[56]

Technology and labor had been organized in the first place for the sake of economic growth and material prosperity, but soon this economic arrangement began to shape all other aspects of social life, in the social structure of capitalism. David Wells believes that capitalism "has reorganized the social structure for the purposes of manufacturing, production, and consumption . . . concentrated the population into cities, and produced massive systems of finance, banking, law, communications and transportation. In short, it has changed the shape of our world. . . . [And] *technology* facilitates the processes of capitalism, and rationalizes all of life."[57]

Like the Industrial Revolution, the French Revolution worked to reconstruct society on the basis of the Enlightenment credo. The cry of the revolution was "Liberty, equality, and fraternity." This slogan was more than words: these ideals led to tremendous bloodshed and then shaped the reforms of the French National Constituent Assembly as it met in 1789. The way to achieve these ideals, the assembly believed, was to abolish the divine right of kings, the privilege of nobility, and the authority of the church—all remnants of an antiquated, hierarchical Christendom. In place of the old order were the inalienable rights of the individual citizen, the subordination of church to state, a constitutional government, administrative and judicial reforms, business legislation, and universal public education. The Declaration of the Rights of Man and the Citizen made a universal statement about the freedom and equality of all human beings, and it became a formative influence throughout the West in the next two centuries.

The changes initiated by the Industrial and French Revolutions transformed society into the modern state, founded on confessional humanism. Andrew Walker notes that, on the one hand, the modern state is a "child of modernity."

Once born, however, this child embodies the faith of modernity: "In the modern world, the state is the single most powerful institutional force in the international community, and probably the most successful institutional carrier of the modernization process."[58]

It would be easy to read this story as the triumph of attractive humanistic ideals over obscurantist religion. However, that would be to misread what really happened. The society that was overturned in the triumph of modernity was not precisely Christian, but rather medieval Christendom—itself a mixture of Christian and pagan elements. Like humanists, Christians are likely to reject the hierarchy of the Middle Ages and the excessive power of the church, but they will do so for different reasons. Most Christians would agree with humanists that various social institutions should be freed from church control, but they might well disagree on the answer to the question, "By what authority should we then shape those emancipated areas of life?" Should it be according to the dictates of reason or according to God's revelation? Moreover, modern humanism continues to live off the accumulated capital of the gospel, for the Christian worldview has played an important role in shaping many of those things that we may now find most attractive, including human rights, freedom, equality, productive change, and education. These were never solely humanist constructions.

Two Different Stories of Progress: Liberal and Marxist

Yet after the revolutions, all was not well. The Industrial Revolution certainly produced ambiguous results. Along with burgeoning wealth came much misery: many of the families that had moved from country to city began to disintegrate; hordes of people crowded into unsanitary living arrangements; men and women and children were shamefully exploited in the factories, where hours were inhumanely long and wages inhumanely short. A sober contrast to the Enlightenment prophecies of Paradise-on-Earth! What had become of the faith and hope of the eighteenth century?

A deeply rooted faith, even faith in a false god, is not easily destroyed. In order to maintain their faith in the Enlightenment story in the face of the grimly growing counterevidence of the Industrial Revolution, true believers in progress found the need to fold all the local evidence of human misery into a greater myth. And two post-Enlightenment narratives arising in the nineteenth century attempt to do exactly that, both maintaining faith in progress through science and technology[59] and interpreting the contrary testimony as part of that story. Those two narratives are liberalism and Marxism.

Liberalism, the first great ideological force unleashed in the nineteenth century, offered a blueprint for society based on the sovereignty of the individual.[60] In its economic form, liberalism prizes the freedom of the individual in economic affairs; in its political form, it prizes individual human rights. To the problem of the nineteenth century's horrific suffering, liberals offered at least two answers. The first was offered by Herbert Spencer (1820–1903), who said simply (and heartlessly) that suffering was the price of evolutionary progress. Other liberals, such as John Stuart Mill and Thomas Hill Green, offered a more socially conscious liberalism, and they struggled to harmonize human freedom with the responsibility of government to pursue justice. But both liberal answers maintained faith in progress, and both explained human suffering as part of the story.

Karl Marx (1818–1883), likewise, offered a progress story that accounted for suffering. One might find Marx more compassionate than the liberals; his writings do evince a moral outrage against the suffering that he encounters. Yet he, like Spencer, offers a rational explanation for suffering that is also dependent on Darwin. In Marx's political thought Darwin's observation of conquest through struggle in the natural world is translated into social terms: history is driven forward by class conflict. The story of progress is a narrative of successive class revolutions that will lead ultimately to equality and the just and equitable distribution of all the wealth created by economic development.

Liberalism and Marxism, contrary notions of historical progress both rooted in the humanism of the nineteenth century, were to take over the world for most of the twentieth century, one finding its center in Washington, DC, the other in Moscow.[61]

The Romantic Reaction (Nineteenth Century)

Since God upholds the order of his creation, holding down a part of his good creation is like holding down a tightly coiled spring: it will eventually spring back with great force. Perhaps this is how best to understand the Romantic reaction of the nineteenth century to those views of life that immediately preceded it. The Enlightenment had made idols of many good aspects of God's creation, while diminishing others. Romanticism was a movement in which some of those dimensions of life that were held down and depreciated in the Enlightenment forced their way back into Western culture. Romanticism was to become a potent force, interacting in complex ways with the Enlightenment vision. It remained subsidiary to the dominant vision of the Enlightenment initially but came to be important again throughout the twentieth century.

Because both Romanticism and the Enlightenment were basically humanist in form, Romanticism was not a challenge to the Enlightenment at the deepest level.[62] But Romanticist humanism was in some measure a rebellion against the reductionism of the Enlightenment. German composer Franz Schubert called the Enlightenment an "ugly skeleton without flesh and blood," since it reduced human beings to the status of merely rational beings.[63] The Romantics believed that this negated the richness of human experience and the complexity of the human person. Emotions, imagination, creativity, and instinct surge back into prominence in the Romantic reaction. The Enlightenment had similarly reduced nature to a lifeless machine, whereas Romantic authors believed that nature must be understood as a complex, living organism. The Enlightenment had reduced our relationship with nature to one of mere observation, experiment, theoretical explanation, and exploitation. The Romantics protested the shabby poverty of such a relationship with nature, believing that one should delight in nature and be awed by it, allowing the emotions and imagination to soak it in. They believed further that humanity does not stand above nature as its master but rather is part of nature.

Whereas the Enlightenment had reduced knowledge to what could be gained by distance from one's subject and by analytical method, William Wordsworth (1770–1850) writes in bitter protest, "Our meddling intellect misshapes the beauteous forms of things—We murder to dissect."[64] Not distance, he implies, but communion with nature and the exercise of the empathetic imagination give a truer understanding of the world; not reason, but imagination, creativity, emotion, and instinct give true knowledge. John Keats says, "I am certain of nothing but of the holiness of the heart's affections and the truth of the imagination. O for a life of sensations rather than a life of thoughts."[65] For the Romantic, knowledge that joins imagination and feeling to reason offers a deeper grasp of creation than does any merely rational method.

The Enlightenment had reduced truth to mere science. For the Romantic, truth is complex, many-sided, plural, and perspectival, and thus science is not the best way to get hold of truth. Instead, poetry, literature, drawing, painting, and music draw out the mysterious intricacies of the world. The Enlightenment's gaze had been turned outward to understand the external world with a view to changing it; the Romantic turns inward to understand the self and the depths of the human soul—its moods and motives, loves and desires, fears and angst, inner conflicts and contradictions, dreams and the subconscious, fantasy and ecstasy. And finally, whereas the Enlightenment tradition had seen only the goodness of humankind, the Romantic, in turning inward, also explores the darker side of humanity, its irrational and evil motives.

All of this meant that Romanticism did challenge the Enlightenment vision of life. Yet, it was not a substitute; in fact, it would live alongside Enlightenment progress. In Romanticism, the goal of being human was to develop the unique potentials of one's own personality: the "whole ideal for man was, not the spread of rational knowledge, but rather the fullest development of the unique potentialities of every man. . . . The whole aim of culture and of life was proclaimed to be the development of the freedom, individuality, and the self-expression of the individual. 'Be yourself; cultivate your personality.'"[66] Thus modern humanism divided into "two cultures."[67] The Enlightenment worldview would continue to dominate cultural development and public life; Romanticism would form a subordinate cultural stream that would influence personal life and would have an increasingly powerful effect in Western culture, with a particular resurgence in the late twentieth century.

Late Modernity: The Gains and Decline of Liberal Humanism (Twentieth and Twenty-first Centuries)

Throughout the twentieth century, scientific or liberal humanism, salted by the gospel, made some remarkable advances for which we can be thankful. Scientific inquiry has advanced the boundaries of knowledge significantly; dizzyingly rapid developments in technology have provided most of us with a much more comfortable life than our parents or grandparents knew. How many of us would want to go back to a time before refrigerators, computers, or modern medical technology? Industrial and economic development has delivered unprecedented material prosperity to many people, especially in the West. Many other political, economic, and educational advances could be named as the milestones of twentieth-century progress. Yet these observations tell only part of the story, for the modern worldview itself is in a crisis that has been deepening throughout the twentieth century, even as material progress has seemed to advance.

The Enlightenment dream began to fade first in Europe as the horrors of two world wars eroded Western nations' confidence in the old prophecies of ever-increasing peace and prosperity. After the "Great War" of 1914–1918, psychologist Carl Jung expressed what many Europeans felt:

> I believe I am not exaggerating when I say that modern man has suffered an almost fatal shock, psychologically speaking, and as a result has fallen into profound uncertainty. . . . The revolution in our conscious outlook, brought about by catastrophic results of the World War, shows itself in our inner life by the shattering of our faith in ourselves and our own worth. . . . I realize only

too well that I am losing my faith in the possibility of a rational organization of the world, the old dream of the millennium, in which peace and harmony should rule, has grown pale.[68]

The situation was markedly different in North America, especially following World War II (1939–1945), when a tremendous spurt of economic growth seemed to confirm the old vision of progress. Whereas Europeans were "not prepared to listen to naively innocent talk about progress and the future," it was different in North America. "In the United States, and similarly in Canada, there was a discernibly different spirit, born of different experiences. In America after 1945 there was a sense of confidence and optimism that was a reaffirmation of historic Western ideas about progress. In the postwar era, America became the new proving ground for the Enlightenment and its faith."[69]

Although more confidence in the myth of progress remains in North America, faith in the modern story is, in the early twenty-first century, waning here as well. Faith in the Enlightenment worldview has receded as the West has gradually begun to understand these five evidences of its profound failure: (1) poverty, (2) environmental degradation, (3) proliferation of weapons, (4) psychological problems, and (5) social and economic problems.

Poverty. In 1960 the United Nations declared the new decade to be a "development decade," a time for developing countries to participate in modern technological and economic progress. Subsequently, the 1970s and 1980s were likewise named "decades of development," but the vision of progress for all the world's people continued to fade as time rolled on. Statistics concerning the gap between the rich and the poor demonstrate how little was actually accomplished during these "decades of development": in 1960, the world's richest 20 percent were thirty times richer than the poorest 20 percent; in 1990, after thirty years of development, the rich were almost sixty times richer[70]; by 1999, the world's richest 20 percent were almost eighty-six times wealthier than the poorest 20 percent; and the gap continues to grow.[71] The dream of material prosperity was, it now seems, only for the few.

Environmental degradation. It is now estimated that if the whole world were to consume natural resources at the same rate as do North Americans, those resources would last for only about ten or twenty years more.[72] Surely, a worldview that would destroy creation if it were lived by all cannot be one that an ethical person should embrace.

Proliferation of weapons. The building up of massive stockpiles of weapons capable of destroying the world is the direct result of modern technological development. And it consumes huge amounts of time, money, and materials.

If one day's worth of global spending on arms were spent on food instead, it could feed the world's hungry for years.[73]

Psychological problems. Kenneth Gergen lists over twenty descriptions of mental or psychological deficits that have come into use only since the beginning of the twentieth century, including anorexia, bulimia, stress, low self-esteem, burnout, and depression. Gergen suggests that it is primarily the technologies of the twentieth century that have contributed to the psychological neediness that these symptoms point to.[74]

Social and economic problems. The breakdown of the family and the rise of crime and unemployment are a few of many symptoms of social breakdown in the modern West that also undermine confidence in the modernist worldview, according to which, such things should be easily overcome. Again, many of these symptoms can be attributed to the increasingly technological culture that has developed within the last century.

As we move toward the second decade of the twenty-first century, it would appear that the modern story has failed to deliver on many of its most important promises. Questions abound:

- Does humanity have the power to renew the world? Or did Jung indeed have his finger on the pulse of Western humanity when he said that faith in humanity had been shattered?
- Can scientific reason in fact give us certain knowledge? Throughout the twentieth century, in such disciplines as anthropology, sociology, history, and linguistics, scholars have emphasized the relativity of human knowledge. Our knowledge is shaped by a host of social factors (tradition, community, language, culture, history, faith) and personal factors (feelings, imagination, the subconscious, gender, class, race). Certainty does not seem so certain anymore.
- Are we really capable of mastering nature to build a better world? Or will we continue to destroy the nonhuman environment until it can no longer sustain us?
- Can technology really deliver us? Has it not dehumanized us, contributed to numerous social problems, advanced environmental degradation, and built weapons of mass destruction?
- Is there a future? Or will our growing pessimism about the future lead us to retreat into a life of "the perpetual present," drown ourselves in entertainment, and seek any and every means of escape from reality?
- Will economic growth and material prosperity really bring a future of happiness? Or is the heavy price we are paying now, in terms

of psychological and relational breakdown, the real return on our investment?

Writing in a different historical context, but one in which the church was also facing tremendous change and challenge, Lesslie Newbigin offered this helpful comment:

> The real question is: *What is God doing in these tremendous events of our time*? How are we to understand them and interpret them to others, so that we and they may play our part in them as co-workers with God? Nostalgia for the past and fear for the future are equally out of place for the Christian. He is required, in the situation in which God places him, to understand the signs of the times in the light of the reality of God's present and coming kingdom, and to give his witness faithfully about the purpose of God for all men.[75]

When we ask what God is doing in the momentous events of our time, the answer that we hear must be the same answer once given by God to the prophet Isaiah: "I am the LORD; that is my name! I will not give my glory to another or my praise to idols" (Isa. 42:8 NIV). Brian Walsh asks "who turned out the lights" on the Enlightenment vision, and he answers his own question this way: "In a sense they turned themselves out. . . . But on an even more ultimate level, who turned out the lights? God did! God is historically turning out the lights of this culture as God always turns out the lights of idolatrous cultures."[76] "We are beginning to notice the modern world, *as we have known it*, disappear in our rear-view mirror as we move on into the unknown."[77]

7

What Time Is It?

*Four Signs of Our Time
in the Western Story*

The rise of postmodernism and globalization and a remarkable swell in the growth of both southern-hemisphere Christianity and Islamic faith—these are some of the touchstones of the early twenty-first century. What view of history could possibly bind such apparently disparate developments together? Is there commonality in the midst of such great diversity?

We believe that there is a common theme here, one that can best be understood by returning to N. T. Wright's worldview question: "What time is it in our culture?" As we have explored already in *The Drama of Scripture*, the fifth "act" of the cosmic drama is already upon us, and we are even now in preparation for the sixth and final act, in which Christ will return to reclaim his creation utterly, restoring it to conform with those plans that he has maintained for it since "before the foundation of the world." In this fifth act of our world's history the rebellious current of what we have been calling the Enlightenment worldview, or (more briefly) modernity, is in serious difficulty. In postmodernity we see modernity's decay, as its internal tensions and radical inconsistencies come under ironic attack, especially in Western nations. Modernity as a worldview was shaped by the myth of progress, which said that humankind would ultimately achieve a paradise on earth by its own industry and capability. Postmodernity suggests that the idol of progress had feet of clay—a revelation that few readers of the Bible would find particularly unexpected. But postmodernity is not the only game in town. In the marketplace modernity still shapes much of our social, political, and economic life. Many cannot or will not bring themselves to believe that the secret of human happiness does not lie in an ever-expanding material prosperity. And thus globalization is a movement that is spreading the modern, liberal story around the world.

Though modernity (and its spread in globalization) and postmodernity (albeit in a very different way) claim to be religiously neutral, we have seen that this cannot be so, since both attempt to establish a sustainable culture on the basis of certain beliefs. They assume humankind's autonomy from God and reject his creational norms for the world. In the place of God they have put human reason, or human language, or material progress, or some other idol—but it is always, and only, an idol. In the twenty-first century we are witnessing a resurgence of both Christianity (especially in the southern hemisphere) and Islam. Although these two religions are fundamentally opposed to one another, they do share a radical antipathy to Western idols. As men and women outside the West's sphere of influence observe the decay of the modernist dream, they seem increasingly to be turning either to biblical faith in the God of creation and redemption or to Islam's alternative (but equally comprehensive) worldview.

If we are to indwell and incarnate the gospel in our own time and place, we must engage in what John Stott has called "double listening"—one ear listening carefully to the Scriptures and the Christian tradition, and the other ear listening to what is going on in the surrounding culture. Only in this way will we be equipped properly to live for Christ. Since a worldview arises out of a story about the world, and stories are concerned with the relationship among events in time, a central question for us is this: "What time is it in our culture?"

In this chapter we will be exploring what is going on in Western culture today, seeking to understand how these events are related to the religious beliefs that drive our culture. Although it may be hard for us to gain critical distance from the complex culture surrounding us, that is essential to our calling as Christians. Failure to know what time it is in our culture will render us unable to discern the crossroads at which we are called to live for Christ. Such failure may well betray us into accepting, however unintentionally, the idols of contemporary culture. It may also cause us to miss the genuinely good things that contemporary life offers.

In this chapter we will survey four "signs of the times" that we, as Christians seeking to live out the implications of a worldview formed and informed by the gospel, must discern clearly: (1) the rise of postmodernity; (2) consumerism and globalization; (3) the renascence of Christianity in the southern hemisphere; and (4) the resurgence of Islam. We begin by considering the phenomenon of postmodernity as we seek to answer the question, "What time is it in our culture?"

Sign 1: Postmodernity

What Is Postmodernity?

The contemporary debate about postmodernism began in the 1950s and 1960s as a reaction to modernism in the arts, and soon it extended to a critique of modern culture as a whole.[1] Modernity, as we have seen, espoused this grand story or metanarrative: progress, based on reason and science, would lead humanity to a new world of peace and prosperity. But event after event in the twentieth century mauled this naïve optimism, until by mid-century the grand story of progress itself appeared to many to be the source of our problems. Some critics of modernity adopted the title "postmodern" to signal their utter rejection of the modernist metanarrative, and Jean-François Lyotard (1920–1998) coined the phrase "incredulity towards metanarratives" as one of the defining elements of the new spirit.[2] For Lyotard, metanarratives are those grand stories or overarching narratives that aim to explain all events and perspectives comprehensively; in fact, this term becomes for Lyotard a near synonym for "worldview-story." His critique was aimed particularly at modernity's trust in reason to explain reality comprehensively, its quest for universally valid criteria by which to order society, and its blind confidence in the ability of science and technology to liberate humankind from all kinds of evil.

Incredulity toward metanarratives has serious implications for those who seek to acquire reliable knowledge. For Lyotard, grand narratives rooted in science and reason were simply no longer believable; instead, he argued, all we have are language games, different linguistic interpretations of the world, and these are always local, never universal. Following Lyotard, the American philosopher Richard Rorty (1931–2007) has argued that all knowledge is "traditioned," and that the concept of the accurate representation of reality that underlies the Western concern with knowledge is a myth.[3] For Rorty, all forms of knowledge are closer to making than to finding, and thus he judges the obsession of Western thinkers with the quest to achieve true knowledge of the world to be part of a worldview that has become simply outmoded.

Postmodern philosophy thus raises all sorts of questions about epistemology: our capacity to know reality, how we know it, and whether we can accurately represent it. The possibility of achieving universal, objective knowledge—the goal so central to modernity—is considered by many postmodern thinkers to be impossible. As Kenneth Gergen says, "We are not dealing here with doubts regarding claims about the truth of human character, but with the full-scale abandonment of the concept of objective truth."[4]

The corollary of this skepticism has been a profound suspicion concerning the hidden agendas of so-called neutral modern knowledge. What had been claimed by modernists to be objective and value-free has come to be seen by many postmodernists as a mask for powerful ideologies.[5] Postmoderns have been very successful in showing that what was presented in modernity as objective truth was in fact loaded down with ideological baggage, including commitments to patriarchy, colonialism, Eurocentrism, rationalism, and anti-Semitism. For example, to say that "Columbus discovered America" is not a neutral historical statement but rather a Eurocentric one, since (according to those who already lived in North America) Columbus did not discover the country but rather invaded it. Jean-François Lyotard and Michel Foucault (1926–1984) view reason itself as inextricably bound up in power games and thus an untrustworthy tool.[6]

The consequence of this skepticism is an awareness of the inevitable pluralism within knowledge. Certainty and truth themselves are now regarded by many with great suspicion. Postmodernism has profoundly challenged the confidence of modernity that the world as it really is can be known through reason and science. For postmoderns, true knowledge of the world is simply unavailable. And, since knowledge of the world is inseparably related to one's view of the world, here too postmodernism has undermined the broad consensus of modernity. In the nineteenth century, historicism emerged in Western culture—the view that there is no God-given order for history, but rather, history is a process of flux and change. All of culture is, according to this view, simply a product of historical forces. Such a view is common among postmodern thinkers. Another common notion is that language is the most fundamental aspect of reality: it is language that defines what reality is. The French philosopher Jacques Derrida (1930–2004) was a leading proponent of this idea.

These approaches, like most postmodern theory, leave little room for any notion of an order in reality that exists apart from human construction. The world is what we make it, and we have made so many different worlds that it is impossible to assert which view of reality is the correct one. Ironically, skepticism about human knowing goes hand in hand with a high view of the human community as that entity which constructs the worlds in which we live. This too reflects a worldview that, at heart, denies the existence of God's creation order for all of reality.

Postmodernism also challenges the modernist notion of what it means to be human. The rationalistic autonomous view of the human that was so dominant in modernity has since been undermined, and many alternatives have been proposed. Rorty, for example, suggests that we should think of the moral self as "a network of beliefs, desires, and emotions with nothing behind it—no substrate behind the attributes. For purposes of moral and political deliberation and conversation, a person just is that network."[7] Emotions, desires, beliefs—aspects of humanity that had been suppressed by the exaltation of reason in modernity—now are finding new life. Human beings do not have a given nature but rather are a construction. Foucault stresses the extent to which our view even of what it means to be human is a construct, a fiction:

> Strangely enough, man . . . is probably no more than a kind of rift in the order of things, or, in any case, a configuration whose outlines are determined by the new position he has so recently taken up in the field of knowledge. . . . Man is only a recent invention, a figure not yet two centuries old, a new wrinkle in our knowledge . . . that will disappear as soon as that knowledge has discovered a new form.[8]

In postmodernity, doubts concerning our ability to know truth, to perceive reality, and even to be sure of what it is to be human undermine the foundations of modernity. The Enlightenment worldview seems in danger of final collapse.

A Christian Response to Postmodernity

How should Christians respond to postmodernity? From its beginnings in the arts and philosophy, postmodernism has now spilled over into every other academic discipline and into popular culture. Whether you are studying literature, psychology, art, theology, economics, law, history, science, medicine, drama, or any other subject, you will find that there is now a body of literature on postmodernism *and* your particular subject. For example, if you study English literature, you will find courses available on critical theory that includes much (often impenetrable) postmodern philosophy. You will also likely find a course on the postmodern novel. Nowadays there is also a whole range of literature dealing with postmodernism and biblical studies. The influence extends throughout popular culture to film, architecture (in postmodern architecture, a collage of styles is brought together), urban design, painting, music, and landscape and garden design, among many others. Postmodernity has captured the imagination of countless people in Western culture.

A Christian approach to postmodernism must not be naïve. There are good and bad aspects to postmodernity. Positively, postmodernity has gone a long way toward exposing modernity as a particular worldview with its own ideological commitments: it is far harder to assume nowadays that modernist scholarship and practices are objective and neutral. Postmodernity has helped to show that everyone does indeed have a worldview, and from a Christian perspective, this is something to celebrate. But postmodernism's strong opposition to affirming any one worldview as true may lead to dangerous relativism. David Harvey observes that whereas modernity had rejected tradition and religious authority, it had held on to the hope that reason alone would lead us to truth.[9] Postmoderns have (rightly) given up on the illusion that human reason will lead us to truth, but they have not recovered tradition, and certainly have not recovered religious authority. Instead, postmoderns courageously celebrate and "play" amidst humanity's limitations and finitude, in a sort of cheerful nihilism. Clearly, this is incompatible with a Christian worldview—it is, in fact, downright dangerous.

So too is there great danger in the view that the world is what we make it. The Christian philosopher Alvin Plantinga traces this aspect of postmodernism back to Kant's idealism, or (what Plantinga calls) "creative anti-realism":

> This is the view that it is human behaviour—in particular, human thought and language—that is somehow responsible for the fundamental structure of the world and for the fundamental kinds of entities there are. From a theistic point of view, however, universal creative anti-realism is at best a piece of laughable bravado. For God, of course, owes neither his existence nor his properties to us and our ways of thinking; the truth is just the reverse. And so far as the created universe is concerned, while it indeed owes its existence and character to activity on the part of a person, that person is certainly not a human person.[10]

One positive contribution made by postmodernity to Western culture has been to bring the topic of religion back into serious academic discussion. Several postmodern thinkers have addressed religious topics in their writings. One now finds topics such as forgiveness and prayer on mainstream academic conference agendas, which would have been unthinkable only twenty years ago. We should welcome these developments, but we must also note that the sort of "religion" articulated by these thinkers is a long way from anything resembling orthodox Christian belief. Postmoderns may have abandoned trust in reason, but that does not mean they have abandoned an idolatrous desire for human autonomy. Nor have they recovered trust in tradition and in the living God—far from it.

In their resistance to worldviews or grand stories, postmoderns reject the possibility of discovering the truth about the world. Many would therefore claim strongly that they do not have a worldview at all, that instead they work from such a collage of elements as they find to be helpful. But it is not so easy to escape having a worldview. Ironically, the postmoderns' very denial of worldviews conceals their own allegiance to a very specific worldview. The person who says "We cannot know the truth" nevertheless wants that claim to be accepted as true and presumes to see that truth clearly![11] Although the postmodernists wear the cloak of humility, their implicit claim—they are the exception to their own rule—is far from humble. For, ironically, postmodernism is absolutely convinced that the proposition "Truth cannot be found" is itself true. Thus, although postmodernism professes to despise worldviews, it is, ironically, precisely that which it professes to despise!

Furthermore, it is very important to note that, from a Christian perspective, the roots of modernity, though attacked by many of these postmodern philosophers, have never been altogether abandoned by them. The ideal of human autonomy, for example, tends to remain as firmly entrenched as ever. As the philosopher of science Mary Hesse perceptively points out, "The liberal consensus has so successfully established itself as the ideology of Western intellectual culture, that it has become almost invisible as the presupposition of every postmodern debate."[12] And postmodernism is primarily a Western and secular phenomenon; even in the West it remains a minority worldview, competing for attention with many alternative worldviews. Take English literature, for example. Attending a literature conference is often more like attending a conference on postmodern philosophy, in which deconstruction and radical feminism and a smorgasbord of alternative ways of reading and writing novels are on offer. But many English professors, lecturers, and writers have resisted the postmodern approach to literature. It is the same in other disciplines: there are now famous examples of postmodern architecture, but by no means have all architects followed this trend. Other styles of architecture persist alongside, and in competition with, and often in reaction to, the postmodern.

One reason that postmodernism remains a minority worldview is that its extreme views are unworkable or unlivable. Life depends on there being an order written deep into the creation; neither scholarship nor daily life can operate for long without this assumption. In philosophy, for example, though the postmodern Jacques Derrida has written some very unusual books—for example, one in which the text is in several columns, each in a different language, or another in which passages from Derrida and other writers are juxtaposed, leaving the reader to fathom out their connections—this simply is not how books are written. Those who write *about* Derrida tend to write clearly and to organize their work in the way books normally operate, with an introduction, clear chapters with logical development, and a conclusion.

Thus, in the twenty-first century West many worldviews compete for dominance. As David Lyon notes, postmodernity is valuable for Christians in that it alerts them to key questions concerning the time in which we live, at the end of the historical period in which the Enlightenment worldview has been so dominant: "Postmodernity offers an opportunity to reappraise modernity, to read the signs of the times as indicators that modernity itself is unstable, unpredictable, and to forsake the foreclosed future that it once seemed to promise."[13] However, postmodernism is also unhelpful to Christians in that although it has abandoned much of modernity's key concepts, it has never abandoned the shaky secular foundations upon which modernity was built. Because of this, postmodernism's own weaknesses are considerable.

Sign 2: Consumerism and Globalization

Consumerism

Ours is a culture in search of meaning. The fragmentation that postmodernism has visited on our culture, and its undermining of modernity, leave Western culture increasingly without a robust center from which to draw its meaning and practices. Postmodernity has reduced the grand story of modernity to "a heap of broken images," mere disconnected fragments. But postmodernism's arrival should not for a moment make us think that modernity has truly departed. "We need to distinguish," says Edward Casey, "the increasingly convincing critique of the modern at the level of theory . . . from the fact that, at a practical level, we remain thoroughly enmeshed in modernity, largely because of the stranglehold that technology, the stepchild of modernity, has on our daily lives."[14]

A vacuum at the center of a culture cries out to be filled, and there are ways in which aspects of modernity, far from vanishing, have remained in or returned to this center. Peter Heslam identifies one such persistent remnant of modernism at the core of Western culture: a pragmatic, consumerist view of human life. He notes that the "ascendant ideologies of capitalism and consumerism . . . are propounded as the only systems that work, and it is 'what works' . . . that is accorded special status in the postmodern worldview."[15] Richard Bauckham perceptively comments, "The alleged incredulity towards metanarratives has a certain plausibility in contemporary Western society, but it can distract from the very powerful, late-modern grand narrative of consumerist individualism and free-market globalization, which . . . enriches the rich while leaving the poor poor, and it destroys the environment. In this way it continues the kind of oppression that the modern metanarratives of progress have always legitimated."[16]

Indeed, Susan White argues that consumerism has become one of the dominant contenders for the position of Western culture's new, defining story, and she traces its outlines in these few deft strokes:

> If there is any overarching metanarrative that purports to explain reality in the late 20th century, it is surely the narrative of the free-market economy. In the beginning of this narrative is the self-made, self-sufficient human being. At the end of this narrative is the big house, the big car, and the expensive clothes. In the middle is the struggle for success, the greed, the getting-and-spending in a world in which there is no such thing as a free lunch. Most of us have made this so thoroughly "our story" that we are hardly aware of its influence.[17]

A consumer culture is one in which increasingly the core values derive from consumption rather than the other way around. In principle, everything becomes a product that can be bought and sold. As Don Slater observes, "If there is no principle restricting who can consume what, there is also no principled constraint on what can be consumed: all social relations, activities and objects can in principle be exchanged as commodities. This is one of the most profound secularizations enacted by the modern world."[18] Sexuality may serve as an example of what Slater means. From a Christian perspective, sexuality is a profound gift of God, to be fully enjoyed within marriage. Although pornography has always turned sex into a marketable product, today's advertising and the Internet have intensified this process in an unprecedented way, so that a huge variety of pornography from any country is immediately available for consumption. Little wonder that addiction to pornography is growing exponentially.

A consumer culture is furthermore one in which freedom is equated with individual choice and private life. Slater notes that freedom to choose whatever product you want in whatever area of life has in large measure replaced the Enlightenment view of reason as a resource that the individual was encouraged to use against the authority of tradition or religion. A good example of how the "freedom to shop" threatens actually to trump the other freedoms of democracy is seen in Wal-Mart's campaign to force its way into Flagstaff, Arizona.[19] The Flagstaff city council had passed an ordinance called Proposition 100, which prohibited the construction of any store larger than 125,000 square feet. Wal-Mart, which wanted to open a large new store in Flagstaff, ran an ad in the *Arizona Daily Sun* comparing Proposition 100 supporters to

Nazi book burners. Anthony Bianco perceptively notes that in "equating a law passed by a city's elected representatives with the violent suppression of free speech, and in elevating discount shopping to parity with the freedoms affirmed by the Bill of Rights, [Wal-Mart] disrespected not only its local opponents but all Americans."[20]

Finally, a consumer culture is one in which needs are unlimited and insatiable. This is ironic, because although consumerism promises to meet our needs in an unprecedented way, its continued existence depends on our needs never quite being met: "Market society is therefore perpetually haunted by the possibility that needs might be either satisfied or underfinanced."[21]

As has often been noted, the result of the dominance of consumerism is that the mall has become the cathedral of our day. In the Middle Ages the cathedral was the center of a city, a symbolic reminder that the life of the city was to be directed to God; by contrast, today's cities are anchored by their shopping malls. As James Rouse (an architect who has designed over sixty malls) notes, "It is in the marketplace that all people come together—rich and poor, old and young, black and white. It is the democratic, unifying, universal place which gives spirit and personality to the city."[22] However, the problem with the mall, as Jon Pahl notes, is that

> it actively encourages us to forget any ideals of collectively meaningful life beyond those that the market creates. The mall creates no enduring community, rests upon no tradition, and promotes no values beyond those determined by corporations to whom consumers are all but anonymous units or marks. We are "united" by the place only in the hierarchy determined by our ability to consume. It is no coincidence that this hierarchy—where the rich get more and the poor get the door—also dominates American politics.[23]

Economic Globalization

The development of consumerism as a worldview since the 1950s is closely bound to globalization, which "encompasses many things: the international flow of ideas and knowledge, the sharing of cultures, global civil society, and the global environmental movement."[24] And, at the heart of globalization, there is a global market, which has been made possible by the communications revolution. Through communications technology the big corporations of the day spread their influence around the world. In the process these corporations are increasingly moving away from the multinational model (based in one country but with branches in other countries) to the transnational, which has no specific ties to any one country but is able to move its offices and factories around the world to maximize profit. Huge amounts of global capital can be moved into a country (electronically) very quickly but can also be withdrawn quickly, which has the potential to inflict great damage, particularly in poorer countries.

At the heart of globalization is market economics, which makes the process of buying and selling a strong contender for the driving motive of Western culture. Consequently, if we are to understand what time it is in our culture today, we need to look closely at the sort of economics that is embodied in consumerism. And a close look reveals, startlingly, that consumerism is anything but postmodern![25]

Christian economist Bob Goudzwaard points out that the modern Enlightenment worldview emerged at a time of great insecurity in Europe. Catholics and Protestants had been battling across Europe, so that religion seemed to offer no stable base for social life. Modernity thus arose as a reaction to fear, in response to the felt need for security: "Modernity, we can say, reinstalled human security. And it did so firstly in the domain of logic and in the certainty of mathematical and mechanical laws. But later on . . . it also sought to overcome this insecurity by a rational and systematic effort to organize, to reorganize, and to recreate human society."[26] And this organizing impetus included the market mechanism that continues to drive globalization.[27]

Classical economic theory (now two centuries old) laid the foundation for the economics that most of Western society has since adopted, and two of its most important principles continue to wield great influence today. The first is utilitarianism, which led to the conclusion that human happiness is best served when a certain amount of labor produces as much output as possible. From this perspective, the source of human happiness lies directly in the amount of goods and services produced and sold in the market. The second principle from classic economic thought is the belief in the inherent rightness of the free market, the conviction that we must follow the market wherever it leads because it will inevitably guide us to a better future. "Indeed, the free working of the market lies close to the centre of Western society's self-definition: in the West it is not government's place to tamper with the market, because this signifies a step away from a 'free-society' and towards a 'totalitarian society.'"[28]

Modern neoclassical economists have been concerned not to be seen to recommend any specific direction for society. Thus "modern economics attempts merely to offer explanations, just as the natural sciences attempt merely to explain reality, as it searches for universally valid laws and undeniable facts that can be linked together in an objective and unbiased fashion." The result is that human needs, motives, and desires are deliberately excluded from economic calculations because "the economist must confine himself or herself to analyzing strictly the processes of the market mechanism."[29] The result is a terribly distorted worldview because it (1) merely accepts all needs as given, (2) believes that human needs are unlimited by nature, (3) sees nature and the environment as "data" and thus excluded from its domain of study, and (4) reduces (human) labor to nothing more than one of several production factors. Goudzwaard and de Lange's critique of this dominant theory is devastating:

> Because it operates in terms of market, it misses entirely the large shards of poverty that the market is unable to register; because it approaches scarcity solely in terms of prices, it cannot assess the economic value of the ecological problem; and because it views labor solely as a paid production factor, it bypasses the problem of the quantity and quality of work. Neo-classical economics was not designed to help solve these problems. It seeks to understand and support only that which relates to production, consumption, income, and money in a market economy. . . .
>
> Our present economy is a "post-care" economy; in it we engage in the highest possible consumption and production and only afterwards attempt to mitigate the mounting care needs with often extremely expensive forms of compensation.[30]

This is not to suggest that globalization is irretrievably evil or that capitalism is all bad. Good things as well as bad have come from globalization.

Globalization is, however, rooted in a view of humankind that privileges human rationality, autonomy, and individualism. Although postmodernism has challenged these beliefs, it has not provided a genuine alternative. Even a thoroughly secularized, autonomous human being, though he or she may despair of being able to know the truth about the world, is still able to consume! Thus postmodernism has, ironically, created space for the dominance of pragmatism, for what works rather than what is reasonable. And, for most Westerners, globalization works: it has increased the items available for consumption and has made the West richer as a whole. The result has been that consumerism, abetted by a commitment to globalization, has become the dominant worldview of our day.

Yet there have been signs that not all is well with globalization. The first significant protest came on November 30, 1990, as the World Trade Organization (WTO) convened in Seattle only to see its trade negotiations (which did not go well, in any case) overshadowed by huge street demonstrations. The mayor of Seattle declared a state of civil emergency and imposed a curfew, while the governor of Washington called up the National Guard. Subsequent meetings of the WTO, though carefully shielded from protestors, did not fare much better; the developing world had awakened to the implications of globalization and was ready to air its grievances.

Although globalization is said to be about "free trade," Joseph Stiglitz argues that "free trade has not worked because we have not tried it: trade agreements of the past have been neither free nor fair."[31] Agriculture provides the clearest example. Much of the developing world is agricultural rather than technological, and Western nations have consistently refused to abandon their protection of domestic agriculture (by means of subsidies), effectively preventing fair competition between their own agricultural producers and those of developing countries. In Europe each cow gets an average subsidy of two dollars per day; tragically, more than half the people of the developing world live on less than that. These subsidies make it impossible for African farmers to compete in world markets: "The United States and Europe have perfected the art of arguing for free trade while simultaneously working for trade agreements that protect themselves against imports from developing countries."[32]

Stiglitz identifies six areas in which globalization is in urgent need of reform: (1) the need to address poverty; (2) the need for foreign assistance and debt relief; (3) the need to make trade fair as opposed to "free"; (4) the need to recognize genuine limits in developing countries' ability to open up their markets to "free trade"; (5) the need to address the environmental crises, including the threat of global warming; and (6) the need for a healthy system of global governance.[33] To Stiglitz's list we would add a seventh item: the need to limit the spread of Western culture, which so often conflicts with indigenous cultural values in the developing world.

To incarnate a Christian worldview today, we must develop a thoughtful critique of globalization and good proposals for reforming it. The market will have to lose something of its autonomy in order to be brought within the context of a more human (and humane) story, and for us that is, of course, the biblical story. Goudzwaard, Vander Vennen, and Van Heemst have begun this kind of work in the biblically sound reforms that they advocate in *Hope in Troubled Times:*

> Why not accept a threshold in our levels of income and consumption and orient ourselves to a level of enough so that our production process can be liberated from extreme stress, turn to meeting the needs of the poor, and invest in the genuine preservation of culture and the environment? Indeed, our businesses, labor unions, political parties, other organizations, and even we ourselves must urgently turn away from infinite material expansion and move instead toward genuinely sustainable economies.[34]

Sign 3: The Renascence of Christianity

Since postmodernism shares many secular humanistic assumptions with modernism, it also shares many of modernism's blind spots. Religion, rendered "private" within the modernist worldview, has rarely (since the Enlightenment) been taken seriously as a cultural force.[35] Although postmodernity has revived religion as a topic of discussion, it has kept religion firmly within those boundaries that had been prescribed by the secular assumptions of modernity.[36] But religion is indeed increasingly a major cultural force in our times: "We are currently living through one of the transforming moments in the history of religion worldwide."[37] One example of such transformation is the renascence of Christianity, especially in the southern hemisphere, where since the mid-twentieth century the number of faithful Christian believers has grown phenomenally. Christians are now a majority or sizeable minority in many of the fastest-growing countries in the world, including the Philippines, Nigeria, Mexico, Brazil, and China. If we extrapolate from present statistics, by the year 2050 "there would be around 2.6 billion Christians, of whom 633 million would live in Africa, 640 million in Latin America, and 460 million in Asia. Europe, with 555 million, would have slipped to third place."[38]

The character of the faith that has grown so vigorously in the developing world is noteworthy, for it is predominantly an orthodox, conservative Christianity with a high view of the Bible and a strong social conscience. Philip Jenkins has explored this in detail in *The New Faces of Christianity: Believing the Bible in the Global South*. As an epigraph to his chapter on "Power in the Book," Jenkins quotes Martin Luther: "The Bible is alive—it has hands and grabs hold of me, it has feet and runs after me." Christians of the southern hemisphere experience Scripture as the living and true Word of God: "Whatever their differences over particular issues, the newer churches see the Bible as a dependable and comprehensive source of authority; and this respect extends to the whole biblical text, to both Testaments."[39] And this high regard for the authority of the Bible has not, in developing countries, been wedded to a political conservatism seeking to entrench the status quo. In fact, it is church leaders who struggle for reform and human rights, even at the cost of their own safety.

Churches of the northern hemisphere have found it hard to orient themselves within postmodernism. How does one live and proclaim the gospel in the midst of a culture where "anything goes," where tolerance is the cardinal virtue and the right of the individual to choose his or her own lifestyle must be respected above all? It is not surprising to find that the most contentious issue in mainstream churches of the northern hemisphere nowadays is what stance to take toward homosexuality. In a profoundly secular culture, which has decided that the freedom to choose is of ultimate significance, any critique of homosexuality is seen as homophobic and as a denial of the equality of the "other." Christianity of the southern hemisphere should help us to gain perspective at this point and to strengthen our commitment to the biblical story, reminding us that our first responsibility is to God and his revelation, while our responsibility to our neighbor is secondary. We cannot allow the demands of our neighbors for free choice—whether it be in sexual orientation or abortion or pornography or consumerism or use of the world's resources— to determine the agenda of Christians today. Before any other consideration, we are called to be faithful to God.

The burgeoning orthodox Christianity of the developing world may challenge the often compromised Christianity of Western nations, especially as faith has been relegated to the sphere of strictly private and personal matters. "For many Christians outside the West, it is not obvious that religion should be an individual or privatized matter; that church and state be separate; that secular values predominate in some spheres of life; or that scriptures be evaluated according to the canons of historical scholarship."[40] Christians of the southern hemisphere are therefore challenging the rest of us to recover the gospel for what it is: a worldview that embraces all of life. So much of Christianity in the northern hemisphere has capitulated to the privatization of religion that it is hard to imagine what a truly living Christian worldview might involve. What does it mean to follow Christ in art, education, politics, marriage and sexuality, economics, business? Although Christians of the southern hemisphere have yet to develop a full-orbed Christian worldview in theory and practice, it certainly is true that they are, as prophets, calling us to recover the comprehensiveness of the Christian faith and to join with them in bringing the whole gospel to the whole world.[41] Jenkins observes that the greatest challenge that the Majority World church may bring to our global world

> is likely to involve our Enlightenment-derived assumption that religion should be segregated into a separate sphere of life, distinct from everyday reality. In the Western view . . . spiritual life is primarily a private inward activity, a matter for the individual mind. For Americans particularly, the common assumption holds that church and state, sacred and profane, are wholly separate enterprises, and should be kept separate as oil and water. In most historical periods, though, such a distinction does not apply, and is even incomprehensible.[42]

Nor is such a distinction comprehensible in Africa, Latin America, and Africa.

What time is it in our culture? The church of Christ in the developing world says that it is time for us to recover a sense of Christ's lordship over all of life, to say with conviction that Jesus "is the secret of heaven and earth, of the cosmos created by God."[43] They demand that we regain a vision of Christ as the clue to the whole of creation and that we pursue that clue relentlessly.

Sign 4: The Resurgence of Islam

In *The Clash of Civilizations and the Remaking of World Order*, Samuel Huntington alerts us to the remarkable recent growth in Islam, which parallels that of Christianity in the southern hemisphere.[44] Islam grew from 12.4 percent of the world's population in 1900 to 19.6 percent in 1993. This resurgence of Islam, which began in the 1970s, now directly affects some one-fifth or more of humanity and has significant implications for the rest of the world. For example, Jenkins notes that of the world's twenty-five largest nations, by the year 2050 twenty will be predominantly or entirely Christian or Muslim.[45] Nine of these countries will be wholly or mainly Muslim, eight others wholly or mainly made up of Christians, and the remaining three will be deeply divided between the two faiths. No less than ten of the world's twenty-five largest states could, by the middle of the twenty-first century, be the site of serious conflict between adherents of Islam and Christianity.

Politically, a major characteristic of resurgent Islam is the turn to Islamic law (Sharia) in place of Western law as the key to a full life and healthy government. Resurgent Islam is deeply critical of the West and is therefore looking for solutions to the challenges of modernity in its own traditions. There is no sacred/secular dichotomy in resurgent Islam; all aspects of life are taken seriously as matters of faith. As Khurshid Ahmad notes, "Islam is not a religion in the common, distorted meaning of the word, confining its scope to the private life of man. . . . Islam provides guidance for all walks of life—individual and social, material and moral, economic and political, legal and cultural, national and international. The Qur'an enjoins man to enter the fold of Islam without any reservation and to follow God's guidance in all fields of life."[46]

Although resurgent Islam is largely within the mainstream, there is also within it a significant radical, fundamentalist or puritan element. Radical Islam feeds Islamic terrorist groups, many of which have expressed "the overall goal of the restoration of a unified worldwide Muslim political community, the *ummah*, ruled by a centralized Islamic authority, the caliphate, governed by a reactionary version of Islamic law, *shari'a*, and organized to wage war, *jihad*, on the rest of the world."[47]

Resurgent Islam presents two major challenges to Christianity. First, it challenges Christianity to rid itself once and for all of the sacred/secular dualism. Islam rejects the dualism that afflicts so much Christian thinking about scholarship and education, for example. Thus, the opening chapter of Chaudhry Abdul Qadir's *Philosophy and Science in the Islamic World* states, "The Islamic theory of knowledge . . . is based upon the spiritual conception of man and the universe he inhabits, while [the Western theory] is secular and devoid of the sense of the Sacred. It is precisely for this reason, according to Muslim thinkers, that the Western theory of knowledge poses one of the greatest challenges to mankind."[48] Islamic belief in the sovereignty of Allah "means that the sense of the Sacred which furnishes the ultimate ground for knowledge has to accompany and to interpenetrate the educative process at every stage. Allah not only stands at the beginning of knowledge, He also stands at the end and He also accompanies and infuses grace into the entire process of learning."[49]

Thus Islam has been far more successful than Christianity in resisting the secularism of modernity. In Islam's response to postmodernism one hears echoes of the concerns voiced by thoughtful Christians, as this passage from the work of Akbar Ahmed illustrates: "The test for Muslims is how to preserve the essence of the Quranic message . . . without it being reduced to an ancient and empty chant in our times; how to participate in the global civilization without their identity being obliterated. It is an apocalyptic test; the most severe examination. Muslims stand at the crossroads."[50]

In one sense, Islam and Christianity stand at the same crossroads, with the same decision before each of them: how to preserve the comprehensive nature of their faith while relating to the ultramodernity of the West. However, Islam has a better record in holding on to the comprehensiveness of its faith. Ziauddin Sardar, a London-based Muslim journalist, gives as one reason why Muslims distrust Christianity that it has "become a handmaiden to secularism. . . . Christianity, it appears, always chooses as secularism wills."[51] Sardar recognizes not only that secularism is itself deeply religious, but also that biblical Christianity is not dualistic and ought to be an "antithesis to secularism."[52] Sardar diagnoses this dualism as evidence of Christianity's historic compromises with Platonism and rationalism, with the result that "the spread of Christianity in the Third world goes hand in hand with the introduction of liberal secularism and Western capitalism into developing societies. . . . Christianity thus serves the interest of secularism in the Third world, despite loud declarations of love and an appearance of authenticity, missionary activity often spreads a dehumanizing form of Western culture and capitalism."[53]

A sense of the resurgence of Islam should help Christians to gain a healthier perspective on postmodernism and globalization. Now, more than ever, we must not accommodate the gospel at every point to secular Western culture, for to do so would leave us with nice people who believe virtually nothing. It is time to recover and stand firm upon the essentials of the faith. The renewal of Islam represents a prophetic challenge to Christians to recover the full dimensions of their faith. Indeed, it is even possible that as Christians do so, they could work with moderate Muslims on how to develop societies that allow for faiths to come into full expression, thereby avoiding the oppressive "freedom of religion" articulated by liberal democracies. However, this could happen only if Islam is up to the challenge of a genuine pluralism that would allow another faith, such as Christianity, to flourish fully alongside its own. "The fundamental question here is whether Islam and Christianity can co-exist."[54]

And this presents the second challenge to Christianity: will Christians and Muslims be able to live together peacefully in a global world? The events of 9/11 have caused many to ask if Islam can find within itself room for tolerance, genuine neighborliness, and a capacity to affirm basic human rights. And although Christianity, as well as Islam, has elements in its history of terrible oppression and coercion, the crucial question is the extent to which coercion is inherent in each of them. Lesslie Newbigin, rightly in our opinion, affirms,

> What is unique about the Christian gospel is that those who are called to be its witnesses are committed to the public affirmation that it is true—true for all peoples at all times—and are at the same time forbidden to use coercion to enforce it. They are therefore required to be tolerant of denial . . . not in the sense that we must tolerate all beliefs because truth is unknowable and all have equal rights. The toleration which a Christian is required to exercise is not something which he must exercise *in spite of* his or her belief that the gospel is true, but precisely *because of* this belief. This marks one of the very important points of difference between Islam and Christianity.[55]

Radical Islam's historical record of violence against those who seek to extend human rights or the rights of women, or those who simply oppose its own political agenda, is not good, to put it mildly. Such radicals engage in militant evangelism but refuse to be evangelized or to allow Muslims the right to convert to another faith. Jacques Ellul argues that "war is a duty for all Muslims. . . . War is inherent in Islam. It is inscribed in its teaching."[56] In order to understand the Islamic attitude toward violence, we must consider the concept of jihad, or struggle, which can be inward or outward and (if directed outward) can be defensive or offensive. Bernard Lewis comments, "For most of the fourteen centuries of recorded Muslim history, *jihad* was most commonly interpreted to mean armed struggle for the defence or advancement of Muslim power."[57] Thinkers such as Peter Riddell and Peter Cotterell find in the Qur'an a tension between defensive and offensive approaches: "Is Islam a religion of peace, as Muslim moderates . . . say, or is it a religion prone to violence and holy war, as statements by radical groups suggest? . . . The answer lies not in an either/or response, but rather in a 'both . . . and' response. The Islamic texts offer the potential for being interpreted in both ways. It depends on how individual Muslims wish to read them."[58]

Radical Islam has received a variety of Christian responses. Some, like Riddell and Cotterell, argue that the heart of the problem is Islamic theology, and that this needs to be sorted out by moderate Muslims if peaceful coexistence between Muslims and others is to be achieved. Others, like John Esposito, recognize the ambiguity in Islamic scripture and tradition and accept the mainstream interpretation of Muslims that terrorism is forbidden and un-Islamic.[59]

We do think that Islam needs to face squarely the extent to which the Qur'an legitimates violence as a means of promoting its faith. At the same time, we assert the vital need to seek to understand the issues that Islamic "terrorists" have raised, while completely eschewing their violent methods of doing so. This will involve becoming more critical of our own role in world affairs and the role of our governments. Like Christ, we need to be passionate about justice. Esposito rightly points out, "The cancer of global terrorism will continue to afflict the international body until we address its political and economic causes, causes that will otherwise continue to provide a breeding ground for hatred and radicalism, the rise of extremist movements, and recruits for the bin Ladens of this world."[60]

Colin Chapman notes, as an example, the injustice that Israel has perpetrated against Palestine: "Elijah predicted a famine; but he also condemned Ahab for murdering Naboth and stealing his vineyard. I find it a very painful experience to visit the West Bank today because there are dozens, or rather hundreds, of Naboth's vineyards—illegal Israeli settlements on every other hill top."[61] He goes on to say, "I personally believe that a serious attempt on the part of the West (and especially the USA) to understand the anger of Palestinians, Arabs and Muslims and to deal with the Israeli-Palestinian conflict in a more even-handed way would go a long way—perhaps even a very long way—towards defusing the anger that many Muslims feel towards the West."[62]

Conclusion

It is a fascinating and complex time in which we live. Modernity is under attack in postmodernism but at the same time is spreading around the world in the process of globalization. Both postmodernism and globalization seem to be feeding a consumer culture. The global growth of Christianity in the southern hemisphere and of Islam brings its own challenges. Contemporary Western culture is, as a result, in a time of crisis and uncertainty.

It is in this context that the church is called to live at the crossroads, at the intersection of the drama of Scripture and the stories of our culture. Clearly, this is no easy task. While postmodernism has subverted the worldviews of modernity and made it easier for a Christian perspective to gain a voice, at the same time postmodernism is deeply intolerant of worldviews per se and certainly finds no place for the Christian claim that the gospel is true. And all this time, while secularism retains its grip on the West, the Christian church is experiencing phenomenal growth in the developing world. How, then, should we live at the crossroads?

8

Living at the Crossroads

A Faithful, Relevant Witness

A Comprehensive Vision of Cultural Engagement

Throughout this book we have emphasized two truths that we believe to be foundational to the cultural task of Christians. The first truth is about who Jesus Christ is: he is the Creator and Redeemer of all things who rules all of history and is moving it to his appointed end (Col. 1:15–20; Rev. 4–5). Jesus is Lord. The second truth is that biblical salvation is comprehensive in scope and restorative in nature: God's purpose in salvation is to restore the whole life of humankind in the context of a renewed creation. If we believe that Jesus is Lord, then we must witness to Christ's lordship in every area of human life and culture. If we believe that salvation is truly comprehensive, then we must embody Christ's salvation in every area of human life and culture. To follow the Lord Jesus and witness to his salvation is to serve him in all things, confessing Christ's rule over the whole of society and culture, taking a stand against all the evil that thwarts that rule.

In the last half century the evangelical church in North America has made significant progress toward reclaiming the comprehensive scope of the gospel. In this it has been moving away from the sort of piety that had severely limited the scope of Christian cultural engagement in the early part of the twentieth century, when evangelicalism had largely become individualistic, otherworldly, and dualistic, confining the gospel to the inward and private dimensions of life.

The motivation for this retreat from cultural engagement was often highly principled: many evangelical leaders sought to avoid what had happened in too many "liberal" churches: the reduction of the gospel to a message of merely social and political activity. Instead of rethinking social and political engagement in the light of the gospel, they abandoned their social calling. Evangelicals ended up adopting a false distinction between "sacred" and "secular" realms of human experience. In limiting its own concerns to the "sacred" matters (prayer, Bible study, evangelism, personal salvation), the evangelical church had largely abandoned Christ's claim to lordship in the "secular" realm. It brings to mind the parable of the man who, afraid of falling off his horse on the left side, leans so far the other way that he falls off his horse on the right side.

The evangelical tradition in the early twentieth century simply did not see the gospel as a transforming power for human culture. David Bosch describes how this desire to withdraw from public life has been a perennial temptation to the church:

> As our concern over rampant secularization increases, we may in fashioning a missiology of Western culture easily be seduced into concentrating on the "religious" aspect [of culture] only, leaving the rest to the secular powers, not least because these powers exert massive pressures on the church to limit itself to the soul of the individual. This is, after all, in keeping with the Enlightenment worldview: religion is a private affair, its truth claims are relative and have no place in the public sphere of "facts." But Christian theology itself also contributed to this notion, as it increasingly individualized, interiorized, ecclesiasticized, and privatized salvation.[1]

About the middle of the century, a number of evangelicals became increasingly uncomfortable with this unbiblical stance. In 1947 Carl F. H. Henry challenged the evangelical (he called it "fundamentalist") community to take seriously once more its social calling in light of the tremendous problems emerging around the world.

> Whereas once the redemptive gospel was a world-changing message, now it was narrowed to a world-resisting message. . . . Fundamentalism in revolting against the Social Gospel seemed also to revolt against the Christian social imperative. . . . It does not challenge the injustices of the totalitarianisms, the secularisms of modern education, the evils of racial hatred, the wrongs of current labor-management relations, and inadequate bases of international dealings.[2]

Yet it would take a few decades before this began to take root. In 1974 at Lausanne,[3] at the largest gathering of evangelical leaders ever held, the official document of that conference (the "Lausanne Covenant") affirmed that social, political, and economic involvement is indeed important to the church's calling. The Lausanne Covenant included a special section on Christian social responsibility and expressed penitence for the church's historical neglect of social concern: "The salvation we claim should be transforming us (2 Cor. 3:18) in the totality of our personal and social responsibilities. Faith without works is dead (James 1:14–26)."[4] A decade later, a statement produced by the World Evangelical Fellowship at Wheaton (1983) reaffirmed the commitment of evangelicals to be engaged in their cultures: "Evil is not only in the human heart but also in social structures. . . . The mission of the church includes both the proclamation of the Gospel and its demonstration. We must therefore evangelize, respond to immediate human needs, and press for social transformation."[5]

A growing number of evangelicals today acknowledge that the mission of the church is as broad as human culture, as broad as creation itself. Social, economic, ecological, and political activity among such Christians has increased dramatically in recent decades. Yet evangelicals sometimes have been selective in the issues that they have addressed, avoiding some areas of life where there is great need for a gospel witness. For example, issues surrounding sexuality, the family, medical ethics, and individual morality are now firmly on the evangelical agenda (as they should be), but the church has not been as critical of the injustices of the capitalistic economic system or of the dangers of humanistic public education and scholarship.[6]

Living at the Crossroads: Insight from Mission

The Christian community living in the fifth act of the drama of Scripture is to be shaped by its mission: to bear witness in life, word, and deed to the coming kingdom of God. But we are also part of a cultural community that finds its identity in another story, a story that is to a large extent incompatible with the biblical story. Since our embodying of the kingdom of God must take cultural shape in our own particular time and place, we find ourselves at the crossroads where both stories claim to be true, and each claims the whole of our lives. How can we be faithful to the biblical story here and now?

The early church struggled to live in a way that was faithful to the gospel in the midst of the pagan Roman Empire. Even after Constantine's conversion to Christianity in the fourth century, faithful Christians in the West found that to live authentically Christian lives and bring the gospel to bear on their cultures often demanded hard choices. During the Middle Ages many public institutions were shaped by the Christian faith, and the monastic orders offered their own faithful versions of Christian life in the midst of sometimes hostile cultures. As exploration and colonization expanded from the fifteenth century onward, serious struggles with the issue of cultural engagement reemerged as first Roman Catholic and then Protestant missionaries moved into cultures hitherto untouched by the gospel. Thus our own situation in the increasingly anti-Christian environment of the early twenty-first century is not unique. Nevertheless, the question of how to live authentically at the crossroads of two cultures remains.

For over half a century, H. Richard Niebuhr's *Christ and Culture* has provided useful categories for wrestling with the question of the relationship of the gospel to culture.[7] More recently, missiology, especially in the burgeoning studies of "contextualization," has offered some excellent insight to those seeking faithfully to relate the gospel to their own culture.[8]

Lesslie Newbigin was among the first to apply the insights of contextualization to Western culture. He had spent forty years as a missionary in India, struggling to contextualize the gospel in the midst of a Hindu culture. He applied the insights achieved from that experience, together with his vast reading in the literature of contextualization, to the task of bringing the gospel to bear on Western culture. Newbigin notes that theological studies on the relationship of gospel and culture, like those by Niebuhr and Tillich, have not been done from the vantage point of those people with real experience in transmitting the gospel to a very different culture.[9] Contextualization studies, on the other hand, have dealt primarily with non-Western cultures and have, as Newbigin says, "largely ignored the culture that is the most widespread, powerful, and persuasive among all contemporary cultures . . . [which is] modern Western culture."[10] He set out to show how the experience of missionaries in the cross-cultural transmission of the gospel, and the reflection on that process (contextualization), could help thoughtful Christians bring the gospel to bear upon their own cultures. We find the literature of contextualization helpful and will draw on its insights as we seek a faithful approach to living at the crossroads.

Some Starting Examples

God's people living at the crossroads are engaged in a missionary encounter where two ultimate and comprehensive stories—the biblical story and the cultural story—collide.[11] If we believe that the gospel offers the true story of the world, and are therefore committed to shaping our entire lives by it, then we will indeed engage with the cultural story being lived out around us. We will live out the good news of Christ's kingdom as a credible alternative to the way of life of our contemporaries, inviting them to turn from the idolatrous beliefs of the Western cultural story and to understand and live in the world in the light of the gospel. But before we reflect more deeply on the dynamics of this missionary encounter, let us consider some concrete examples of Christians faced with difficult choices at the crossroads of culture.

(1) A Christian businesswoman works in middle management for a large company. It becomes increasingly evident to her that the profit motive dominates her company to the exclusion of every other consideration—the bottom line is all that really matters. But she recognizes that this drive for profit means upholding unjust economic structures that exacerbate poverty in developing countries and ransack the natural environment. How is this businesswoman to respond if she wants to keep her job and address this injustice?

(2) A Christian graduate student is working on his PhD in a public university. It becomes increasingly obvious to him that relativism shapes the very foundations of his subject. His professors and fellow students dogmatically refuse even to consider the possibility that any true metanarrative, including the biblical one, exists. Yet their own view of the world is itself a deeply committed one, from which they roundly and passionately condemn what they see as the "sins" of heterosexism, patriarchy, racism, and ethnocentrism. They demand dogmatically that all scholars should play the game according to their rules. How is a thoughtful Christian student to make his way in this academic world?

(3) A Christian social worker takes a position at a psychiatric hospital. She becomes aware that hospital policy has been shaped throughout by an understanding of the human being that categorically denies the fact of human sinfulness. All problems, according to this culture's view, may be attributed to one's environment; no person is ever to be held accountable for any part of his or her own predicament. But this Christian social worker is convinced that the medical culture's approach is stripping human dignity from the people she serves and in fact is getting in the way of solving their problems. She believes that an approach that takes seriously humanity as being made in God's image and yet being sinful would be much more fruitful. Yet her whole professional culture rejects such an approach. How can she function in such an environment of conflicting commitments?

(4) A Christian teacher takes a position teaching history in a local public elementary school. It is made clear to her that she must not in any way allow

her faith to "interfere" with her task: she is to teach history precisely as it is narrated in the textbook. But that textbook, she soon discovers, tells a story that is out of keeping with the story that would be told if one started with the gospel. The official "history" to be taught in her school assumes the progress and evolution of humanity, especially through science and technology. What does she do?

(5) A Christian athlete finally fulfills his dream of making it to the professional level of baseball. He loves the competition and sees it as a gift of God, but increasingly he is uncomfortable with the economics of professional sports. Is anyone worth the tens of millions of dollars that they are being paid? Can such enormous salaries be justified in a world in which so many people struggle merely to survive? He begins to see that salaries are negotiated not from a sense of the athletes' real need (or an awareness of how short their careers may be); instead, salary demands are driven by egocentrism and naked greed. He wonders what, in this environment, it could possibly mean to play baseball "for the glory of God."

(6) A Christian enters politics and is elected to public office. She wants to enact laws that truly contribute to public justice. Yet as she becomes more and more involved in the political process, she realizes that the pervading liberal ideology, which upholds the freedom of the individual at all costs, actually is contributing to injustice. She sees also that the making of policy is more often influenced by money and political pressure than it is by a real concern for justice. No one around her seems troubled by these facts—they are merely the assumptions of political life. Can this woman withstand the pressure to conform and still be an effective politician?

These six examples of Christians seeking to live and to choose faithfully at the crossroads of culture all come from true stories. These are real people, known by us personally. Theirs are the real struggles of Christians living now in Western culture, trying to negotiate what faithfulness to the gospel looks like at the crossroads. They raise the issue that we want to address in this chapter: how can a Christian remain faithful to the biblical story while living in a culture that has largely been shaped by a very different story?

"In the World but Not of It": Critical Participation

If we are to live faithfully in the biblical story, we must become critical participants in the cultures that surround us. As participants, our relationship to culture is positive: we are part of it and identify with it, seeking (as members, fellow citizens, participants) to "love and cherish all of its created goodness."[12]

As critical participants in culture, however, we will often find ourselves standing in opposition to it, rejecting and challenging the idolatry that twists and distorts its development. There are thus two sides to this faithful engagement: affirmation and rejection, participation and opposition, solidarity and separation. This has often been expressed as being "in the world" but not "of the world" (John 17:13–18).

Our participation and solidarity are required by two strands of the biblical story. God has created human beings to live in social and cultural cohesion (Gen. 1:26–28), and thus as communal creatures, the people of God should joyfully and willingly engage in their roles in society by contributing toward cultural development. Furthermore, because Jesus is Lord, we are called in his service to struggle for all that he claims as his own. Abraham Kuyper has stated this forcefully: "There is not a square inch of the entire domain of human life of which Christ the Sovereign does not say, 'That is mine!'"[13] If Christ is indeed Lord of every human culture, then his followers must not simply withdraw; rather, they must uphold his rightful claims there. Yet the biblical story demands the other side as well. The apostle Paul commands us not to "conform to the pattern of this world" (Rom. 12:2). For Paul, "world" is culture disfigured by idolatry. Thus our affirmation of culture must be accompanied by rejection.

The cross wonderfully illustrates the two-sided responsibility of Christian participation in culture. On the one hand, the cross was God's ultimate expression of his love for the world, an act of solidarity with the corrupt and suffering world that he loved and came to save. But the cross was also the ultimate expression of God's judgment against the sin and idolatry of the world, his utter rejection of all that seeks to destroy the *shalom* of his creation.[14] Believers who have heard the call to take up the cross and follow Jesus must assume the same relation to the world that is illustrated by that very cross. "We must always, it seems to me, in every situation, be wrestling with both sides of this reality: that the Church is for the world against the world. The Church is against the world for the world. The Church is for the human community in that place, that village, that city, that nation, in the sense that Christ is for the world. And that must be the determining criterion at every point."[15] How does the Christian businesswoman stand opposed to the enshrinement of profit motive and yet in favor of a healthy business life? How does the Christian university student stand against the idol of relativism yet affirm the many insights into creation offered by "secular" scholarship?

"An Unbearable Tension"

The starting point for the church's relation to culture is affirmation: we live in solidarity with our cultural contemporaries. Since God loved the world, we must too. This positive affirmation does not, however, lessen the deep sense of what Newbigin calls the "unbearable tension" that comes from being a member of two communities anchored in "two different and incompatible stories."[16] This "unbearable tension" exists between the gospel and the cultural story. Hendrik Kraemer believes that if the church is to be faithful, it must cultivate an awareness of this tension and fully embrace it. "The deeper the consciousness of the tension and the urge to take this yoke upon itself are felt, the healthier the Church is. The more oblivious of this tension the Church is, the more well established and at home in this world it feels, the more it is in deadly danger of being the salt that has lost its savour."[17] Yet many Christians in Western culture have lost this sense of tension between the gospel and their cultural story.[18] This may occur when we begin to accept, consciously or otherwise, the myth that contemporary Western culture is really a "Christian" culture and so poses no threat to Christian faith. But that is indeed a myth: no culture is (or ever has been) truly Christian. We may also lose the healthy sense of the tension between the gospel and culture by accepting another dominant myth of our time: that contemporary culture is religiously neutral, either because it is secular or pluralistic.[19] Yet this too is a myth, for Western culture (like all human cultures) has been shaped by ultimate beliefs. As Newbigin puts it, "No state can be completely secular in the sense that those who exercise power have no beliefs about what is true and no commitments to what they believe to be right. It is the duty of the church to ask what those beliefs and commitments are and to expose them to the light of the gospel."[20] Indeed, the fundamental beliefs of humanism are masked by precisely this claim to religious neutrality. Years ago, T. S. Eliot warned that the majority of Christians of his day were unconscious of the fact that they were living in a culture that was dangerous to Christianity.

> The problem of leading a Christian life in a non-Christian society is now very present to us. It is not merely the problem of a minority in a society of individuals holding an alien belief. It is the problem constituted by our implication in a network of institutions from which we cannot dissociate ourselves; institutions the operation of which appears no longer neutral, but non-Christian; and *as for the Christian who is not conscious of his dilemma— and he is in the majority—he is becoming more and more de-Christianized by all sorts of unconscious pressures*; paganism now holding all the most valuable advertising space.[21]

Unfaithful Ways to Resolve the Tension

Christians could, of course, avoid the tension of living in two cultures by the strategies of withdrawal, accommodation, or dualism. We could attempt to withdraw from "secular" culture altogether into a Christian ghetto, abandoning the West to its idols. But since God made us to be cultural creatures and enjoined his people to be salt and light in the present world, withdrawal is not a faithful option. We could accommodate ourselves to modern culture, reminding ourselves that God loves his world and shutting our eyes firmly to the equal and opposite truth that God does not love the sin that has twisted and thwarted human culture from its foundations upward. No Christian can find accommodation to be a faithful option.

The third approach, to adopt a kind of dualism, is dangerously seductive and also quite widespread. The kind of dualism that we have in mind here makes a firm distinction between "contentious ground" and "neutral territory" in the conflict of competing worldviews. Thus, whereas we may be forced to admit that Christianity has some definite (and difficult) things to say about, for example, medical ethics, perhaps the contemporary economic practices of capitalism are neutral. Although we oppose abortion, public education is considered a neutral area. We engage culture in certain areas, but in others we simply fit in. This sort of dualism is blind to the fact that the religious beliefs upon which cultures are founded are all-encompassing. Human rebellion against God's purposes for creation has shaped economics, politics, and education just as surely as it has shaped contemporary ethical standards. If we are truly to embody a biblical worldview, we cannot (by adopting the double-mindedness of dualism) surrender large chunks of the territory claimed by our King.

A Faithful Approach

If we reject these three approaches, how do we live faithfully in this "unbearable tension" of stories, affirming the cultural development that God loves, while rejecting the idolatry that has twisted it even as it has developed?

A helpful starting point is to recall the important distinction, mentioned in chapter 3, between structure and direction, or creational design and spiritual power. All cultural products, institutions, relationships, and patterns manifest something of God's original creational design or structure. Sin never twists or destroys any cultural product or societal institution so badly that nothing of the creational goodness remains in it; God faithfully upholds his creation by his word. At the same time, a spiritual power that stands in opposition to Christ has touched and tainted every one of those same cultural products, institutions, relationships, and patterns. Thus, for example, in the political arena we recognize much of God's creational design for the government to pursue public justice, yet we can see how the spiritual power of a liberal ideology may corrupt that design and lead to injustice. In the economic arena we can recognize in business something of God's design for a stewardly and efficient sharing of the world's resources, yet at the same time we perceive how the spiritual powers of economic idolatry and the profit motive have distorted economic life, so that natural resources are consumed wastefully and poverty is exacerbated. In academic life we can recognize much truth and insight in the scholarship of those whose work does not start with the gospel, but we can see also how the spiritual powers of rationalism, naturalism, and relativism have twisted the insights of many scholars. In whatever we examine critically we will discover something of God's good creational structure and also evidence of how it has been deformed by sin. A faithful embodiment of the gospel in our own cultural settings demands that we discern between the creational structure and design in all things and the religious misdirection and rebellion that pervert God's good world.

Much can be learned here from the cross-cultural missionary experience of the past two hundred years. When a missionary goes to a culture where the controlling faith assumptions are rooted in a religion obviously hostile to the Christian faith, she must carefully analyze that culture with a view to understanding its controlling assumptions and foundational religious beliefs. She will be aware that in, for example, a Hindu or a Muslim culture, the core cultural beliefs will be incompatible with the gospel; the antithesis will be clear. But at the same time, she will seek to embody the gospel by looking for ways in which the prevailing cultural structures affirm creation. Since she knows that her task is to witness to the gospel in a culture that is at odds with the gospel, she will be careful not to be absorbed into that culture's controlling assumptions; but since she wants to embody good news to that people in their culture, she will want the gospel to be at home there as well. And thus she will live with the tension of being simultaneously at home and at odds with the cultural story. This constant awareness will produce in her an inner dialogue between the scriptural story and the cultural story, a dialogue that will help to guard against the twin dangers of withdrawal and absorption. She will learn to live so fully within both traditions and both communities that the debate between them becomes internalized. As a Christian, she will be committed to live fully in the biblical story, making that story her story, so she can see her host culture through the lens of the Bible. This inner dialogue will become for her a way of life, a state of mind, a constant in her engagements with culture. Thus a sustained tension may become the anchor of faithfulness.

For a missionary, this tension is essential. Compromise and accommodation would leave her with no gospel to share, no further reason to be a missionary. Yet if her presentation of the gospel makes it appear utterly alien to the people of the culture that she brings it to, it would be rejected. The gospel must shine through the missionary's own life and words, in forms familiar to those whose lives she seeks to illumine. Thus, having a missionary consciousness means being alert to good creational design on the one hand, and idolatry on the other.

New Testament Examples of Faithful Contextualization

The apostle Paul was a cross-cultural missionary. He approached the idolatrous Roman culture of his day by distinguishing between creational design and cultural idolatry.[22] The primary social institution of the Roman Empire was the *oikos*, a word normally translated "household" but with the sense of economic relationships and political authority in an extended family structure. The father (*paterfamilias*) held absolute power: he was the *kyrios* or lord of the home. The entire *oikos* was shaped by the Roman Empire's abusive and hierarchical view of authority.

Instead of simply rejecting or affirming the cultural institution of the Roman household, Paul discerns the creational relationships within it—husband and wife, parent and child. Then he works to transform them, to reshape them by the power of the gospel. We can read Ephesians 5 in this light. Paul's exhortation to husbands—to love their wives sacrificially, to nurture their children lovingly, and to treat their slaves with respect—was utterly radical for that time and place and people. Paul is urging the *paterfamilias* to use his authority in a loving and sacrificial way. When Paul speaks to women and slaves, he restores dignity to them by exhorting them to choose to submit themselves. And the motivation of all members of the *oikos* is to become new: all this is to be done for the sake of the Lord. The *oikos* is to be "no longer a patriarchal institution but . . . [is to be] redefined by Christ's sacrificial love for the church . . . a visible alternative to the dominant cultural model."[23] Thus Paul's missionary strategy was to call the church to live within the existing institutions of culture, yet with a critical and transforming presence.

What Paul calls for within the social institutions of the Roman Empire, John does with language, the very words and thought forms of Hellenistic culture. He begins with the announcement, "In the beginning was the *logos*"

(John 1:1). To a Greek reader, this *logos* would seem to refer to an imaginary, invisible rationality that permeated the world, giving it order. John begins with the affirmation that the *logos* is indeed responsible for creating and maintaining order in the world. But then he subverts the idolatrous Greek concept, declaring that this *logos* is not the idol of the Greeks but rather is the man Jesus Christ. The *logos* became flesh (*sarx*), says John (John 1:14). Thus John affirms the creational reality of order expressed in the term *logos* but goes on to challenge and contradict the mistaken religious understandings of this concept that had developed in the classical world. In this way John is both relevant and faithful: relevant because he uses familiar categories to express existential struggles, faithful because he challenges the idolatrous worldview that has shaped those categories.

The gospel says both yes and no to each cultural form: yes to the creational design or structure, no to the idolatrous religious power that has distorted that design.

Discerning Creational Design, Cultural Idolatry, and Healing Action

Thus faithful contextualization demands discernment in three dimensions: (1) creational design, (2) cultural idolatry, and (3) healing potential. Consider the examples at the beginning of the chapter. For the businesswoman struggling with the profit motive that drives her company, the first question is, "What is the creational design or characteristic responsibility of business?" She might conclude something like this: business is to love one's neighbor by providing goods and services in a stewardly and just manner. For the doctoral student struggling with humanistic scholarship, the question might be, "What is the purpose and calling of scholarship?" He might conclude that it is to gain systematic and historical insight into God's world. For the Christian politician, the question would be, "What is the specific obligation of the government?" She may answer that it is to administer the public affairs of a certain territory according to just laws. Of course, these are just thumbnail descriptions, and they would need to be worked out in much more detail. Nevertheless, implicitly or explicitly, our starting point for faithful Christian involvement in culture will be to achieve some understanding of the purpose for which the particular cultural institution exists and a picture of what healthy art, sports, international relations, labor, marriage, or the family might look like if they were to be oriented to that purpose.

Faithfulness at the crossroads will involve, in the second place, insight into cultural idolatry and the way that it corrupts God's creation. All businesses, places of learning, and governments embody human responses to God's intended purposes for them, and in these responses obedience will be intertwined with disobedience. Every business will provide goods and service with some measure of stewardship and justice, but every business will also betray how it has been shaped by the underlying idols of its culture. Profit is one legitimate aspect of the business enterprise when it is properly subordinated to other motives, but when profit becomes the sole motive for business, its idol, then that business will be warped by its own idolatry. All scholarship bears some insight into God's world, but when the illusion of scientific objectivity and neutrality, or the postmodern idol of relativism, provides the framework for scholarship, its insights will be distorted. Every government may seek more or less to implement just laws, but the understanding of justice in every human government will to some degree be disfigured by its underlying idolatry. When the freedom of individuals—by itself a necessary consideration of public justice—comes to dominate the agenda, as it does in liberalism, other aspects of justice (like the rights of community, the poor, and of the nonhuman creation) are apt to be neglected. In each case one must discern not only the created order of the social institution being considered but also how that cultural structure has been deformed by idolatry.

Finally, a faithful witness will discern what healing action might look like in each particular situation. The businesswoman will pay attention to the glimmers of justice and stewardship manifest in the way her business provides goods and services and will seek to strengthen and develop them. The doctoral student will strategically seize the genuine insights that his discipline affords, while rejecting the false premises on which some of the theorizing may rest. The politician will struggle to discern where public justice is legally embodied. The task is to struggle to move in a direction of more stewardship, more insight, more public justice. Here the task will be highly contextual. What must be done will depend on the position that the Christian holds, the degree of distortion evident in his or her cultural arena, and the opportunities that may exist for faithful witness to an alternative worldview. But the Christian who works in the midst of an alien culture may take heart in reflecting that God holds his creation together in harmony, and that joy and *shalom* in human life depend on conforming to his wisdom.

Countering Four Dangers

The view of cultural engagement that we have outlined to this point is open to at least four potential criticisms. The first is that this view is individualistic, emphasizing the calling of individual believers in society and neglecting the communal witness of the church. Second, in attempting to bring the various social and cultural institutions into greater conformity with God's design, there is the danger that those marginalized by such institutions may be forgotten. Third, this approach may make Christians more vulnerable to the temptations of triumphalism and coercion: it is tempting to try to build the kingdom here and now, using various methods of force to construct a "Christian" society. And finally, there is the ever-present danger of compromise: as the believer seeks to engage culture from within, it is perilously likely that he or she will be transformed by the powerful idols at work there instead of bringing the transforming power of the gospel to bear on the culture. It is especially those from the Anabaptist and liberationist traditions who have pressed these valid concerns; responding to them will deepen our understanding of what is involved in living at the crossroads.

A Communal Witness

Two of the leading missiologists of our time have strongly affirmed the importance of the calling of individual believers in culture. "A missionary encounter with the West will have to be primarily a ministry of the laity," says David Bosch,[24] echoing Lesslie Newbigin: "The primary witness to the sovereignty of Christ must be given, and can only be given, in the ordinary secular work of lay men and women in business, in politics, in professional work, as farmers, factory workers and so on."[25] Though we fully agree with Newbigin and Bosch on the importance of individual Christians bringing the gospel to bear where their lives engage the surrounding culture, we also want to take seriously the warnings voiced by other Christian thinkers.

Darrell Guder and his coauthors are concerned that there is a danger of reducing the cultural mission of the church to the witness of the individuals within it. They target Niebuhr's *Christ and Culture* as a primary example: "Niebuhr's analysis has no real place for the church. His primary actor is the individual Christian, who must make choices concerning Christ and culture. By implication, the church is simply a collection of individual Christians."[26] Guder and company rightly point out that the witness of the church should be a communal as well as an individual affair. The church is, after all, called to witness to the life of the kingdom, as Newbigin himself acknowledges: "The most important contribution which the Church can make to a new social order is to be itself a new social order."[27] Standing against the idolatry of our culture, the church is called to embody a different form of life, to be an alternative community, a countercultural body, "a visible, beckoning, hope-giving, guiding sign of the shalom of the kingdom."[28]

This alternative community will experience God's presence in a secular world; it will pursue justice in a world of economic and ecological injustice; it will exercise generosity and simplicity in a consumer world; it will give itself selflessly in a world dominated by selfishness; it will witness to truth (with boldness and humility) in a world of relativism; it will hold out hope in a world that has lost a vision of the future; it will express praise, joy, and thanksgiving in a world convinced of its own entitlement.

The cultural witness of the church may be communal in a second way, that of establishing separate organizations of believers to carry out a faithful witness in, for example, politics, trade unions, media, and education. This tradition has been much more prominent in continental Europe than in the United Kingdom and North America. Herman Ridderbos is correct when he says that the mission of the church "bears primarily a communal character." He continues, noting that "without a proper organizational association we cannot meet our common responsibility in various respects." It will be difficult to meet our Christian responsibility especially in scholarship and politics "without associating ourselves organizationally with one another."[29] The complexity and size of the task demands that we pursue fresh initiatives and imaginative ways of bearing witness together in public life.

And finally, there is a third dimension to the cultural witness of the church, as in worship and education the congregation seeks to "equip its members for active and informed participation in the public life of society in such a way that the Christian faith shapes that participation."[30]

A Merciful Witness

In our zeal to effect God-honoring changes in the social structures of our surrounding cultures, we must be careful not to forget the very people who have been marginalized and oppressed by those structures:

> If we allow ourselves to be persuaded that "ambulance work" is something to be treated with contempt, we have surrendered the basic Christian position and left the field to those who destroy the human person for the sake of social planning. We must do both: we must care for the victim of disaster or injustice, and we must also undertake those measures of social engineering or revolution which are needed to prevent disaster and injustice from happening.[31]

There is no doubt that Jesus privileged the poor and marginalized in his mission, reaching out to them in mercy.[32] Therefore, for those who follow Jesus in his mission, concern for the poor and oppressed will be essential to their own mission.[33] Mercy will walk hand in hand with justice, and the pursuit of structural transformation will go together with compassion for the marginalized.

A Tolerant and Suffering Witness

In his parables Jesus countered several misunderstandings of the kingdom of God. In the parable of the sower (Matt. 13:1–9) Jesus indicates that the kingdom comes not by force and coercion but rather by the weakness of a message about the kingdom. The Messiah resembles not an arrogant warrior, but a humble sower. The kingdom comes by the Word of God: embodied in life, demonstrated in deed, and announced in word. And in the next parable (Matt. 13:24–30) Jesus tells about an enemy who sows weeds where the sower has sown good wheat. Should these weeds be uprooted? Jesus answers no; these weeds are to be allowed to grow until the end of the age has arrived. Here Jesus is correcting the common misunderstanding of his day that the kingdom of God would irrupt fully and at once, destroying all opposition to it in a single, decisive stroke. But this is not the kingdom that Jesus heralded; his mission was, as ours must be, a mission of tolerance that does not enforce the kingdom in any way other than by embodying and communicating God's Word in an appealing way. As the well-known hymn "Lead On, O King Eternal" puts it, "For not with swords' loud clashing nor roll of stirring drums; with deeds of love and mercy the heavenly kingdom comes."

This is not the sort of agnostic "tolerance" that is promoted in the Western cultural story as the great virtue of a pluralist society, a tolerance that relegates all truth claims (other than its own) to the private sphere; rather, this is a tolerance that recognizes that people do live out of different faith commitments and must be allowed the freedom to live out of them. In what has been termed "principled pluralism"[34] or "committed pluralism,"[35] we would acknowledge that each community within a culture has the right to claim its own understanding, its own faith commitment, to be true for all. The way forward toward public truth would be by the way of respectful dialogue and struggle among differing points of view and competing truth claims.

Nor should believers use their power in an attempt to usher in or build the kingdom of God in a coercive way. The kingdom of God will come fully only when Christ returns; until then, Christian social activity is primarily witness to what will be. Our witness within culture remains provisional at best, an enacted prayer that the kingdom will come.

Carrying out our mission in the overlap of the ages means also that there may be suffering. The history of this time between the times will not be one of smooth progress toward the coming kingdom. Nor will our mission be one that resembles a steady victorious march toward the end in which culture is gradually transformed. Rather, this redemptive era is one of fierce conflict with many casualties. Our mission will be one that is costly and may involve suffering. Paul states, "Everyone who wants to live a godly life in Christ Jesus will be persecuted" (2 Tim. 3:12; cf. Acts 14:22). How close our understanding of mission is to the New Testament's may perhaps be in part judged by the place that we accord to suffering in our understanding of the calling of the church.

Suffering is the result of a missionary encounter with the idolatrous powers of our culture. Every cultural story seeks to become not merely the dominant story, but the exclusive one. If we as the church want to be faithful to our equally comprehensive story, we will find ourselves faced with a choice: either accommodate ourselves as a minority community and modify the comprehensive claims of the gospel or remain faithful and experience some degree of conflict and suffering.[36]

Ours is a mission under the cross. The good news may call forth opposition, conflict, and rejection. We announce and embody a victory that remains hidden until the final day. And so that victory often is embodied in what appears to the world as weakness, even foolishness. Yet the victory of the cross is assured in the resurrection. Until that resurrection life comes, the church's mission will remain one of conflict and suffering. Newbigin notes, "If we take seriously our duty as servants of God within the institutions of human society, we shall find plenty of opportunity to learn what it means to suffer for righteousness' sake, and we shall learn that to suffer for righteousness' sake is really a blessed thing."[37]

A Faithful Witness

In engaging the structures of society, the Christian will face pressure to play by the cultural rules of the game—to conform, to compromise with cultural idolatry. For example, the businesswoman will be under constant pressure to conform to the profit motive, and the price of maintaining her integrity might well be the loss of her job, or at least her promotion. It would be easier to invoke the same biblical truths that we have emphasized—the goodness of creation to be enjoyed, the importance of the creation mandate, the lordship of Christ over all of cultural life, the mandate to be involved in all of culture—and turn them to selfish purposes. Then we would say "Christ is Lord of business" in order to enter the realm of business, not to engage the powerful idolatries that shape it but rather to make as much money as possible and to enjoy the comfortable life that it may afford.

Facing the rigors of a missionary encounter (especially when there is rejection and suffering) and discerning creational design from idolatrous misdirection is a demanding calling. Our faithful response will depend in large part on the support that we receive from a (church) community of like-minded believers, and on a healthy spirituality.

Too often, Western Christians have engaged in frantic social, political, and economic activity on behalf of the kingdom without rooting their work in prayer. N. T. Wright comments,

> If the church is indeed to be Jesus' agent in bringing his whole agenda to his whole world, it needs his own Spirit. Indeed, if the church attempts to do what has to be done without constantly seeking to be filled and equipped by Jesus' own Spirit, it is committing blasphemy each time it opens its mouth. This is not a plea that all Christians should enlist in the charismatic movement. Rather, it is a plea that all Christians, particularly those involved at the leading edge of the church's mission to bring healing and renewal to the world, *should be people of prayer*, invoking the Spirit of Jesus daily and hourly as they go about their tasks, lest they be betrayed into the arrogance of their own agendas or into the cowardice of relativism.[38]

The mission of the church is not first of all about organization, strategy, cultural power, or worldview analysis, as good as these things may be. Instead, it is about a healthy life of prayer and meditation, immersion in Scripture as the true story of the world, and hearty participation in the life of the congregation; it is here that the life of the kingdom is known, experienced, and shared. Newbigin expresses it well: "If there is a committed people as the sign and agent and foretaste of what God intends, it can only be insofar as their life is continually renewed through contact with God himself."[39] The church that wants to be faithful in its missionary encounter will need to develop and nourish a vital spirituality.

If the church is to be faithful to the gospel, it will need to be part of a supportive community to its people. In an urgent plea to fellow pastors Lesslie Newbigin once asked,

> Are we taking seriously our duty to support [our lay people] in their warfare? Do we seriously regard them as front-line troops? . . . What about the scores of Christians working in offices and shops in that part of the city? Have we ever done anything seriously to strengthen their Christian witness, to help them in facing the very difficult ethical problems which they have to meet every day, to give them the assurance that the whole fellowship is behind them in their daily spiritual warfare?[40]

The people of God need to be nourished with the life of Christ through the various means God has provided: the Word, the Lord's Supper, prayer, worship, and fellowship. The people of God need to be supported in their callings in active encouragement, intercessory prayer, counsel, and perhaps even financial support when hardship comes as a result of members' faithfulness. And God's people need to be equipped for their tasks, perhaps by meeting and struggling together with other Christians who share their task—for example, a group of Christian lawyers might meet to discuss how best to bring a kingdom vision to their vocational setting.

Salt, Light, a City on a Hill

There were in Jesus' day at least four seemingly reasonable, and yet fatal, alternatives to a faithful witness to God's kingdom. The Essenes withdrew from society, the Sadducees compromised with the Roman Empire, the Pharisees retreated into organized religion, and the Zealots used every possible means, including violence, to usher in the kingdom in their own strength. It was in the vivid context of these unfaithful approaches to culture that Jesus spoke the words of the Sermon on the Mount:

> You are the salt of the earth. But if the salt loses its saltiness, how can it be made salty again? It is no longer good for anything, except to be thrown out and trampled underfoot. You are the light of the world. A city on a hill cannot be hidden. Neither do people light a lamp and put it under a bowl. Instead they put it on its stand, and it gives light to everyone in the house. In the same way, let your light shine before others, that they may see your good deeds and glorify your Father in heaven. (Matt. 5:13–16)

Helmut Thielicke observes, "Salt and light have one thing in common: they give and expend themselves—and thus are the opposite of any and every kind of self-centered religiosity."[41] If we truly understand our cultural calling in the light of the gospel and carry it out faithfully, not only will we point to the rightful Lord of creation and renewal, but we will also love our neighbor. It is the justice, peace, joy, and righteousness of the kingdom of God that provide for the flourishing of human life, and it is these gifts to his creation that God has entrusted to us for the sake of our neighbors.

9

Life at the Crossroads

Perspectives on Some Areas of Public Life

The gospel needs to be made incarnate in every area of life. In this final chapter we explore how reflection on what a Christian worldview means for six areas of contemporary life might equip us for that task. Of course, there are many other areas that we could have written about, and much more could be said about each of the areas that we have chosen, but these six will give a good indication of what a Christian worldview "with legs" might look like today.

Business

There is nothing new about business. Buying and selling were as common in the Old Testament as they are today, and God gave Israel many laws to regulate business justly.[1] Here is one example: "Do not have two differing weights in your bag—one heavy, one light. . . . You must have accurate and honest weights and measures, so that you may live long in the land the LORD your God is giving you. For the LORD your God detests anyone who does these things, anyone who deals dishonestly" (Deut. 25:13–15). The laws in Deuteronomy were given to the Israelites as they prepared to enter the promised land, and God wanted their business practices to reflect his own character, in honesty and justice.[2] The one doing business who owns two sets of weights intends to use the heavy weights when buying (thus getting more for his money) and the light weights when selling (thus making a bigger profit on what he sells). The assumption in the Deuteronomy text is that business—the exchange of goods—will take place among the Israelites, and that this is a fundamentally good thing, provided that it is just and honest. In Proverbs 11:1 (NIV) the creational structure of business is affirmed ("accurate weights are [the LORD's] delight"), and sinful misdirection of business is condemned ("the LORD abhors dishonest scales").

The woman of Proverbs 31 exemplifies the fear of the Lord that is the foundation of wisdom (cf. Prov. 1:7; 31:30). Although she does not engage in any overtly "religious" activities, this godly woman's zealous commitment to the Lord shows itself in her daily activities as homemaker and businesswoman. She buys a field and plants a vineyard out of her earnings (v. 16). She sells linen garments and sashes for profit (vv. 18, 24). She makes clothing of fine linen and "purple," a luxurious cloth made with a costly Phoenician murex dye.[3] All these details combine to give a clear picture of her relationship to God: in her business activities she embodies the fear of the Lord.

Clearly, from a biblical point of view, business is a field into which we are called to serve the Lord. But the Bible is also aware of how easily business can be distorted so that it becomes oppressive and idolatrous. The Old Testament prophets cry out against such distortions (e.g., Amos 8:4–6; Mic. 6:10–11), but perhaps the strongest critique of misdirected business comes in the book of Revelation, in its condemnation of the political and economic excesses of first-century Rome. Richard Bauckham observes,

> Rome is . . . "the great city that rules over the kings of the earth" (17:18), whose vast consumption sucked in all the produce of the empire. . . . In this world system Rome was the centre growing rich through the impoverishment of her periphery. This is the nearest thing to contemporary economic globalization that we could reasonably expect from the first century of our era. John's list of cargoes shipped to Rome ends emphatically with "slaves—that is, human lives" (18:13, my translation): a comment on the whole list. In view of the child slave labor that produces in some Asian countries the cheap goods wanted by the wealthy consumers of the west, the same comment on the contemporary globalized economy would surely be appropriate.[4]

Clearly, the Bible has much to say about business as it was conducted in the culture of the ancient Middle East, but a contemporary Christian perspective on business also needs to take seriously the historical development of culture since that time, as well as in our contemporary situation. The Industrial Revolution and especially globalization have increased the power and influence of business far beyond anything previously known. While there are similarities as well as important differences between the biblical world and our own world, nevertheless, two convictions rooted in the truth of Scripture will help us to develop a Christian perspective on business. The first conviction is that business is fundamentally good: since it provides the means by which needed commodities may be exchanged, healthy business is motivated at its core by the loving service of one's neighbor. Through my labor I provide what my neighbor needs, and in the process I am also able to provide for my family's needs. If I do my work well and if I work hard, profit may result; this is a good thing, but it will not be my primary motivation for business. The second biblical conviction is that business, as it is practiced by sinful men and women in our good but fallen world, is easily misdirected toward wrong goals. My motive for doing business may turn to selfish or dishonest gain, and my business itself become a means of oppression.

A healthy and just business community will genuinely serve the needs of citizens and nations rather than making a small minority very rich while oppressing the poor. A Christian perspective on business must therefore include thoughtful critique of contemporary abuses of business, not least in the global corporate world, and the development of positive, healthy businesses managed so as to honor the Bible's injunctions concerning trade. A faithful Christian critique will consider the ways in which business is structured today and will be aware of how easily we can be caught up in these structures and thus become complicit in what is done through them. We now know, for instance, that some corporations consistently use cheap labor in foreign countries, which allows them to produce their products very inexpensively and then sell them for a huge profit in their home countries. As Christians, we need to arm ourselves with good information against being involved as consumers in oppressive business practices.

Since the lives of business corporations are entwined with our lives—in our buying and selling, our being employed, our investing—we need to become aware of who these companies are and what sort of ethics govern their practices at home and abroad. We can then decide whether or not to buy their products, and we can encourage others to do likewise. We need to work with fellow Christians and draw on the research of others. A church or group of churches could, for example, appoint a committee to work in this area. Corporate executives in our churches could be invited to be interviewed about their practices. Christians should support just business practices at home and abroad, and there are organizations such as Fairtrade to help educate us and alert us to those products that have come to our markets as a result of unfair trade.[5] Those of us involved in business can focus on building healthy local businesses that embody the biblical principles that we have discussed, businesses that model wholesome practices and are responsible to their local communities.

In February of 2006 a remarkable program was shown on South African television, *Bread: Feeding the Nation.* Wessel van Huyysteen discovered that four large companies monopolize the making of bread in South Africa today. These companies produce bread on a large scale in a highly mechanized way; they do not employ a great many workers. Their flour production is such that nearly all of the good elements of the wheat are destroyed so that the final product is pleasant but not particularly healthy. Van Huyysteen also discovered that there are many small producers of bread in South Africa, many of them using healthy flour and employing a higher proportion of workers and providing bread locally at a lower price. The conclusion seems simple enough: decentralize bread production in South Africa. The product would be healthier by far, employment would increase, bread prices would be lower, and local communities would be better served. But this course of action would not serve the interests of the large companies!

In *The Unsettling of America,* Wendell Berry—English professor, Kentucky farmer, poet, essayist, and novelist—delivers a sobering critique of farming in America, noting how the development of huge mechanized farms has been bad for rural communities, bad for the land, bad for animals, and bad for consumers.[6] But Berry's message is fundamentally positive: he encourages us to be aware of and to support local production, to grow for ourselves whatever we can, and to be aware of whom we are buying from and to check that their practices are healthy and good. Berry argues strongly that businesses should be connected with and responsible to local communities.

It is hard to work with integrity within a misdirected structure: a business operating in defiance of biblical principles will likely be a very difficult place for a committed Christian to work. One important way forward for the Christian community will be for Christians and like-minded individuals to create new businesses, structured so as to serve and provide for the needs of their neighbors. Undoubtedly, such businesses will often be called to "live at the crossroads," since they will stand against the dominant view that the only real motive for doing business is to make the largest profit possible. Nevertheless, it is exhilarating to imagine a host of businesses springing up whose core motivation is to lovingly serve the needs of fellow citizens.

Business, when it provides for the needs of our neighbors, can be a delightful, fulfilling vocation in which to serve the Lord God. Christians need to be discerning in developing and supporting businesses that truly honor God and genuinely serve their neighbors. Surely here is one of the most challenging, and rewarding, mission fields in the world.

Politics

When you think about politics, you soon realize that much about government has to do with our world being fallen and broken. Think, for example, about the decision by George Bush and Tony Blair to wage war in Iraq. Whether this decision was right or wrong, it would have been unnecessary in an unfallen world, where people and nations live at peace with each other. Because so much of politics has to do with arbitrating between conflicting views, some argue that government as an institution developed only in response to the fall. Others, however, argue that the institution of government is part of the created order and would have developed whether or not there had been a fall. This latter view emphasizes the positive role of government in ordering a society justly. We believe that government is part of God's created order, but whichever view one takes, it is clear that the Bible is full of teaching about government and politics. In the Old Testament the government that is most in view is that which rules over Israel. God shaped the Israelite development of monarchy so that it was to be the sort of rule that facilitated God's own rule over his people (see Deut. 17:14–20; 1 Sam. 8–12). Although several kings stand out as exemplary in this respect (David, Solomon, Josiah, Hezekiah), the history of monarchy in the Old Testament is a sad one, and the potential of government to facilitate the Lord's own reign over his people remains largely unfulfilled.

Even as we recover the political dimension of the Old Testament, we need to be alert to the difference between the status of Israel in the Old Testament and the status of the church in the New Testament. Israel was a theocracy, a nation in covenant relationship with the Lord and thus unlike any modern nation. Israel had formally agreed to live fully as God's people, and the intention was that every aspect of their life—economic, political, familial, and the rest—would be lived under God's reign. After Pentecost all this changed: God's people, the church, were scattered among all nations. The church is a theocracy, but the nations in which Christians live are not.

A New Testament text that is central to teaching about government is Romans 13:1–7. Here Paul recognizes that as an institution, government has a unique and important role to play. In language reminiscent of the Sermon on the Mount, in Romans 12:14–21, the immediate context of Romans 13:1–7, Paul instructs the Roman Christians to bless those who persecute them and not to take revenge. They are to leave room for "God's wrath." Government itself is intended to be "God's servant, agents of wrath to bring punishment on the wrongdoer," a God-ordained institution for maintaining justice. It is for this purpose that government "bears the sword"; that is, it has the power to enforce the law of the land (Rom. 13:4). Thus, although Christians are not to take revenge into their own hands (but rather are to love and show compassion even to those who would wrong them), they are to look to government to play its God-given role of imposing justice in societies. The result is that, as Paul says, Christians will have a positive approach to the state, honoring it and being good, tax-paying citizens (Rom. 13:5–6).

So far, so good. But does Romans 13 legitimate whatever governments do even when they are unjust and oppressive? The sense of the biblical text has often been misappropriated in this way. During the period of oppressive racial apartheid in South Africa, when Michael Cassidy (representing the National Initiative for Reconciliation) went to see President P. W. Botha, Botha had the Bible in his hands open at Romans 13. Botha's symbolic action was meant to imply that resistance to or criticism of the state was unbiblical, anti-Christian.

But the whole Bible, including Romans 13, denies this implication. Romans 13:4 and 6 describe the ruler as "God's servant," thus conveying both nobility (since the ruler is *God's* servant) and responsibility (God's *servant*). In the context of the Roman Empire, to describe a ruler as a servant was to put an end to the notion that rulers could do whatever they liked. A servant was there to obey his or her master. Thus Romans 13 cannot be read as legitimating whatever governments choose to do, for they are to serve God in serving justice; should they fail to do this, they become subject to God's judgment.

In the Old Testament the narratives of the plagues in Exodus and the stories of the miracles in the times of Elijah and Elisha demonstrate unequivocally that it is the Lord (not Caesar or Ahab and Jezebel) who is in charge. In Exodus 1 the midwives Shiphrah and Puah are commended for civil disobedience: "The midwives . . . feared God and did not do what the king of Egypt had told them to do; they let the [newborn Israelite] boys live. . . . So God was kind to the midwives. . . . And because the midwives feared God, he gave them families of their own" (Exod. 1:17–22). The biblical story thus gives important principles by which we may work out a solidly Christian approach to government and politics: (1) government has been instituted by God for our good and must conform to God's design; (2) its role is to maintain public justice in society, and it is entitled to use force to do so; (3) yet governments can be corrupted by various idolatries;[7] (4) Christians should be model citizens and should honor and respect government; and yet (5) they can never give uncritical allegiance to any human government, since their first loyalty is to Jesus, the Son of Man.

How do these insights come into play today? Once again, as we have stressed repeatedly in this book, it is important in developing a Christian worldview not only to indwell the biblical story but also to relate that story to our situation today. An obvious example here is that the dominant form of government today is democracy, a model completely unknown to the biblical world. Christians today live in pluralistic societies in which several worldviews compete, and consequently we cannot simply apply Old Testament laws to contemporary culture. Take the death penalty, for example. Even if we can affirm its validity, it is by no means clear how those crimes that merited the death penalty in the Old Testament (e.g., adultery, idolatry, homosexuality) relate to legislation in our own pluralistic culture.

Thus, developing a Christian worldview in relation to politics today is no easy enterprise. We suggest that the following will be key elements of such an approach. First, the biblical clues must be taken seriously.[8] As Oliver O'Donovan notes, if Scripture is God's Word, then we have to make the journey from what God said to Abraham to how to handle Iraq today (noting that Abraham lived in what is today Iraq). O'Donovan goes on to say that whereas a preacher may make this journey in under twenty minutes, a scholar may take a lifetime to do so.[9] Relating the biblical story to politics today is complex, and we help no one by formulating simplistic views buttressed by a few proof texts.

Second, we need to become familiar with the long Christian tradition of political reflection. Oliver O'Donovan and Joan Lockwood O'Donovan rightly lament our ignorance of, for example, the rich reflection in Christian thought on what constitutes a just war.[10] Christians need to really know this tradition, so that its resources may become part of our own critical reflection as we participate in our nations' decisions of when and when not to go to war.

Third, we need to know something of the story of politics, of how it has developed over the centuries and how we have inherited the institutions of our own day. This will put them in historical and cultural context and enable us to respond to them with insight.

Fourth, gifted Christians need to enter politics as politicians, as scholars, and as leaders in society, exerting influence on government directly but also instructing fellow Christians in how to think through contemporary political issues from a Christian perspective. A good example of this is the work that the relatively small Center for Public Justice (CPJ) has done over the past years on welfare reform under the leadership of Jim Skillen. Government legislation (promoted by CPJ) known as "Charitable Choice" has opened up great avenues for Christian and other religious groups to receive government funding for welfare work while retaining their religious integrity—a major step in undermining an unhealthy secularized state-church divide.[11]

In our comfortable middle-class communities it is hard to realize how much is at stake in healthy politics. But if we were to live in Rwanda during the genocide there, or in Iraq or Darfur today, we would soon wake up to the vital importance of healthy politics.[12] Government is from God, but the biblical drama calls us to do what we can to direct politics in such a way that it brings glory to God and blessing to all peoples.

Sports and Competition

If one embraces a narrow, world-negating view of the gospel, one will have little place for sports and athletic competition. But since the gospel is a gospel about the kingdom of God, sports and competition cannot so easily be jettisoned from a Christian view of things, for these too are gifts of God in creation, to be richly enjoyed with thanksgiving. It delighted God to give them; he created the potential in the creation for humanity to discover, develop, and enjoy them. He delights when we receive them as gifts, honor him in our use of them, and thank him for them. An ascetic and dualistic spirituality that diminishes sports shows ingratitude for one of God's good gifts. The movie *Chariots of Fire* has it right when Eric Liddell says, "God made me fast. When I run I feel his pleasure. . . . It's not just fun. To win is to honor him."

The whole area of sports is rooted in creation in two ways. First, sports find their source in who we are as God's image, created with a diversity of functions and abilities, and made to be social creatures, to develop and enjoy a diversity of relationships, including those of play, leisure, and competitive interaction. God has also made us to be imaginative creatures. As Bart Giamatti (former commissioner of Major League Baseball) put it, sport is "part of our artistic and imaginative impulse."[13] In sports as in the arts, we are able creatively to construct imaginary worlds with their own goals, rules, and obstacles, and to enter them for a time.

Sports are also rooted in the creational calling that God gave humanity in the beginning, the so-called cultural mandate (Gen. 1:26–28; 2:15). Humanity was given the delightful task of exploring, discovering, and developing the potential that God put in the creation in loving communion with himself. God's gift of sports was not given, of course, fully developed—the garden of Eden was not equipped with squash courts and baseball diamonds! Instead, God gave humanity the formative power to explore, discover, and develop the potential of the creation in diverse ways. It is out of this foundational task that sports and athletics have arisen as one cultural product.

Although many would agree that sports and athletics are gifts from God, perhaps fewer would agree that competition is also a good gift. Marvin Zuidema rightly notes that competition is a "basic ingredient" of sports and athletics and that "no one can play responsibly to lose," and he goes on to address a view of many in the Christian community concerning this aspect of sports: "Competition is morally wrong because it pits one player or team against another in rivalry which often results in hate."[14] Zuidema and others argue that rivalry is not what competition is about. John Byl believes that "overcoming unnecessary obstacles" is at the heart of sports and athletics.[15] Frey and his fellow authors elaborate: "Obstacles provide hindrances which prevent the player from using the most efficient way of accomplishing the goal. The joy in the game is in creating tactics to overcome the obstacles and accomplish the goal."[16] In sports, teams or individuals agree cooperatively to oppose one another within the stated goals, rules, and obstacles of the game. In other words, cooperation, not rivalry, is at the heart of competition.

Competition can enhance the joy and emotional intensity of the whole athletic experience, helping to sharpen one's skills and produce satisfying physical exertion. Thus an opponent is not first of all a rival but rather someone who provides the opportunity for a more delightful experience of sport. Competition is an enriching part of God's gift. One loves one's neighbor in sport by providing stiff competition to enhance the athletic experience. Many athletes can resonate with Zuidema's belief that "competition can bring out co-operation, celebration, respect, and even love."[17]

Yet competition can be twisted by sin and thus turn ugly. It is necessary, therefore, to discern what healthy and normative competition is. A competitor is not to be regarded as a mere hindrance, an object whose resistance must simply be overcome, like the resistance of a barbell in weightlifting. Human beings are created in God's image, and therefore even in the heat of competition they must always be treated with love, dignity, respect, and appreciation. There is no room in a Christian appreciation of sport for sentiments such as those expressed in Vince Lombardi's infamous observations: "Winning isn't everything; it's the only thing" (a quote he took from "Red" Sanders)[18] and "To play [football] you must have fire in you, and there is nothing that stokes that fire like hate."

Sports and athletics are part of the creation and can bring delight as gifts of God. They do not need to be justified because they bring physical fitness, refreshment for work, or psychological release, or because they build character and self-discipline, or because they serve as bridges for evangelism. These side benefits may or may not be worthy, but in any case they are incidental.[19] The existence of sports and athletics is justified simply because God gave them as gifts to enjoy. As Edward Shaughnessy puts it, "Essentially sport has no purpose at all: it is an end in itself. . . . Its possible uses are incidental, like those of the fine arts, religion or friendship."[20]

There are organic connections between athletics and other aspects of God's creation; there are physical, emotional, economic, social, and aesthetic components in all athletic activity. On the one hand, this means that play suffers when other aspects of creation are weakened. For Byl, social and psychological harmony are essential conditions for sports, but there are many other conditions as well.[21] Can you imagine a competition where the athletes could not count, where they did not have the physical fitness to last longer than five minutes, or where they were incapable of emotional expression? Could sports develop in a culture where economic conditions required people to spend all their waking hours making a living or where dishonesty abounded? Good sports thrive when other cultural conditions are in balance, and, reciprocally, other dimensions of our lives suffer when there is no place for play.

When the sound of any one instrument in the orchestra is too weak, the whole harmony suffers; when play and leisure are muted and sports are depreciated, culture as a whole suffers. But the other danger for an orchestra is that any one instrument might become too loud, which also will destroy the harmony. When one part of creation is idolized, given significance beyond its due, the harmony of creation is destroyed. And it is precisely this kind of idolatry that is so abundantly evident in sports and athletics in our own day. Charles Prebish identifies sport as the fastest growing religion in America, far outdistancing whatever is in second place.[22] Sports, athletics, and competition are good, then, when seen as one valid part of God's world and when they conform to God's creational design, but they can easily become idols, taking on a place of worship that is not theirs by right.

Scholarship can help in discerning the creational design intended for wholesome sport and recreation: "Academic inquiry into what is going on in our play is both legitimate and important. It can be helpful in deepening, enriching, and broadening our critical insight into recreational practices. It can help to account for leisure time habits. In so doing, it can also help in correcting and reforming this dimension of life."[23] In the same way that sociologists might make a contribution to understanding the creational design of marriage, or psychologists to understanding the role of emotions, there is a need for scholars to deepen the Christian community's understanding of God's original intent for sport. Of course, a big part of understanding God's creational design for sports and competition is to understand how sin has corrupted and polluted them. No athletic contest simply embodies the goodness of God's original design. Exploring God's creational design will mean becoming sensitive to those cultural idols that have perverted sport in numerous ways, including a "win at all costs" mentality, idolatrous economic motives, and a hedonism that elevates athletics to the place of the highest good.[24]

Different parts of God's creation bring joy to different people because people are "wired" differently. For some it may be music, for others carpentry, for still others books. These things that especially bring delight can be occasions that remind us to return to God the thanksgiving and praise that are due for every part of our lives. Years ago Gordon Spykman began a convocation address with these words: "Nothing matters but the kingdom." Here he paused, letting the truth of that observation sink in. Then he continued with "But because of the kingdom, everything matters." Since "the kingdom" is God's power in Jesus Christ by the Spirit to restore all of creation to live again under his liberating rule, everything matters. Sports, athletics, and competition matter because Christ created them and is restoring them. When we stand before the judgment seat of Christ, where only gold, silver, and precious stones will last through the fire of God's judgment (1 Cor. 3:12–15), there will be athletic acts of gold and silver that will last. Spykman, making reference to Revelation 21:24–26, rightly says that the "treasures of the nations will go into the new Jerusalem. Among those treasures . . . is good, sound, healthy leisure"[25] and, we would add, good, sound, healthy sports.

Creativity and Art

Christians sometimes associate artistic creativity only with "high art" such as opera, ballet, painting, and sculpture and then wonder what any of this has to do with the gospel and evangelism. Such Christians can generally see a place for creativity only if it serves the church by focusing on overtly Christian topics with a strong message or by helping decorate the church bulletin or by fleshing out the church service with a skit. High art has its own important place in culture, but to reduce creativity to it alone, or to say that creativity is valid only when it is put to the service of "sacred" activities, is to trivialize creativity and to miss out on this important way in which God has made us to glorify him. Creativity, in the fullest sense, is expressed in the way a house is designed and decorated, the setting of a table for a meal, the clothes and jewelry that we wear, the way we arrange our work area, how we organize our garden, the style of the car we drive, the stories we tell, and the music we listen to.[26] Creativity, or what we might call the aesthetic dimension of life, fills our world.

For the Christian, creativity is rooted in the doctrine of creation. Hans Rookmaker wrote a small book called *Art Needs No Justification*, in which he argues that we do not need to justify art by seeing it as valuable only if put to some "good" (evangelistic or ecclesiastic or even commercial) purpose.[27] The justification for art lies in the way God has made us. God's workmanship in the creation is extraordinary, his creativity overwhelming. Ponder, for example, the fact that no two snowflakes are identical—a truly amazing thing, given the unimaginable number of them. Part of being made in the image of God is that he has graced us with something of his own capacity for creativity, the "possibility both to create something beautiful, and to delight in it."[28]

Creativity is a gift. This truth is confirmed in texts such as Genesis 4:21–22, in which the normative development of culture is suggested in the observations that Jubal is the father of all who play the flute and harp and Tubal-cain forges tools out of bronze and iron.[29] The psalms are wonderful poetry (many having intriguing headings, such as "For the director of music. To the tune of . . . "), and the whole collection climaxes in Psalm 150, with its exhortation to praise the Lord with a whole variety of musical instruments and with dance.[30]

Although art needs no evangelistic or "church" justification, it is still valuable and important to ask why God has given us this marvelous capacity for creativity.[31] Artists, including painters, sculptors, writers, and filmmakers (among many others), help us to experience and see the world in fresh ways. Sometimes those "fresh ways" are also new ways, but this need not be the case. In his discussion of the capacity of artworks to project a world, Nicholas Wolterstorff notes, "Over and over when surveying representational art we are confronted with the obvious fact that the artist is not merely projecting a world which has caught his private fancy, but a world true in significant respects to what his community believes to be real and important."[32] The novelist Joseph Conrad says that the task of a novelist "is, by the power of the written word to make you hear, to make you feel—it is, before all, to make you *see*."[33] Leland Ryken notes, "The world of the literary imagination is a highly organized version of the real world. It is a world in which images, characters, and story patterns are presented stripped of distracting complexities."[34] Literature and other art often invite us into a reduced world in order that we may focus on particular aspects of the real world. "Art does not try to give a photographic copy of life; it rearranges the materials of life in order to give us a heightened perception of its qualities. Art is life at the remove of imaginative form."[35]

A good example of this is the film *Extremities*, in which Farrah Fawcett plays the role of a rape victim. The film gives the viewer a jarring sense of the sheer horror of rape in a way that statistics and reports about rape can never do. Similarly, a classic novel such as Alan Paton's *Cry, the Beloved Country* evokes for the reader the painful realities of apartheid in South Africa by telling the story of a young black man and a young white man and the interaction of their families, thereby enabling one to see the relational horror of apartheid. A film such as *Off the Black* enables us to feel the pain of a teenager whose mother has left his father (with whom he lives), as well as the redemptive relationship that the teenager develops with his coach. *Ordinary People*, an older film, evokes the relational pain that often lies hidden behind respectable family facades, while also holding out hope for growth and relational redemption.

Art also expands our individual experience. As C. S. Lewis observes, "We seek an enlargement of our being. We want to be more than ourselves. Each of us by nature sees the whole world from one point of view with a perspective and a selectiveness peculiar to himself. . . . We want to see with other eyes, to imagine with other imaginations, to feel with other hearts, as well as with our own. . . . This, so far as I can see, is the specific value or good of literature . . . it admits us to experiences other than our own."[36] Art stirs and develops our imaginations. In a technological world in which analytical reason is so highly valued, we easily lose the imaginative capacity that we had as children. And yet, even if we are not artists, imagination is a vital part of our being. Albert Einstein developed his theory of relativity from imagining himself on a light beam![37] Recent studies have distinguished between the analytical left side of our brain and the imaginative right side. In Western culture (and especially in academia) the left side of our brain tends to be overdeveloped, while the playful, imaginative right side is shrunken and underdeveloped. Exposure to art and involvement in creativity helps to stir our imaginations and to bring the different sides of our selves into harmony. Thus, although neither the businessperson nor the scientist is called to be an artist, effective business and scientific work requires creativity and imagination, things that the arts can help us to develop in ourselves.

Art also encourages our sense of play, another thing that adults often leave behind with childhood. The psychiatrist Carl Jung found in his midlife crisis that part of his healing involved a return to playing. During a critical period in his life he worked each day at building a model village, and this became a major part of his healing.[38] C. S. Lewis asserts, "Our leisure, even our play, is a matter of serious concern. There is no neutral ground in the universe: every square inch, every split second, is claimed by God and counterclaimed by Satan. . . . It is a serious matter to choose wholesome recreations."[39]

Of course, creativity and art are never neutral, and once we start to see how powerful art can be, we also become aware of how seriously it can be misdirected. Ryken notes, "Artists aim to make the audience share their vision—to see what they see, feel what they feel, and interpret life as they do."[40] Keith McKean says, "Literary reality is a carefully framed and controlled kind of actuality, with every element displaying the artist's own beliefs, his own values."[41] The artist's choice of both subject matter and medium is always shaped by the artist's worldview and always presents a particular perspective: both the worldview and the perspective need to be understood for what they are.

Extreme examples of the abuse of art can be seen in the symbols and imaginative portrayals of themselves that evil regimes have employed to propagate their ideology. Adolf Hitler's regime during the 1930s and 1940s gives good examples of this in the spectacular propaganda films that Joseph Goebbels produced, and in the carefully orchestrated displays of public enthusiasm and military power that the Nazis regularly staged. The imaginative aspect of their efforts was extremely vivid and strong, but it was turned to unthinkably evil purposes. Less obvious misdirections of creativity are much more common and closer to home. When we reduce God's gift of artistic expression to Christian bumper stickers, or to pencils and even breath mints with Bible verses printed on them, we trivialize the gospel and bring Christ into disrepute. When Christian drama is reduced to nothing more than shabby evangelistic performances in the church, we imply that the gospel is a small and insignificant entity. And when Christian films are melodramatically produced and focused on the rapture in order to scare audiences into conversion, we fail to do justice to the huge breadth of creativity that God built into his creation.

Historically, the church has a great tradition of art and creativity. The Bible itself contains much extraordinarily beautiful literature in poetry, parables, tragic and comic narratives, biographies, and dream visions. The church was once the center of artistic creativity, where decorated and illuminated manuscripts, paintings and sculpture, stained glass, poetry and drama, literature, music, and architecture joined to proclaim the glory of God. It is a rich legacy that we need to recover. How might we do this?

First, we need to recognize the possibilities for creativity in all the different areas of our lives. Although not all of us are called to be artists, all of us are called to be creative. Making our home, apartment, or dorm room a relaxed and health-giving place in which to live, developing a garden into a pleasurable area with many indigenous plants so that birds feel at home there too, setting the table in a special way on special occasions, telling stories to our children with skill and imagination, developing an appreciation of good music, developing taste in clothing, learning to appreciate the beauty of nature—all these are small but significant ways in which to cultivate God's gift of artistic creativity in our lives. The opportunities are endless.

A second way to recover our Christian artistic legacy is by taking seriously God's calling of some of us to be artists. If the Christian community as a whole is genuinely committed to participating in God's redeeming of the arts, then it is vital that we recognize the calling of the artist to be a legitimate full-time Christian calling. Those gifted with artistic abilities have often found the church a hard community in which to flourish, especially in those periods in which an unbiblical dualism has relegated artistry to the "lower" or less-spiritual orders of life. We need to change that. The church has a responsibility to recognize artists and to encourage them to serve Christ within the vocation that he has given them. We long for the day when the yearly church meeting includes not only reports on the services and finances of the church but also some discussion of how the full-time service of artists (and others, of course) has been going.

Not all of us are called to be artists, but all of us should be ready to receive the gifts that artists bring. It is of little use firing up Christians to become artists in Christ's service if no one is interested in supporting their initiatives, visiting their galleries, hearing their music, and buying what they produce. We should take an interest in all good art and support it (whether it is done by Christians or not), but certainly we should have a particular commitment to supporting Christian artistic endeavors. You, your church, or your company could commission a painting or sculpture, attend a poetry reading of a local Christian poet, or organize an arts and crafts festival. You could take a course in art history or art appreciation. You could visit a gallery. You could try your hand at something to stimulate the artistic side of you, whether sketching, woodworking, origami, autobody repair, or working in stained glass.

Third, we need to develop discernment about art and creativity. The fall of humankind runs through all of creation, and that includes the arts; they are as capable of being misdirected as any other structure in God's creation. Pornography is only one obvious example of how God's artistic gifts can be perverted to serve sinful purposes. To see that pornography is misdirected is fairly straightforward; likewise, it is easy to see that the reduction of Christian art to Bible verses stamped on pencils is tragic. But with much creativity and art it is far more difficult to discern good from bad, and all the gradations in between.

A nuanced critique of art is not easily achieved; it requires reflection and a growing acquaintance with art. However, it is an essential resource if we are to fill our lives with what is true, noble, pure, lovely, admirable, excellent, and praiseworthy (Phil. 4:8). There are forms of misdirected and perverted creativity that should be rejected, but we need to make sure that we do not arrogantly dismiss art without careful and informed reflection.

Only thus will we play a positive role in the redemption of this great gift of creativity that God has embedded in his creation. In the vision of the new Jerusalem with which the book of Revelation concludes, we read that "the kings of the earth will bring their splendor into it" (21:24). This gives us an inkling of how the treasures of creativity will be taken up as part of the new creation.

Scholarship

George Marsden, in *The Outrageous Idea of Christian Scholarship*,[42] notes that genuine Christian scholarship is rare because Christian scholars have, by and large, been trained to keep their religious beliefs private as the price of their acceptance into the academic community. Graduate students find that the Christian worldview must be tailored to fit the modern humanist worldview or else their scholarship will not be taken seriously. Authentic Christian scholarship is "outrageous," Marsden argues, because it defies this notion and declares that the gospel has a formative role in scholarship.

The dearth of robust Christian scholarship is distressing for two reasons. First, it means that Christians' scholarly work has become "conformed to this world" (to use the language of Paul in Rom. 12:2). For Paul, "this world" referred to a culture twisted by idolatry; thus, to the degree that a Christian's scholarly endeavor is not shaped by the gospel, it is unfaithful, compromised with idolatrous unbelief. The second reason for concern is the power of the modern secular university and of the ideas disseminated from that institution. Twenty-five years ago Charles Malik spoke of the power of the university, and his observations remain true today:

> This great Western institution, the university, dominates the world today more than any other institution: more than the church, more than the government, more than all other institutions. All the leaders of government are graduates of universities, or at least of secondary schools or colleges whose administrators and teachers are themselves graduates of universities. The same applies to all church leaders. . . . The professionals—doctors, engineers, lawyers, etc.—have all passed through the mill of secondary school, the college and the university. And the men of the media are university trained. . . . The universities, then, directly and indirectly dominate the world; their influence is so pervasive and total that whatever problem afflicts them is bound to have far-reaching repercussions throughout the entire fabric of Western civilization. No task is more crucial and urgent today than to examine the state of mind and spirit of the Western university.[43]

Al Wolters, in *Ideas Have Legs*, has given us a helpful picture of the power of ideas originating in scholarship: "Ideas have legs in the sense that they are not the disembodied abstractions of some ivory-tower academic, but are real spiritual forces that go somewhere, that are on the march in someone's army, and that have a widespread effect on our practical, everyday lives."[44] He quotes the influential twentieth-century economist John Maynard Keynes: "The ideas of economists and political philosophers, both when they are right and when they are wrong, are more powerful than is commonly understood. Indeed, the world is ruled by little else. Practical men, who believe themselves to be quite exempt from any intellectual influences, are usually the slaves of some defunct economists."[45]

Wolters gives examples of erroneous distinctions that have made their way into common life and now unconsciously direct people's thoughts and actions, such as the distinctions between facts and values, and theory and practice. As we unconsciously employ these distinctions, we unconsciously interpret the world according to the view of some long-forgotten but still influential thinker. Wolters concludes, "In such seemingly innocent-looking words and phrases a whole idolatrous perspective on the world, a whole distorted mind-set and humanistic thought-pattern, is subliminally propagated in our civilization."[46] Brian Walsh and Richard Middleton have done similar work in *The Transforming Vision*, showing the pernicious effect of the doctrines of behaviorism on the discipline of psychology, and of neoclassical theory on economics.[47] Ideas are indeed important weapons in the spiritual battle for creation. Christian scholarship can help equip Christians of any age for a faithful witness to God's kingdom in all of life. Contrarily, the absence of genuine Christian scholarship will inevitably encourage us to adopt the reigning worldview of our culture.

Christian scholars and communities of higher education must recognize that they participate in two venerable scholarly traditions. The first is the Western academic tradition that stretches back to ancient Greece; the second is the Christian tradition of involvement in higher education that had its beginnings with the church fathers. Christian academic institutions must not attempt to create an academic ghetto by devising some new kind of "Christian scholarship" from scratch. Instead, Christian academics should aim to be critical participants in our culture and its tradition of scholarship, sharing in the academic task even with those of our colleagues who do not share our religious commitments. Our own contributions to the cultural stream of academic work will flow from the Christian tradition. This will involve a deep commitment to the truth of the gospel as the light that illumines the world of scholarship. Thus, although Christian academics should feel "at home" in the

Western academic tradition, they must never lose sight of the fact that they are also "at odds" with it. The story of the Bible offers a comprehensive view of the world that is bound to conflict with the views held in the surrounding culture, and this conflict is bound to shape the work of Christian scholars.

This twofold cultural stance means two things when it comes to dealing with scholarship that is shaped by other religious commitments. On the one hand, since God is faithful to his creation, much true insight into God's world will come to us from the non-Christian academic community; on the other hand, the idolatry that underlies Western scholarship will be at work to distort that insight. The task of the Christian scholar is to embrace and to celebrate true insights into the world from whatever source they come, but also to uncover the idolatry that has twisted them.

In the task of Christian scholarship we must be particularly careful in how we base our own work upon Scripture, rejecting the easy answers of both biblicism and dualism. The approach of the biblicist is to attempt to make the Bible answer questions that it was never meant to answer. The Bible becomes a handbook or answer book that gives direct answers to contemporary questions within various disciplines. This approach recognizes neither the fundamental redemptive purpose of Scripture (2 Tim. 3:15–16) nor the cultural gap between Scripture and our time. Biblicism creates a deceptively simple line between the biblical text and contemporary scholarship. The second problematic use of Scripture is the sort of dualism by which the Bible is kept entirely separate from scholarship. In the dualist view, since the purpose of the Bible is to address "spiritual issues" only, its authority applies to theology or religion but no further; the broader reaches of scholarship are beyond the Bible's writ. Such a view clearly negates the Bible's own claims regarding the cosmic scope of redemption and thus ultimately denies the possibility of faithful *Christian* scholarship. Without a biblical worldview at the center of the Christian scholar's theorizing, the idolatrous cultural story certainly will fill the vacuum.

We turn instead to three positive and legitimate ways in which Scripture can function in scholarship, approaches that take seriously the peculiar nature of Scripture and the cultural distance between the biblical world and the modern world. First, and most broadly, Scripture offers the true story in which we find the meaning of our lives and the calling by which we carry out our academic tasks. Second, the biblical story may be articulated in terms of a worldview where the categories of creation, fall, and redemption are elaborated with respect to their significance for scholarly endeavors. For example, developing the notion of creation order may help to stand against the naturalism of the natural sciences and the relativism of the social sciences. Opening up the notion of idolatry may help with spotting theories that reduce their explanation to one aspect of creation.

The third way in which Scripture might function in our scholarship is in revealing various themes and norms that would guide the scholar. Sidney Greidanus gives several practical examples:

> In political science one would be guided by such biblical themes as the sovereignty of God, the God-given authority of government, the task of the government to promote (the biblical norms of) justice, liberty and peace, and the required obedience of citizens. In sociology one would take into account the biblical norms for marriage, family, and other societal structures. In psychology one would view man not as an animal that can be conditioned, nor as a machine that can be programmed, but as a creature of exceptional worth because man alone is made in the image of God. . . . In economics one would want to take into account the biblical ideas of justice and stewardship, of ownership, of work and play.[48]

Faithful Christian scholarship will be characterized by both an acknowledgment of the insights of the Western cultural tradition of scholarship and a critique of the ideological settings in which those insights are embedded. Since all academic work is an accounting of the order of creation, and since God has upheld that order and upheld the image of God in humanity, scholarship will always give insight into God's world. And since human sin and idolatry affect all cultural endeavors, academic insights into God's creation order will always be distorted to some degree. Christian scholars should work to uproot theories from their idolatrous soil and replant them in the soil of the gospel, where they can bloom more fruitfully. Christian scholars should attempt to distinguish the creational insight and structure from the idolatrous religious direction in all theories, including their own, working humbly, faithfully, and prayerfully to redirect theoretical work in alignment with a biblical worldview.[49]

Thus, in psychology the theory of behaviorism promotes a naturalistic reductionism that does not account for the rich complexity of human functioning. A Christian psychologist, while perhaps finding much rich insight into human behavior from the work of behaviorists, must in his or her own scholarship work to extract those insights from the deterministic worldview that diminishes human responsibility. For the Christian economist, the Marxist preoccupation with economic forces as the overriding explanation of human history and life may open up many insights into human culture and society, but the Bible teaches clearly that economic forces are not the deepest dynamic of human history and behavior: religious commitment is the bedrock foundation. Further, the biblical story shows that since creation is rich and manifold, there are many factors—emotional, aesthetic, political, ethical—that combine to shape human history. Thus, Marxist analysis may contribute much to the work of the Christian economist, but a biblical worldview will correct the distortions of ideological Marxism. A Christian scholar may profit from feminism's insight into the way sinful patriarchalism has shaped so much of human history and society and yet not accept that gender is somehow the only human quality with real significance. A Christian literary scholar who works with Romantic literature is bound to appreciate what that tradition has revealed to us about the workings of the imagination but should resist Romanticism's idolatrous elevation of the imagination to a place of ultimate authority. A Christian economist studying the powerful global ideology of the free market will find insights into the way economic life should function but may well be called to speak out against the unjust structures that have shaped the market internationally.[50]

Scholarship, like all other aspects of human life, is on the field of battle between the kingdom of God and the kingdom of darkness. Both powers vie to shape and direct scholarship for their own ends. This is a vital place for Christians to be involved in culture.

Education

The tension between worldviews, the struggle that we must engage in if we are to live faithfully at the crossroads of two cultures, is abundantly evident in the area of education. Lesslie Newbigin expresses this tension as the "secular-apostolic dilemma": how can a Christian remain faithful to his or her apostolic identity, bearing witness to the true story of the gospel, and yet be involved in the public life of a culture that has been shaped by a wholly different story?[51] In Newbigin's view, a Christian who seeks to be involved in the public school system must negotiate between two fundamentally different understandings of the purpose and goal of human life. The state mandates education for its own purposes and is willing to support Christian education if it falls in line with those purposes. The gospel, however, holds up an entirely different purpose and goal for human life. There are two different goals and thus two entirely different understandings of education's purpose. From the standpoint of the state, the gospel nurtures children in ways that may threaten national unity. From the standpoint of the Christian, the state seeks to inculcate a worldview wholly foreign, and often inimical, to a biblical worldview. How can the Christian be involved in cultural development and yet remain faithful to the gospel?

Contemporary public education has largely been formed by the Enlightenment worldview. The implications of this worldview for education were articulated in Condorcet's *Sketch for a Historical Picture of the Progress of the Human Mind*. In the view of Condorcet, education was to be a primary instrument for the implementation of the Enlightenment vision. According to Enlightenment thought, only universal public education that was not dominated by the church could bring equality of opportunity. Ignorance was the enemy of that progress, and education was to serve the humanist vision of life by transmitting a unified body of universal scientific knowledge to the next generation, equipping them to build a more rational society of freedom, justice, truth, and material prosperity.

It would take more than two centuries for the Enlightenment vision to fully shape Western governments' policies on education. Not until fairly recently has the worldview undergirding much of Western educational philosophy come under serious challenge, and the effects of this paradigm shift may prove to be particularly significant for education, as Brian Walsh suggests:

> Consider the role of the Western story of progress in education. Again, Usher and Edwards are helpful: "Historically, education can be seen as the vehicle by which modernity's 'grand narratives,' the Enlightenment ideals of critical reason, individual freedom, progress and benevolent change, are substantiated and realized." Take away this story of civilisational progress and the modern mass education loses a central dimension of its *raison d'etre*.[52]

If education has been guided for more than two hundred years largely by a story of "progress through science and technology," a story that society no longer believes to be true, then what new goal will society substitute for the one that has been lost? If, according to the Enlightenment view, the purpose of education was to pass along a unified body of universal knowledge, but society now suspects that there is no such thing to pass along, then what will society choose as the new purpose of education?

Economism and consumerism have such palpable influence in our late-modern and postmodern world that it is not surprising to hear Neil Postman speak of economic utility, consumerism, technology, and multiculturalism as the "gods" of Western society.[53] In a world such as this the purpose of education is merely to provide useful information and marketable skills that will enable students to compete and survive in the jungle of the global market. According to this view, the growth of the population, the shrinking of goods, and the unforgiving severity of the competitive market all demand that students find some advantage over their competitive peers; education can provide such a service by giving them what they need to live in and contribute toward this consumer world. "The issue is not *whether* education is rooted in a grand story, but *which* grand story it shall be rooted in? If the tale of capitalist progress is beginning to fray at the edges then perhaps this is an evangelistically opportune time for Christian education to offer another story—one that replaces the self-salvation of economic progress with the tale of the coming Kingdom of redemption."[54] How do we bring the gospel to bear on an educational system that has been formed by the modern humanist story? How can we infuse education with a biblical vision of life?

We need to be reminded of our calling to be critical participants in our culture, including the culture of education. That is, we are to be both engaged with our culture (as participants) and disengaged from it (as those who maintain a critical distance from the presuppositions on which modern Western culture is based).

Let us consider our role as participants first. Some Christians have chosen to form separate Christian schools or to pursue home-based education—options that we wholeheartedly support—and thus have opted out of direct participation in the public culture of education. The danger of these paths is that they may isolate us from our neighbors and may cause us to forget that we are to be participants in our culture's development. We share with our non-Christian neighbors the common task of transmitting insight from one generation to another in order to prepare our children for living in this world. Stuart Fowler comments on our responsibility to be engaged with the surrounding culture of education no matter what particular means of educating our own children we choose:

> We are not called to establish closed Christian communities in the world, but to penetrate as salt into the world. Our Christian communities deserve the label "Christian" only so far as they facilitate penetrating this world in keeping with Jesus' words to his Father concerning his disciples in all ages: "As you have sent me into the world, so I have sent them into the world" (John 17:18). It is valid to maintain Christian schools and colleges as manifestations of our community in Christ. They are not valid if they function within a closed Christian educational network. To be authentic they must be open to other educational communities in the world around us. We do not maintain our Christian integrity by isolating ourselves from the world around. Rather, such isolation denies our calling and falsifies our witness.[55]

We are also to be critical participants in our culture. To offer an educational witness that has genuine integrity, we must affirm that our view of education is founded on a worldview very different from that of the surrounding culture, one that yields fundamentally different faith commitments. Our task is to struggle with the tradition of education as it has developed in our culture, seeking to translate the gospel (and the gospel's implications for education) faithfully in this milieu. We must seek to take hold of the legitimate insights that have arisen from the Western secular educational tradition and transplant them into the soil of the gospel.

This, obviously, is a task of years, not hours. It is also quite clearly a communal task, beyond the resources of any one person or family, and a task that crosses cultures and generations. So each of us may play only a small role in advancing the goal of faithful Christian education. We often will find that we are making only slow progress along a path already traveled by faithful Christians of earlier generations. Nevertheless, we are called to be faithful, and small progress is much better than no progress. How, then, are we to proceed?

The most concentrated reflection on how the gospel may be brought to bear on education has taken place within the Christian school movement. There is no comparable body of literature either from those who work within the public system or from those in the home-educating community. The Christian school movement has indeed made progress in the task of articulating educational theory from the vantage point of a Christian worldview. There is a rich body of literature on such topics as Christian (or biblical) perspective in teaching and learning, the formation of Christ-centered curriculum, and inculcating a Christian world-and-life view. The insights gained from such perspectival research have been brought to bear on questions of educational purpose, pedagogy, curriculum, leadership, and institutional structure.[56] These reflections from the perspective of professional Christian educators offer much to all Christians who are involved or seek to be involved in education, whether in Christian schools, within the public system, or in home-based education.

The title of an article by John Hull enables us to sharpen our focus on a central issue in this literature: "Aiming for Christian Education, Settling for Christians Educating."[57] Christian education is (or should be) a distinct alternative to the public school system, one that rejects the cultural idolatry (and specifically the humanist worldview) that has shaped much of public education. Christian education must be based on a distinctive and comprehensive philosophy that transforms the entire enterprise in its purposes, goals, curricula, pedagogy, evaluation, and leadership. But Hull warns that in place of genuine Christian education we often settle for Christians educating; that is, we compromise by accepting a close likeness to public school education and then tack on some attention to issues of moral integrity, devotional piety, and biblical insight on specific topics such as Genesis 1 and the question of the earth's origins. This approach does little more than to maintain the humanist status quo in education. Thus Hull helpfully distinguishes between the kind of education that has truly been shaped by a Christian worldview and the kind of education that (although carried out by committed and well-meaning Christians) remains heavily influenced by the prevailing humanist paradigm.

Jack Mechielsen's *No Icing on the Cake* makes the same distinction very clear: "Relating the gospel to education is not simply a matter of putting religious icing on an otherwise secular educational cake. Those who confess the Name of Christ are called to develop learning and teaching which is based on the Word of God. Recognising Christ's creation-wide redemption, Christians will produce fresh and new approaches in education: a brand new cake!"[58] The problem with the icing-on-the-cake approach or with the compromise position of "Christians educating" is that these models tacitly adopt the faulty premise of the Enlightenment, that education is religiously neutral and thus can be separated from religion.[59]

Any fruitful discussion of Christian education must consider the overall purpose or goal of education itself. In *The End of Education*, Postman describes this topic as central to the crisis in public education in the late twentieth and early twenty-first centuries. What are we educating *for*? Hence Postman's title and its play on words: if we no longer agree on the end (the goal or purpose) for education, it may be that we have reached the end (the termination) of education. He observes that for all our talk about pedagogy, educational structures, processes, and politics, we rarely consider the reason for education itself—its goal. But education, Postman insists, cannot proceed without serving some god, without finding its place within "a comprehensive narrative about what the world is like, how things got to be the way they are, and what lies ahead . . . [for] without a narrative, life has no meaning. Without meaning, learning has no purpose. Without a purpose, schools are houses of detention, not attention."[60] The lack of conscious reflection on the goal or purpose of education leads us to accept by default those purposes, those "gods" that have been shaped by a culture in crisis.

Both modern and postmodern thinking about the purpose of education has opened up insights into why we educate our children. We can agree with most public educators that education ought to equip students to play positive and productive roles in society; surely, to build a better society is a worthwhile goal toward which Christians can direct their energies. Although Christians may well differ on what this "better society" should look like, they can affirm the educational goal of transmitting insight in order to shape good citizens. Likewise, most Christians will affirm the more recent articulation of education's purpose: to give children the insight and skills they need to care for themselves and provide for their families. The ability to earn a living and to care for our needs is a legitimate goal that Christians can share with their non-Christian neighbors.

Nevertheless, the idolatry within much current educational theory and practice must be recognized and rejected. The Enlightenment's scientism, which trusts in science to bring us to a better society, is an idol whose failure to deliver what it promised is now clear. Consumerism must similarly be rejected: educating our children to play the consumer game would be like capitulating to Canaanite idolatry as Israel did in the promised land.

As we seek to articulate a truly biblical goal and purpose for education, we may consider any number of helpful suggestions offered by Christian educators within the past few years, such as educating for responsive discipleship,[61] for freedom,[62] for responsible action,[63] for *shalom*,[64] or for commitment.[65] Another formulation that seeks to affirm a biblical basis for education would be to say that its purpose is to educate for witness. As God's people, we are called to witness in the whole of our lives to the coming rule of God. Education is for the purpose of equipping students to witness faithfully to the gospel in the whole of their lives.

One important thing that the word *witness* is intended to highlight is the antithetical posture of the Christian in culture. Too often Christian education unwittingly trains students not to challenge the existing culture but rather to accommodate themselves to it, to fit in. Too often the goal of Christian educational institutions is merely to establish themselves and to gain recognition according to prevailing standards, even when those standards are derived from worldviews that we cannot endorse. We have sometimes allowed the standards of a secular worldview to shape our thinking on what educational excellence is all about. Witness is a reminder that in all areas of life, including education, our fundamental faith assumptions will clash with those of our non-Christian neighbors. Witness demands a missionary encounter. And witness is as wide as human experience: we witness to Christ in the whole public arena, including education. Authentic Christian education is *for* witness.

We should also think of Christian education *as* witness, in and of itself. This observation is meant to guard against a danger faced especially by both home-educators and Christian schools: it is perilously easy for us to hide our educational light under a bushel. It is much safer and more comfortable to withdraw into our educational enclaves in distant safety from the public schools than to show who we are and whose we are. Those who dare to challenge the dominant patterns of education may invite hostile scrutiny, loss of funding or recognition, marginalization. We may be faced with hard questions that we cannot answer. However, our way of educating should be a witness in itself. In other words, we must not merely prepare students *for* witness, but in the very enterprise of educating in a way that is faithful to the gospel, we must function *as* educational witnesses. In a dark world where education is losing its way, we need to offer the light of Jesus Christ.

If the goal of witness is firmly embedded in our hearts and discourse, then our decision-making about curriculum, pedagogy, leadership, and all the other facets of the educational task will be guided by our educational purpose. As we grapple with government regulations concerning curriculum, we will consider also what needs to be taught to equip students for lives of witness. As we engage the prevailing educational structures, pedagogical practices, and evaluative procedures, we will consider how this can best be achieved within a school whose focus is Jesus Christ. In each case we must enter the cultural arena of education to participate in the ongoing cultural tradition, while yet seeking to be faithful to the all-encompassing story of Scripture. We may learn much from those of our neighbors who share with us the task of education but who are working out of different faith commitments. We must work critically—from within the gospel, a Christian worldview, and Christian educational philosophy—to discern the idolatrous foundations of the culture that surrounds us and how those foundations have dictated the shape of public education as it now is.

Christians differ among themselves concerning how best to relate to the public school system, the primary institutional carrier of the Enlightenment vision. Since the public school system has been shaped from top to bottom by this worldview—a vision of life and of education that is incompatible with the gospel—the question is, "Must we part ways with the public schools; and if so, how?" Some Christian educators and learners have responded by continuing to carry out their calling within the public school system, and of these, some (perhaps many) have done so by accommodating themselves to the Enlightenment story that makes religion a private matter, thus perpetuating the myth of religious neutrality. Some justify this sort of accommodation by appealing to a somewhat narrow definition of evangelism: they will say that they are afforded opportunities to speak the gospel to their fellow students and workers. The danger of such an approach is that it neglects the fact that the whole public school system, while having much that is good and true, has been shaped by the various idols of humanism. But there are many Christians who understand this danger very well and have worked hard to be faithful to the gospel while remaining within the public school system; they see this as the best way to seize the evangelistically opportune time. Still other Christians have decided that the juggernaut of the humanistic tradition in the public schools is too powerful to be resisted from within; these have opted out, either by forming separate Christian schools or by taking the task on themselves in some form of home-based education. Yet, whether in public schools, in separate Christian schools, or in home education, the task of the believing community is to bring the gospel to bear on education.

We believe that each of these approaches may offer clear benefits. Each also is beset by dangers. And thus we will conclude this section of the book with some questions for each of the groups, questions intended to help each to remain faithful witnesses on whichever path they have chosen.

To the home-educating community: What forms of community will enable you to fulfill the difficult task of educating Christianly? What is your real motive in home-educating? Is it to build character, to give a more rigorous education than the schools can give, to protect your children from the evils of the world? These may be laudable goals, but they are not enough. Is it your goal to prepare faithful disciples to witness to the gospel in all of life? If the story of the coming kingdom is really to shape our education, it will be an enormous task. Again, what forms of community will help to equip parents and families to accomplish it?

To the Christian school community: How can an educational alternative to the public school paradigm be realized? Both John Hull and Ken Badley have questioned whether Christian schools are actually that much different from their public counterparts.[66] Hull, after studying thirteen Christian high schools in Canada and in the process "sifting through dozens of surveys, interviews, and observation notes," concludes that "on the whole, there was nothing distinctively Christian about these schools in terms of their curricular design, pedagogy, evaluation procedures, organizational structure, or the lifestyle of its students."[67] Even more disheartening is an earlier comment he makes: "As far as I can tell, Christian schools do not provide an alternative Christian education, if by that term we mean that our biblical perspective on life leads to a biblical model of education."[68] Perhaps Hull is too pessimistic in his conclusions. But, in any case, he makes it clear that implementing a distinctively Christian vision of education is extremely difficult. The power of the humanist tradition; the expectations of parents; the limited time, ability, and training of many teachers; the pressures of governmental expectations; and the pervasive understanding of educational "excellence" that has been shaped by a thoroughly humanist worldview all conspire against the endeavor. The issue for Christian school advocates is to face this matter squarely and to ask what is needed to overcome these formidable obstacles.

To those Christians who choose to remain part of the public school system: What forms of community will enable you to educate your children in a truly Christian way? This question assumes two things: first, that we acknowledge that the public system is built on fundamental commitments that are not neutral but rather are to some degree in opposition to the gospel; second, that it is very difficult for any individual to stand against the power of the humanist tradition within the public school system. Thus, how can you pursue the task to which you have been called, in company with others who share the same convictions?

If God's people are to be faithful in their educational callings, then community and cooperation are essential. Whichever path is chosen, there is a need for members of the Christian community to walk alongside one another for strength, for encouragement, for practical everyday support, for prayer. In many ways the future witness of the church in Western culture is dependant on today's faithfulness in this task.

Pastoral Postscript

As we have sought to spark Christians' imaginations with the magnitude of a Christ-centered worldview in various settings around the world, we have found that many are excited by a larger vision of the Christian faith than they had known before, and yet they may feel overwhelmed by the enormity of what needs to be accomplished. Worldview studies can make us more fully aware not only of the comprehensive scope of the gospel and of our mission, of the religious power and all-embracing reach of our own culture's secular "faith," but also of the unbearable tension that comes with living at the crossroads where these two stories intersect. Thus to feel both exhilarated and overwhelmed should not be unexpected. Often this growing awareness moves us to consider the size, complexity, and difficulty of the task of bearing witness to the gospel in the public square. We may be tempted to think that we can usher the kingdom in tomorrow, or we may become discouraged and ask, "Who is equal to the task?" The triumphalism of the former response soon discovers how hard it can be to bear witness to the kingdom in a fallen, broken world. The answer to the latter question, of course, is that no one is equal to such a task. So what now? Four concluding pastoral remarks may help us to gain perspective as we take up our challenging and exhilarating calling to witness to the kingdom of God.

First, we are not sent out into the world alone and without human support. Jesus made provision for the communication of the gospel through history and into all cultures of the world by forming and sending not a collection of individuals but rather a community. "As the Father has sent me, I am sending you" (John 20:21), and here the "you" is emphatically plural. Our witness to the good news of the kingdom within our cultures is a communal witness.

Witness simply cannot happen in isolation. We need each other in many ways. Each of us will need to make a commitment to be involved in a local congregation where we are nourished in the gospel of the kingdom and supported both for a missionary encounter with the culture and for the inevitable suffering that such an encounter will bring. We will need to meet for prayer, reading, study, and discussion with others of like mind within the local congregation, those who are also serious about a faithful witness in public life, and also with those whose callings (occupations, professions, interests) are like ours. We will need to become familiar with and make use of the growing body of resources available on the Internet, at conferences, and in books and journals that can help us think through issues in Christian worldview.

Moreover, only a vigorous spirituality can sustain us in our task.[1] Eugene Peterson captures what is involved in witnessing to the kingdom in a quotation from Nietzsche. Peterson says that Christians need "a long obedience in the same direction."[2] Consider, for example, how William Wilberforce labored all his adult life for the abolition of slavery. Only deep roots in Christ will sustain us in this kind of work. As Jesus prepared his disciples for their mission in the world (John 13–17), he made it clear that there would be no fruit apart from abiding in him (John 15:1–11). The apostle Paul employs a similar horticultural metaphor, then adds one from architecture, as he exhorts the Colossian church members in their mission to continue to live their lives in Christ, with roots deep into Christ and built on the foundation of the gospel (Col. 2:6–7). There has been a vigorous tradition in the history of the Christian church of wrestling with the relationship between the contemplative life and the active life, balancing the life of prayer and that of cultural involvement—*ora et labora*.[3] But in practice the two can all too easily come apart. If we are to be sustained in a faithful and active witness to the lordship of Christ in public life, we will need to cultivate a vibrant spirituality so that the contemplative life can nourish the active, and vice versa. As the Catholic document *Starting Afresh from Christ* puts it,

> An authentic spiritual life requires that everyone, in all the diverse vocations, regularly dedicate, every day, appropriate times to enter deeply into silent conversation with him by whom they know they are loved, to share their very lives with him and to receive enlightenment on the daily journey. It is an exercise which requires fidelity, because we are constantly being bombarded by the estrangements and excesses which come from today's society, especially from the means of communication. At times fidelity to personal and liturgical prayer will require a real effort not to allow oneself to be swallowed up in frenetic activism. Otherwise it will be impossible to bear fruit.[4]

We cannot sustain a faithful witness without taking spiritual nourishment from Scripture, prayer, meditation, and fellowship.

Furthermore, we need to understand that our witness is first of all a work of God's Spirit. Those who have been most vocal in calling for an engagement and encounter with culture have often been those infected by the disease of activism. A bishop from eastern Europe once commented to Mike that what struck him most about North American Christianity was that so much of it seemed driven by humanistic self-confidence. This kind of implicit trust in human strength is a sure recipe for burnout and discouragement. We most definitely are not called to build God's kingdom; that metaphor is never used in Scripture, despite its popularity in some circles. The word *witness*—in life, word, and deed—much better describes what we need to do and to be. And we are not responsible for the success of our witness: we are not the primary authors of history, and we are not called to direct it to its final goal. These matters are safely in the hands of our sovereign God.

In missionary circles the language of *missio Dei* (God's mission) has lately become commonplace, and this is a welcome emphasis.[5] In the nineteenth and early twentieth centuries, cross-cultural missions were corrupted to some degree by the same confidence in human planning and effort that had infected Western culture from its very roots in the modernist concept of progress. More recently, a chastened missionary community has rediscovered Scripture's teaching that we as a church have been taken up into what *God* is doing in history. The Father has a long-term purpose to restore the creation, and he has been pursuing this purpose since the beginning (and thus mostly without our help!). He sent his Son to accomplish his work in a decisive way. Now at his invitation and command we are sent in the power of the Spirit to witness to what he has done, is doing, and yet will do. It is no accident that Jesus said to the newly formed Christian community that their mission would *begin* when the Holy Spirit was poured out (Acts 1:8).

This is all much bigger than our time in history, our geographical location, our small piece of the world, our feeble efforts. God is at work, and his purposes will be accomplished. We are called only to witness, by the power of his Spirit in our lives, words, and actions, to what he is doing. Thus we can work—and rest—with joy. Such restful and confident joy is in short supply among activists. Perhaps it should not be a surprise that as Jesus was preparing his people to take up their mission in the world, he explicitly gifted them with his peace (John 14:27; 16:33) and his joy (John 15:11; 16:20–24; 17:13).

Finally, we can engage the powers in the public square in hope. We can be sure that because of what Christ has done, the end of universal history is sure: God's kingdom will come in its glorious fullness. However, that day has not yet come, and so sometimes it can seem like a mirage, a mere dream. Our lives must be characterized by what Wendell Berry calls "difficult hope."[6]

No wonder then that the Bible repeatedly calls believers, no matter how hard their circumstances, to live in hope. Hope is the confident certainty and secure assurance that because of what Jesus has accomplished, God's purposes for his creation surely will be realized.

Jesus stands at the end of history as its final judge, and what he has accomplished will be the basis of that final judgment. In this regard, Scripture assures us of three things. First, we are promised that those who stand on the side of Christ will ultimately be vindicated: we can be sure that if we give ourselves fully to the work of the Lord and seek his kingdom first, our labor will not be in vain (1 Cor. 15:58). Second, we know that we will be judged not on the basis of whether or not we were successful (by human standards) but rather on the basis of whether or not we were faithful. Karl Marx concluded one of his books with these words: "The philosophers have only interpreted the world, in various ways; the point is to change it."[7] But in believing that humanity had it in its own power to change the world, Marx was simply mistaken. We Christians long to see the world changed by the gospel, and we know that one day, when Jesus returns, it will indeed be changed. Until that day, we hope that our own efforts may have some salting effect for good. However, we must not make change the motive for what we do. Our efforts may impact the world, or they may not. And even if they do make an impact, it may be temporary. Surely, all human effort eventually will be buried beneath the rubble of history. Our aim must be to remain faithful to the gospel, leaving the results to the work of God's Spirit.

Third, although human efforts are finite, we can be confident that what is done for the sake of Christ and his kingdom will last. Paul employs one of his favorite metaphors from architecture when he speaks of his own calling from God (and each of us can apply his observations to our own callings in culture). Paul says that each of us should build on the foundation of the gospel of Jesus Christ. The materials that we should use are gold, silver, and costly stones, because (unlike wood, hay, and straw) they will last through the fires of judgment. The fires of God's judgment will test the quality of each person's work, and faithful endeavors in keeping with God's kingdom will not be destroyed (1 Cor. 3:10–15). And all faithful cultural effort will find its place on the new earth (Rev. 21:26). Jim Skillen puts it well:

> We can work with true expectancy in politics [and, we would add, in every other area of public life] as those who know that our works will follow us. . . . Moses prays in Psalm 90: "Lord establish the work of our hands." In the apostle John's vision of the final revelation of Jesus Christ, God's blessing comes to those who die in the Lord, as the Spirit says, "that they may rest from their labours, for their deeds follow them!" (Rev. 14.13). What we do in the Lord, by the power

of His Spirit, in politics and in every other earthly occupation will be brought
to perfection in the final Sabbath. We can be confident that our deeds of justice
now are kingdom deeds that will never be lost. Christ is gathering them up into
His great storehouse of treasures. They are gold that will not be destroyed by
the fire because they are fruits of God's redeeming work in us.[8]

We may confess this with joy and confidence, faith and hope:

> Our hope for a new earth is not tied
>   to what humans can do,
>   for we believe that one day
>   every challenge to God's rule
>   and every resistance to his will shall be crushed.
> Then his kingdom shall come fully,
>   and our Lord shall rule forever.
>
> We long for that day
>   when Jesus will return as triumphant king,
>   when the dead will be raised
>   and all people will stand before his judgment.
> We face that day without fear
>   for the Judge is our Savior.
> Our daily lives of service aim for the moment
>   when the Son will present his people to the Father.
> Then God will be shown to be true, holy, and gracious.
> All who have been on the Lord's side will be honored,
>   the fruit of even small acts of obedience will be displayed. . . .
>
> We rejoice in the goodness of God,
>   renounce the works of darkness,
>   and dedicate ourselves to holy living.
> As covenant partners, called to faithful obedience,
>   and set free for joyful praise,
>   we offer our hearts and lives
>   to do God's work in his world.
> With tempered impatience, eager to see injustice ended,
>   we expect the Day of the Lord.
> And we are confident
>   that the light which shines in the present darkness
>   will fill the earth when Christ appears.
>
> Come, Lord Jesus!
> Our world belongs to you.[9]

Notes

Preface

1. This was an area of importance for Mike during his high school years. Read about one of his attempts to struggle with this area in light of the gospel in "Delighting in God's Good Gift of Competition and Sport," in *Engaging the Culture: Christians at Work in Education*, ed. Richard Edlin and Jill Ireland (Sydney: National Institute for Christian Education, 2006), 173–86.

2. See Michael W. Goheen, "Mission and the Public Life of Western Culture: The Kuyperian Tradition," *The Gospel and Our Culture Network Newsletter (U.K.)* 26 (Autumn 1999): 6–8. Here Newbigin is compared with the Kuyperian tradition, articulating places where there can be mutual enrichment and correction.

3. This refers to the Dutch Calvinist tradition that stems from Abraham Kuyper. See chap. 2, the section titled "The Appropriation of Worldview in Christian Thinking."

4. Christian Worldview Network ceased its activities some time ago, but much of its published material is available at http://thebigpicture.homestead.com/.

5. Among South African evangelicals there were, of course, some notable exceptions, such as Michael Cassidy, the founder of African Enterprise. However, such evangelicals were in the minority.

6. See Richard Mouw, *The Smell of Sawdust: What Evangelicals Can Learn from Their Fundamentalist Heritage* (Grand Rapids: Zondervan, 2000).

7. Herman Bavinck, *The Philosophy of Revelation* (1909; repr., Grand Rapids: Baker Academic, 1979), 242.

8. N. T. Wright, *The New Testament and the People of God*, Christian Origins and the Question of God 1 (London: SPCK, 1992), 40 (italics added).

9. We might also mention an unpublished work written by a team of authors in the UK, headed up by Jonathan Chaplin, entitled "An Introduction to a Christian Worldview" (Open Christian College, 1986). This work used Brian Walsh and Richard Middleton, *The Transforming Vision: Shaping a Christian World View* (Downers Grove, IL: InterVarsity, 1984), as well as Albert Wolters, *Creation Regained: Biblical Basics for a Reformational Worldview* (Grand Rapids: Eerdmans, 1985), to teach a distance-learning course. The structure of the course followed Walsh and Middleton, and so it too dealt with worldview in a comprehensive way.

Chapter 1 Gospel, Story, Worldview, and the Church's Mission

1. The biblical basis for this section is explored in detail in Craig G. Bartholomew and Michael W. Goheen, "Act 4: The Coming of the King: Redemption Accomplished," in *The*

Drama of Scripture: Finding Our Place in the Biblical Story (Grand Rapids: Baker Academic, 2004), 129–70.

2. Christopher J. H. Wright, *The Mission of God: Unlocking the Bible's Grand Narrative* (Downers Grove, IL: InterVarsity, 2006), 54–55.

3. Erich Auerbach, *Mimesis: The Representation of Reality in Western Literature*, trans. Willard R. Trask (Princeton, NJ: Princeton University Press, 1968), 15.

4. N. T. Wright, *Jesus and the Victory of God*, Christian Origins and the Question of God 2 (London: SPCK, 1996), 198.

5. Lesslie Newbigin, *The Gospel in a Pluralist Society* (Grand Rapids: Eerdmans, 1989), 15.

6. Wright, *Mission of God*, 17.

7. Wright, *Mission of God*, 51.

8. Wright, *Mission of God*, 22–23.

9. Christian Reformed Church, *Our World Belongs to God: A Contemporary Testimony* (Grand Rapids: CRC Publications, 1987), paragraphs 32, 44–45 [also available at http://www .crcna.org/pages/our_world_main.cfm].

10. Newbigin, *Gospel in a Pluralist Society*, 15–16 (italics added).

11. "Missionary encounter" is the language frequently employed by Lesslie Newbigin. See, for example, *Foolishness to the Greeks: The Gospel and Western Culture* (Grand Rapids: Eerdmans, 1986), 1.

12. Lesslie Newbigin, *The Other Side of 1984: Questions for the Churches* (Geneva: World Council of Churches, 1983), 23.

Chapter 2 What Is a Worldview?

1. We are indebted to Roy Clouser for pointing us to this wonderful metaphor.

2. For a definitive treatment of this topic, see David Naugle, *Worldview: The History of a Concept* (Grand Rapids: Eerdmans, 2002).

3. Naugle, *Worldview*, 59.

4. Albert M. Wolters, "On the Idea of Worldview and Its Relation to Philosophy," in *Stained Glass: Worldviews and Social Science*, ed. Paul A. Marshall, Sander Griffioen, and Richard J. Mouw, Christian Studies Today (Lanham, MD: University Press of America, 1989), 15.

5. Naugle, *Worldview*, 55.

6. Peter Heslam, *Creating a Christian Worldview: Abraham Kuyper's Lectures on Calvinism* (Grand Rapids: Eerdmans, 1998), 89.

7. See Naugle, *Worldview*, 76, 81.

8. Sander Griffioen, "The Worldview Approach to Social Theory: Hazards and Benefits," in Marshall, Griffioen, and Mouw, *Stained Glass*, 87. Griffioen offers an excellent six-point summary of Dilthey's views.

9. From H. A. Hodges, *Wilhelm Dilthey: An Introduction* (New York: Oxford University Press, 1945), quoted in Dorothy Emmet, "The Choice of a World Outlook," *Philosophy* 23, no. 86 (July 1948): 208.

10. Wilhelm Dilthey, *Selected Writings*, ed. and trans. H. P. Rickman (Cambridge: Cambridge University Press, 1976), 141.

11. Griffioen, "Worldview Approach," 87.

12. Dilthey, *Selected Writings*, 141.

13. James Orr, *The Christian View of God and the World* (1893; repr., Grand Rapids: Eerdmans, 1947), 4.

14. Orr, *Christian View*, 378.

15. Orr, *Christian View*, 4, 5, 17, 18.

16. Subsequently published as *Lectures on Calvinism* (Grand Rapids: Eerdmans, 1931).

17. Kuyper, *Lectures on Calvinism*, 11.

18. Kuyper, *Lectures on Calvinism*, 11.

19. Abraham Kuyper, *Principles of Sacred Theology*, trans. J. Hendrick de Vries (1898; repr., Grand Rapids: Baker Academic, 1980), 154.

20. See Carl F. H. Henry, *God, Revelation, and Authority*, vol. 5, *God Who Stands and Stays: Part One* (Waco: Word, 1982), chap. 20, "Man's Mind and God's Mind."

21. There is some debate about whether or not Schaeffer was a rationalist. See B. A. Follis, *Truth with Love: The Apologetics of Francis Schaeffer* (Wheaton: Crossway, 2006), chap. 3, "Rationality and Spirituality."

22. See Alasdair MacIntyre, *Whose Justice? Which Rationality?* (Notre Dame, IN: University of Notre Dame Press, 1988).

23. See, for example, J. F. Sennet, ed., *The Analytic Theist: An Alvin Plantinga Reader* (Grand Rapids: Eerdmans, 1998); Nicholas Wolterstorff, *Reason within the Bounds of Religion* (Grand Rapids: Eerdmans, 1976). For an introduction to so-called Reformed epistemology, of which Plantinga and Wolterstorff are leading figures, see Dewey J. Hoitenga, *Faith and Reason from Plato to Plantinga: An Introduction to Reformed Epistemology* (Albany: State University of New York Press, 1991).

24. Francis A. Schaeffer, *The Complete Works of Francis A. Schaeffer: A Christian Worldview*, 2nd ed., 5 vols. (Wheaton: Crossway, 1982).

25. Albert M. Wolters, *Creation Regained: Biblical Basics for a Reformational Worldview* (Grand Rapids: Eerdmans, 1985). A second edition, with a postscript coauthored by Michael W. Goheen, was published in 2005.

26. Brian J. Walsh and J. Richard Middleton, *The Transforming Vision: Shaping a Christian World View* (Downers Grove, IL: InterVarsity, 1984). See also J. Richard Middleton and Brian J. Walsh, *Truth Is Stranger Than It Used to Be: Biblical Faith in a Postmodern Age* (Downers Grove, IL: InterVarsity, 1995); Brian J. Walsh, *Subversive Christianity: Imaging God in a Dangerous Time* (Bristol: Regius, 1992).

27. James W. Sire, *The Universe Next Door: A Basic Worldview Catalog*, 4th ed. (Downers Grove, IL: InterVarsity, 2004).

28. Arthur F. Holmes, *Contours of a World View*, Studies in a Christian World View 1 (Grand Rapids: Eerdmans, 1983).

29. N. T. Wright, *The New Testament and the People of God*, Christian Origins and the Question of God 1 (London: SPCK, 1992), 38–44, 122–44.

30. Charles Colson and Nancy Pearcey, *How Now Shall We Live?* (Wheaton: Tyndale, 1999).

31. See Nancy Pearcey, *Total Truth: Liberating Christianity from Its Cultural Captivity* (Wheaton: Crossway, 2004).

32. See John R. W. Stott, ed., *Making Christ Known: Historic Mission Documents from the Lausanne Movement 1974–1989* (Carlisle: Paternoster, 1996), chaps. 1 and 7 for the Lausanne Covenant; and, on the relationship between evangelism and social engagement, see the 1982 Grand Rapids Report, *Evangelism and Social Responsibility: An Evangelical Commitment*, ed. John R. W. Stott, Lausanne Occasional Papers 21 (Exeter: Paternoster, 1982).

33. John R. W. Stott, *Christian Mission in the Modern World* (London: Falcon, 1975).

34. John R. W. Stott, *New Issues Facing Christians Today* (London: Marshall Pickering, 1999).

35. T. Dudley-Smith, *John Stott: A Global Ministry* (Leicester, UK: Inter-Varsity, 2001), chap. 9.

36. James Sire, *How to Read Slowly: Reading for Comprehension* (Downers Grove, IL: InterVarsity, 1978).

37. Sire, *Universe Next Door*, 16.

38. Sire, *Universe Next Door*, 16; see also idem, *Naming the Elephant: Worldview as a Concept* (Downers Grove, IL: InterVarsity, 2004), 12.

39. Sire, *Naming the Elephant*, 122.

40. Sire, *Naming the Elephant*, 122; see also idem, *Universe Next Door*, 17.

41. Sire, *Naming the Elephant*, 124.

42. Somewhat obscurely, Sire comments, "A worldview is not a story or a set of presuppositions, but it can be expressed in those ways" (*Naming the Elephant*, 126).

43. Romano Guardini, *The World and the Person*, trans. Stella Lange (Chicago: Henry Regnery, 1965); originally published as *Welt und Person: Versuche zur christlichen Lehre vom Menschen* (Würzburg: Werkbund-Verlag, 1939). Another good resource is the set of CDs by Scott Hahn, *Building a Catholic Biblical Worldview* (West Covina, CA: St. Joseph's Communications, 1999).

44. Alexander Schmemann, *For the Life of the World: Sacraments and Orthodoxy*, 2nd ed. (Crestwood, NY: St. Vladimir's Seminary Press, 1973).

45. Naugle, *Worldview*, 52, quoting Schmemann, *For the Life of the World*, 20–21.

46. Harry Blamires, *The Christian Mind* (London: SPCK, 1963), 189.

47. Thomas Merton, *Contemplative Prayer* (London: Darton, Longman & Todd, 1969), 85.

48. Karl Barth, *Church Dogmatics*, vol. 3, *The Doctrine of Creation: Part 1*, ed. G. W. Bromiley and T. F. Torrance (Edinburgh: T&T Clark, 1958), 343.

49. Francis Schaeffer, *Escape from Reason: A Penetrating Analysis of Trends in Modern Thought* (Downers Grove, IL: InterVarsity, 1968), 21.

50. Wright, *New Testament and the People of God*, 41–42.

51. On Ecclesiastes 3:11, see Craig G. Bartholomew, *Ecclesiastes* (Grand Rapids: Baker Academic, forthcoming).

52. Richard Middleton and Brian Walsh have helpfully phrased four worldview questions: Where am I? Who am I? What's wrong? What's the remedy? (*The Transforming Vision*, 35). N. T. Wright has suggested that we change the singular "I" to the plural "we" to indicate the communal sharing of worldview beliefs. He has also suggested the addition of a fifth question, "What time is it?" to indicate that worldview is a narrative in which we find our place (*Jesus and the Victory of God*, Christian Origins and the Question of God 2 [London: SPCK, 1996], 443n1; see also 467–72). Also, missiologist J. H. Bavinck suggests that the human being, "by virtue of his place in the world, must always and everywhere give answers to the same questions. He has to struggle with the basic problems which his existence itself entails" (*The Church between Temple and Mosque: A Study of the Relationship between the Christian Faith and Other Religions* [1966; repr., Grand Rapids: Eerdmans, 1981], 31). He formulates those questions in terms of five magnetic points that are found in all world religions. He speaks of "I and cosmos," "I and the religious norm," "I and the riddle of my existence," "I and salvation," and "I and the Supreme Power." We have found it helpful to speak here of four questions that summarize these magnetic points: What is the nature of ultimate reality? How can I achieve salvation? What is the meaning of human life? What is the source of order and how can it be known? (Bavinck, *The Church between Temple and Mosque*, 32–33). We already referred to the diagnostic questions posed by James Sire.

53. See James Olthuis, "On Worldviews," *Christian Scholar's Review* 14 (1985): 153–64; also published under the same title in Marshall, Griffioen, and Mouw, *Stained Glass*, 26–40.

54. Roy Clouser, *The Myth of Religious Neutrality: An Essay on the Hidden Role of Religious Beliefs in Theories* (Notre Dame, IN: University of Notre Dame Press, 1991), 1.

55. As with John Calvin, *Institutes of the Christian Religion*, ed. John T. McNeill, trans. Ford Lewis Battles, 2 vols., Library of Christian Classics 20–21 (Philadelphia: Westminster, 1960), 1:3–5, which was the purpose of his *Institutes*.

56. S. MacDonald, "Augustine, *Confessions*," in *The Classics of Western Philosophy: A Reader's Guide*, ed. Jorge J. E. Gracia, Gregory M. Reichberg, and Bernard N. Schumacher (Oxford: Blackwell, 2003), 103.

57. See especially Oliver O'Donovan, *The Desire of the Nations: Rediscovering the Roots of Political Theology* (Cambridge: Cambridge University Press, 1996).

58. See O'Donovan, *The Desire of the Nations*; see also Craig Bartholomew et al., eds., *A Royal Priesthood? The Use of the Bible Ethically and Politically: A Dialogue with Oliver O'Donovan*, Scripture and Hermeneutics 3 (Grand Rapids: Zondervan, 2002).

Chapter 3 A Biblical Worldview: Creation and Sin

1. See Christopher J. H. Wright, *The Mission of God: Unlocking the Bible's Grand Narrative* (Downers Grove, IL: InterVarsity, 2006), 105–21.

2. John Henry Newman, *The Idea of a University* (1873; repr., London: Longmans, Green, 1923), 50–51.

3. Herman Bavinck, *The Doctrine of God*, ed. and trans. William Hendriksen, Twin Brooks Series (Grand Rapids: Baker Academic, 1977), 89. The first and last sentences in quotation marks are from John Calvin, *Institutes of the Christian Religion* I.V.1, 5.

4. Quoted in Newman, *The Idea of a University*, 36.

5. The Vulgate is an early fifth-century translation of the Bible into Latin partly translated and revised by Jerome. It became the definitive and official Bible of the Roman Catholic Church and exercised great influence on the church and culture during the Middle Ages.

6. See Paul G. Schrotenboer et al., *God's Order for Creation* (Potchefstroom: Institute for Reformational Studies, 1994); Albert M. Wolters, "Creation Order: A Historical Look at Our Heritage," in *An Ethos of Compassion and the Integrity of Creation*, ed. Brian J. Walsh, Hendrik Hart, and Robert E. VanderVennen (Lanham, MD: University Press of America, 1995), 33–48; David Koyzis, *Political Visions and Illusions: A Survey and Christian Critique of Contemporary Ideologies* (Downers Grove, IL: InterVarsity, 2003), 194–201.

7. Bruce Milne, *Know the Truth: A Handbook of Christian Belief* (Leicester, UK: InterVarsity, 1984), 74.

8. Abraham Kuyper, *Lectures on Calvinism* (Grand Rapids: Eerdmans, 1931), 78.

9. Kuyper, *Lectures on Calvinism*, 53.

10. Albert M. Wolters, *Creation Regained: Biblical Basics for a Reformational Worldview*, 2nd ed. (Grand Rapids: Eerdmans, 2005), 17.

11. Wolters, *Creation Regained*, 29.

12. Gerhard von Rad, *Old Testament Theology*, trans. D. M. G. Stalker, 2 vols. (New York: Harper & Row, 1962–1965), 1:418.

13. Gordon Spykman, *Reformational Theology: A New Paradigm for Doing Dogmatics* (Grand Rapids: Eerdmans, 1992), 180.

14. Gerhard von Rad, *Wisdom in Israel*, trans. James D. Martin (Nashville: Abingdon, 1972), 71.

15. Wolters rightly notes: "'Submit yourselves for the Lord's sake to every *authority instituted* among men' (1 Pet. 2:13); the italicized words translate the Greek word *ktisis*, the regular biblical word for 'creation' or 'creatures.' It seems plain, therefore, that civil authority is founded on an ordinance of God" (*Creation Regained*, 25–26).

16. Bernard Zylstra, "Thy Word Our Life," in *Will All the King's Men . . . : Out of Concern for the Church, Phase II*, ed. James Olthuis (Toronto: Wedge, 1972), 157.

17. Hendrikus Berkhof, *Christian Faith: An Introduction to the Study of the Faith* (Grand Rapids: Eerdmans, 1979), 523, 543; idem, *Christ the Meaning of History* (Grand Rapids: Baker Academic, 1966), 188–92.

18. See Gunnlaugur Jónsson, *The Image of God: Genesis 1:26–28 in a Century of Old Testament Research*, trans. Lorraine Svendsen, rev. Michael S. Cheney, Coniectanea biblica: Old Testament Series 26 (Stockholm: Almquist & Wiksell, 1988), 143–44; J. Richard Middleton, *The Liberating Image: The Imago Dei in Genesis 1* (Grand Rapids: Brazos, 2005), 93–145.

19. Henri Blocher, *In the Beginning: The Opening Chapters of Genesis*, trans. David G. Preston (Downers Grove, IL: InterVarsity, 1984), 82.

20. See Anthony Hoekema, *Created in God's Image* (Grand Rapids: Eerdmans, 1986), 100; Richard J. Mouw, *When the Kings Come Marching In: Isaiah and the New Jerusalem* (Grand Rapids: Eerdmans, 1983), 47.

21. Blocher, *In the Beginning*, 85.

22. Blocher, *In the Beginning*, 96.

23. For an interpretation of these words as blessing, see Clarence Joldersma, afterword to *Educating for Life: Reflections on Christian Teaching and Learning*, by Nicholas Wolterstorff, ed. Gloria Goris Stronks and Clarence W. Joldersma (Grand Rapids: Baker Academic, 2002), 296; John Stek, "What Says the Scripture?" in *Portraits of Creation: Biblical and Scientific Perspectives on the World's Formation*, by Howard J. Van Till et al. (Grand Rapids: Eerdmans, 1990), 251.

24. Lynn White, "The Historical Roots of Our Ecologic Crisis," *Science* 155 (1967): 1203–7.

25. Jonathan Chaplin et al., "An Introduction to a Christian Worldview" (unpublished course material, Open Christian College, 1986), 53.

26. Spykman, *Reformational Theology*, 178.

27. Nicholas Wolterstorff stresses this aspect of *shalom*: "Shalom incorporates *delight* in one's relationships. To dwell in shalom is to find delight in living rightly before God, to find delight in living rightly in one's physical surroundings, to find delight in living rightly with one's fellow human beings, and to find delight even in living rightly with oneself" (*Educating for Shalom: Essays on Christian Higher Education* [Grand Rapids: Eerdmans, 2004], 23).

28. Cornelius Plantinga Jr., *Not the Way It's Supposed to Be: A Breviary of Sin* (Grand Rapids: Eerdmans, 1995), 10.

29. Plantinga, *Not the Way It's Supposed to Be*, 7.

30. Gerhard von Rad, *Genesis: A Commentary*, trans. John H. Marks (Philadelphia: Westminster, 1961), 78.

31. Plantinga, *Not the Way It's Supposed to Be*, 30.

32. Bruce Waltke observes, "As a result of the Fall and God's judgment upon them, the woman desires to rule her husband, and he seeks to dominate her (Genesis 3:16B)" ("The Role of Women in Worship in the Old Testament," http://www.ldolphin.org/waltke.html [accessed February 14, 2008]). See also Susan T. Foh, "What Is the Woman's Desire?" *Westminster Theological Journal* 37 (1975), 374–83; idem, *Women and the Word of God: A Response to Biblical Feminism* (Phillipsburg, NJ: Presbyterian & Reformed, 1979), 68–69.

33. G. C. Berkouwer, *Sin*, trans. Philip C. Holtrop, Studies in Dogmatics (Grand Rapids: Eerdmans, 1971), 235; see also 235–322; see also Plantinga, *Not the Way It's Supposed to Be*.

34. Chaplin et al., "An Introduction to a Christian Worldview," 64.

35. See Jeremiah 3 and the book of Hosea.

36. Brian J. Walsh and J. Richard Middleton, *The Transforming Vision: Shaping a Christian World View* (Downers Grove, IL: InterVarsity, 1984), 67.

37. Berkouwer, *Sin*, 235, 240, 259.

38. Plantinga unfolds sin in its corrupting power in a threefold way: sin perverts or twists the creation so that it serves an unworthy end; sin pollutes and contaminates the creation; sin brings disintegration and deterioration.

39. Berkouwer, *Sin*, 262. He is summarizing Bavinck's discussion in *Gereformeerde Dogmatiek*, III, 125.

40. There is a long history, going back to Augustine, of reflection on sin in terms of *privatio*. Augustine said that the evil "has no existence except as a privation of the good" (*Confessions* 3.7.12). See the discussion in Berkouwer, *Sin*, 256–67.

41. Plantinga, *Not the Way It's Supposed to Be*, 89.

42. C. S. Lewis, *Mere Christianity* (New York: Macmillan, 1952), 49.

43. Herman Bavinck, *Gereformeerde Dogmatiek*, III, 126, quoted in Berkouwer, *Sin*, 262.

44. Wolters, *Creation Regained*, 53–68.

45. Bob Goudzwaard, *Aid for the Overdeveloped West* (Toronto: Wedge, 1975), 14.

46. Goudzwaard, *Aid for the Overdeveloped West*, 15.

47. G. C. Berkouwer writes, "Life on this earth does not yet disclose the full consequences of sin. Calvin speaks of 'common grace' and, in this connection, he discusses virtues to be seen also in the lives of unbelievers. He did not wish to ascribe these phenomena to a left-over

goodness in nature as if apostasy from God were not so serious but rather he discerned here the power of God in revelation and in grace preserving life from total destruction" ("General and Special Divine Revelation," in *Revelation and the Bible*, ed. Carl F. H. Henry [Grand Rapids: Baker Academic, 1959], 20–21).

Chapter 4 A Biblical Worldview: Restoration

1. For a seven-page summary of this story, see Craig Bartholomew and Michael Goheen, "The Story-Line of the Bible," http://www.biblicaltheology.ca/blue_files/The%20Story-Line%20of%20the%20Bible.pdf (accessed February 14, 2008).

2. Christopher J. H. Wright, *The Mission of God: Unlocking the Bible's Grand Narrative* (Downers Grove, IL: InterVarsity, 2006), 23.

3. See Michael W. Goheen, "(Re)New(ed) Heavens and Earth: The End of the Story," http://www.biblicaltheology.ca/blue_files/(Re)New(ed)%20Creation-The%20End%20of%20the%20Story.pdf (accessed February 14, 2008); J. Richard Middleton, "A New Heaven and a New Earth: The Case for a Holistic Reading of the Biblical Story of Redemption," *Journal for Christian Theological Research* 11 (2006): 73–97 [also available at http://www.luthersem.edu/ctrf/JCTR/Vol11/Middleton_vol11.pdf]; Michael Williams, "A Restorational Alternative to Augustinian Verticalist Eschatology," *Pro Rege* 20, no. 4 (June 1992): 11–24.

4. Albert M. Wolters, *Creation Regained: Biblical Basics for a Reformational Worldview*, 2nd ed. (Grand Rapids: Eerdmans, 2005), 49.

5. Wolters, *Creation Regained*, 77.

6. Middleton, "A New Heaven and a New Earth," 75–76.

7. See the fine book by Michael Williams, *As Far as the Curse Is Found: The Covenant Story of Redemption* (Phillipsburg, NJ: Presbyterian & Reformed, 2005).

8. See Wolters, *Creation Regained*, 40.

9. Gerhard von Rad, *Wisdom in Israel*, trans. James D. Martin (Nashville: Abingdon, 1972), 159.

10. David Bosch, *Transforming Mission: Paradigm Shifts in Theology of Mission* (Maryknoll, NY: Orbis, 1991), 33.

11. E. H. Scheffler argues that in Luke salvation has six dimensions: economic, social, political, physical, psychological, and spiritual ("Suffering in Luke's Gospel" [DD diss., University of Pretoria, 1988], 57–108; cited in Bosch, *Transforming Mission*, 117).

12. Colin Gunton, *Christ and Creation* (1992; repr., Eugene, OR: Wipf & Stock, 2005), 17–18.

13. John Driver, *Understanding the Atonement for the Mission of the Church* (Scottdale, PA: Herald, 1986), 71–86.

14. Lesslie Newbigin, *The Gospel in a Pluralist Society* (Grand Rapids: Eerdmans, 1989), 179. Newbigin uses the past tense—"privatized," "talked," "culminated"—but we have changed these for literary purposes to the present tense. Compare the biting criticism of Christians by the nineteenth-century nihilist philosopher Friedrich Nietzsche: "The 'salvation of the soul'—in plain English: 'the world revolves around me'" (*The Antichrist*, aphorism 43).

15. The Spirit as a gift that brings the end-time kingdom is a well-established concept in biblical and theological scholarship. See, for example, Neill Q. Hamilton, *The Holy Spirit and Eschatology in Paul*, Scottish Journal of Theology Occasional Papers 6 (Edinburgh: Oliver & Boyd, 1957), 17; Hendrikus Berkhof, *The Doctrine of the Holy Spirit* (Richmond: John Knox, 1964), 105.

16. See Lesslie Newbigin, *Mission in Christ's Way: A Gift, a Command, an Assurance* (New York: Friendship Press, 1987).

17. Herman Ridderbos, *The Coming of the Kingdom*, ed. Raymond O. Zorn, trans. H. de Jongste (Philadelphia: Presbyterian & Reformed, 1975), 354–56.

18. Lesslie Newbigin, *Household of God: Lectures on the Nature of the Church* (New York: Friendship Press, 1954), 153.

19. Quoted in George Marsden, *Fundamentalism and American Culture: The Shaping of Twentieth-Century Evangelicalism, 1870–1925* (New York: Oxford University Press, 1980), 38.

20. Lesslie Newbigin, "The Bishop and the Ministry of Mission," in *Today's Church and Today's World: With a Special Focus on the Ministry of Bishops*, ed. John Howe (London: CIO Publishing, 1977), 242.

21. Bosch, *Transforming Mission*, 35.

22. Lesslie Newbigin, "Abiding in Him," in World Council of Churches, Faith and Order Commission, *Uniting in Hope: Reports and Documents from the Meeting of the Faith and Order Commission, 23 July–5 August, 1974, University of Ghana, Legon*, Faith and Order Paper 72 (Geneva: Commission on Faith and Order, World Council of Churches, 1975), 141. See also Lesslie Newbigin, *The Good Shepherd: Meditations on Christian Ministry in Today's World* (Grand Rapids: Eerdmans, 1977), 140–44.

23. See Albert M. Wolters, "The Reformational-Evangelical Worldview and the Future Mission of Institutions of Christian Higher Education in a North American Context," in *Vision and Mission: 25 Years; The Reformational-Evangelical Vision of Life and the Future Mission of Christian Higher Educational Institutions in World Perspective* [also in Afrikaans], ed. B. J. van der Walt (Potchefstroom: Potchefstroomse Universiteit vir Christelike Höer Onderwys, 1989), 87.

24. We borrow this image from Wolters, *Creation Regained*, 45–46.

25. This is not to deny either that there is a heaven or that when we die we go to heaven until the resurrection of the body. For a simple yet helpful elaboration of this, see David Lawrence, *Heaven: It's Not the End of the World! The Biblical Promise of a New Earth* (London: Scripture Union, 1995); on the biblical notion of heaven, 48–59; on the "intermediate state" between death and resurrection, 60–74.

26. Lawrence, *Heaven*, 17–18. See also Paul Marshall and Lela Gilbert, *Heaven Is Not My Home: Learning to Live in God's Creation* (Nashville: Word, 1999); Michael Wittmer, *Heaven Is a Place on Earth: Why Everything You Do Matters to God* (Grand Rapids: Zondervan, 2004); Nathan Bierma, *Bringing Heaven Down to Earth: Connecting This Life to the Next* (Phillipsburg, NJ: Presbyterian & Reformed, 2005).

27. Lawrence, *Heaven*, 17.

Chapter 5 The Western Story: The Roots of Modernity

1. Lesslie Newbigin, "Gospel and Culture—But Which Culture?" *Missionalia* 17, no. 3 (November 1989): 214.

2. Friedrich Nietzsche, *The Gay Science*, trans. and ed. Walter Kaufmann (New York: Vintage, 1974), 181–82 (paragraph 125).

3. *Humanist Manifesto I* (1933). Since this document first appeared, two further manifestos have followed: *Humanist Manifesto II* (1973) and *Humanism and Its Aspirations: Humanist Manifesto III* (2003). The texts are available at http://www.americanhumanist.org/about/ (accessed February 18, 2008).

4. Corliss Lamont, *The Philosophy of Humanism*, 8th ed. (Amherst, NY: Humanist Press, 1997), 309. The entire book is available at http://www.corliss-lamont.org/philos8.pdf (accessed February 18, 2008).

5. This is the form of humanism held by Lamont (see *Philosophy of Humanism*, 317).

6. The labels *liberal* and *communist* could be included here to describe the two principal forms taken by humanism in the twentieth century. Of course, since the collapse of the Soviet Union in 1991, it has been liberal humanism that has dominated the Western world.

7. Alan D. Gilbert, *The Making of Post-Christian Britain: A History of the Secularization of Modern Society* (London: Longman, 1980), 153.

8. Michael Polanyi, *Personal Knowledge: Toward a Post-critical Philosophy* (Chicago: University of Chicago Press, 1958), 265–66. We have borrowed and altered Polanyi's image. Polanyi speaks of the "combustion of the Christian heritage in the oxygen of Greek rationalism."

9. Christopher Dawson, *Religion and the Rise of Western Culture* (New York: Image, 1958), 16.

10. Dirk H. Th. Vollenhoven, *The Problem-Historical Method and the History of Philosophy*, ed. Kornelis A. Bril (Amstelveen: De Zaak Haes, 2005), 29–88. Vollenhoven died before people began to speak of postmodernity. He spoke of only three periods: pagan, synthesis, and antisynthesis. We have added neo-pagan. See John Kok, *Patterns of the Western Mind: A Reformed Christian Perspective*, 2nd ed. (Sioux Center, IA: Dordt College Press, 1998), 27.

11. Speaking of Western culture, Lesslie Newbigin says, "It is a pagan society, and its paganism, having been born out of the rejection of Christianity, is far more resistant to the gospel than the pre-Christian paganism with which the cross-cultural missions have been familiar. Here, surely, is the most challenging missionary frontier of our time" (*Foolishness to the Greeks: The Gospel and Western Culture* [Grand Rapids: Eerdmans, 1986], 20).

12. We are aware of the difficulty and danger of this enterprise, especially of attempting it in just one chapter. Yet we do it because we believe that it is essential for faithful Christian living. We certainly invite others to correct and improve on this narrative.

13. James Shiel, *Greek Thought and the Rise of Christianity*, Problems and Perspectives in History (New York: Barnes & Noble, 1968), 5.

14. This includes things such as the distinction between deduction and induction; the syllogism; distinction between material, efficient, formal, and final causes; distinctions between subject-object, essential-accidental, matter-form, potential-actual, universal-particular, genus-species-individual; and ten categories of substance, quantity, quality, relation, place, time, position, state, action, and affection.

15. Richard Tarnas, *The Passion of the Western Mind: Understanding the Ideas That Have Shaped Our World View* (New York: Ballantine, 1991), 62.

16. See, for example, Rodney Stark, *The Victory of Reason: How Christianity Led to Freedom, Capitalism, and Western Success* (New York: Random House, 2005).

17. The story of his conversion is found in Augustine's renowned *Confessions*. *Confessions* is a series of thirteen autobiographical works written in 397–398. In the first ten works Augustine tells his own story, and in the last three works he offers reflections on the biblical book of Genesis.

18. Tarnas, *Passion of the Western Mind*, 147.

19. Hans Küng, *Christianity: The Religious Situation of Our Time*, trans. John Bowden (London: SCM, 1995), 417.

20. Fernand van Steenberghen, *Aristotle in the West: The Origins of Latin Aristotelianism*, trans. Leonard Johnson (Louvain: E. Nauwelaerts, 1955), 67.

21. Küng, *Christianity*, 426.

22. Brian J. Walsh and J. Richard Middleton, *The Transforming Vision: Shaping a Christian World View* (Downers Grove, IL: InterVarsity, 1984), 115.

23. Lesslie Newbigin, *Sign of the Kingdom* (Grand Rapids: Eerdmans, 1980), 47.

24. Lesslie Newbigin, *The Household of God: Lectures on the Nature of the Church* (New York: Friendship Press, 1954), 1.

25. Lesslie Newbigin, *Priorities for a New Decade* (Birmingham: National Student Christian Press and Resource Centre, 1980), 6.

Chapter 6 The Western Story: The Growth of Modernity

1. Lesslie Newbigin notes, "'Enlightenment' is a word with profound religious overtones. It is the word to describe the decisive experience of Buddha. It is the word used in the Johannine writings to describe the coming of Jesus. . . . The leading thinkers of the mid-eighteenth

century felt themselves to be at such a moment of enlightenment." This feeling of exhilaration at finding the light that marked this period "came from the conviction that things which had been previously obscure were now being 'explained.' In place of 'dogmatic' or 'unscientific' explanations which no longer satisfied the mind, the true explanation of things was now coming to light" (*The Other Side of 1984: Questions for the Churches* [Geneva: World Council of Churches, 1983], 7–8).

2. Perhaps the German humanist Christoph Cellarius (1638–1707) was the first to actually employ this division, which he did in his seventeenth-century work *Universal History, Divided into Ancient, Medieval, and Modern Time Periods*. See Geoffrey Barraclough, *History in a Changing World* (Oxford: Blackwell, 1955), 54.

3. Johan Huizinga, *Men and Ideas: History, the Middle Ages, the Renaissance; Essays*, trans. James S. Holmes and Hans van Marle (New York: Harper & Row, 1970), 243–87.

4. John Dewey, *Reconstruction in Philosophy*, enlarged ed. (Boston: Beacon, 1957), 47–48.

5. See Romano Guardini, *The World and the Person*, trans. Stella Lange (Chicago: Henry Regnery, 1965); originally published as *Welt und Person: Versuche zur christlichen Lehre vom Menschen* (Würzburg: Werkbund-Verlag, 1939). Guardini helpfully formulates three starting points of the modern world that emerged in the late medieval period and especially at the Renaissance: nature, subject, and culture. The key to understanding these three is autonomy, by which Guardini refers to an understanding of creation, human life, and cultural development as existing apart from God and his authority. Guardini's nature, subject, and culture correspond roughly with our points 2 through 4 on the Renaissance worldview.

6. Guardini, *The World and the Person*, 9.

7. J. B. Ross and M. M. McLaughlin, eds., *The Portable Renaissance Reader* (New York: Penguin, 1977), 478.

8. Guardini, *The World and the Person*, 11.

9. Bob Goudzwaard, *Capitalism and Progress: A Diagnosis of Western Society*, trans. and ed. Josina Van Nuis Zylstra (Toronto: Wedge; Grand Rapids: Eerdmans, 1979), 134.

10. Guardini, *The World and the Person*, 11.

11. Ronald A. Wells, *History through the Eyes of Faith: Western Civilization and the Kingdom of God* (San Francisco: Harper & Row, 1989), 75.

12. Crane Brinton, *The Shaping of the Modern Mind: The Concluding Half of Ideas and Men* (New York: New American Library, 1953), 22.

13. Richard Tarnas, *The Passion of the Western Mind: Understanding the Ideas That Have Shaped Our World View* (New York: Ballantine, 1991), 321.

14. For a full discussion of the secularizing impact of the Reformation from a position that is not sympathetic to Christianity, see Tarnas, *Passion of the Western Mind*, 237–47.

15. Roland H. Bainton, *Here I Stand: A Life of Martin Luther* (1950; repr., New York: Penguin, 1995), 144.

16. Lesslie Newbigin, *Foolishness to the Greeks: The Gospel and Western Culture* (Grand Rapids: Eerdmans, 1986), 15, 22.

17. *Novum Organum*, book 1, aphorism 3.

18. *Novum Organum*, book 1, aphorism 129.

19. See Peter A. Schouls, *Descartes and the Enlightenment*, McGill-Queen's Studies in the History of Ideas 13 (Kingston: McGill-Queen's University Press, 1989). Schouls demonstrates that the thought of Descartes, especially his view of freedom, mastery, and progress, is fundamentally similar to that of the Enlightenment *philosophes*.

20. René Descartes, *Discourse on Method*, 3rd ed., trans. Donald A. Cress (Indianapolis: Hackett, 1993), 3.

21. Pope's epitaph for Newton.

22. Donald H. Kobe, "Copernicus and Martin Luther: An Encounter Between Science and Religion," *American Association of Physics Teachers* (March 1998): 192. These words were not

written by Luther but rather were quoted from memory by one of his friends from a discussion. Kobe's article shows the historical development of Luther's original remark and how it has been exaggerated and misused to promote the warfare metaphor between science and religion. I owe this reference, along with some clarification on Luther's quotation, to Dr. Paul Brown, professor and coordinator of environmental studies at Trinity Western University, Langley, BC.

23. Max Wildiers, *The Theologian and His Universe: Theology and Cosmology from the Middle Ages to the Present*, trans. Paul Dunphy (New York: Seabury, 1982), 140 (originally published as *Wereldbeeld en teologie: Van de middeleeuwen tot vandaag* [Antwerp: Standaard, 1977]).

24. Tarnas, *Passion of the Western Mind*, 261.

25. Carl Becker, *The Heavenly City of the Eighteenth-Century Philosophers* (New Haven: Yale University Press, 1932), 31.

26. Immanuel Kant, *Criticism of Herder* (1785), quoted in F. S. Marvin, *The Living Past: A Sketch of Western Progress*, 4th ed. (Oxford: Clarendon, 1928), 217.

27. Cited in Becker, *Heavenly City*, 145.

28. William Goodwin, *Enquiry Concerning Political Justice and Its Influence on Morals and Happiness* (Toronto: University of Toronto Press, 1946), 2:528, quoted in Goudzwaard, *Capitalism and Progress*, 41.

29. Becker, *Heavenly City*, 31.

30. Quoted in John B. Bury, *The Idea of Progress: An Inquiry into Its Origin and Growth* (London: Macmillan, 1920), 173.

31. Lawrence Osborn, *Restoring the Vision: The Gospel and Modern Culture* (London: Mowbray, 1995), 46.

32. Osborn, *Restoring the Vision*, 57.

33. Ronald Wright, *A Short History of Progress*, CBC Massey Lecture Series (Toronto: House of Anansi Press, 1994), 4; cf. Christopher Dawson, *Progress and Religion: An Historical Inquiry* (London: Sheed & Ward, 1929), 3.

34. Becker, *Heavenly City*, 31; cf. Goudzwaard, *Capitalism and Progress*, 38.

35. Tarnas, *Passion of the Western Mind*, 323.

36. See Bury, *The Idea of Progress*, 197; Goudzwaard, *Capitalism and Progress*, 49.

37. Alexander Pope ridicules the view that pursuit of self-interest would coincide with the purposes of God for economic life: "Thus God and Nature formed the general frame; And bade self-love and social be the same" (*An Essay on Man: In Epistles to a Friend*, 4 vols. [London: J. Wilford, 1733–1734], Epistle 3, 317–18).

38. Marvin Perry et al., *Western Civilization: Ideas, Politics, and Society*, 5th ed. (Boston: Houghton Mifflin, 1996), 439.

39. Paul Tillich, *Perspectives on 19th and 20th Century Protestant Theology*, ed. Carl E. Braaten (London: SCM, 1967), 33.

40. George Soros and Jeff Madrick, "The International Crisis: An Interview," *The New York Review of Books* (January 14, 1999): 38. Cited in Bob Goudzwaard et al., *Globalization and the Kingdom of God*, ed. James W. Skillen (Washington, DC: Center for Public Justice; Grand Rapids: Baker Academic, 2001), 24.

41. Newbigin, *Foolishness to the Greeks*, 31.

42. Paul Hazard, *European Thought in the Eighteenth Century: From Montesquieu to Lessing*, trans. J. Lewis May (Cleveland: World Publishing, 1963), 145; originally published as *La pensée européenne au XVIIIème siècle: De Montesquieu à Lessing*, 3 vols. (Paris: Boivin, 1946); see also idem, *The European Mind: 1680–1715*, trans. J. Lewis May (New York: World Publishing, 1963), 269–70; originally published as *La crise de la conscience européenne, 1680–1715*, 3 vols. (Paris: Boivin, 1935).

43. A. P. d'Entrèves, *Natural Law: An Introduction to Legal Philosophy* (London: Hutchinson's University Library, 1951), 55.

44. Newbigin, *The Other Side of 1984*, 12. Newbigin's reference to Montesquieu (1689–1755) is from his famous first chapter in *De L'esprit des lois* (*On the Spirit of Laws*), an essay on government, first published in 1748.

45. Eduard Heimann, *History of Economic Doctrines: An Introduction to Economic Theory* (London: Oxford University Press, 1945), 49, quoted in Goudzwaard, *Capitalism and Progress*, 20.

46. Peter Gay, *The Enlightenment: An Interpretation*, 2 vols. (New York: Knopf, 1966–1969), 1:149.

47. Hazard, *The European Mind*, 256.

48. In a sense, these are two routes that we see taken in capitalist and communist societies— the two forms that the Enlightenment worldview eventually would take. The communist form of humanism attempts to eliminate the Christian faith, while the capitalist form relegates the Christian faith to the private realm.

49. Tarnas, *Passion of the Western Mind*, 306–7.

50. Tarnas, *Passion of the Western Mind*, 286.

51. Goudzwaard, *Capitalism and Progress*, 50–51.

52. The American Revolution too could be considered here as a revolution that implemented the Enlightenment worldview.

53. Stephen Monsma et al., *Responsible Technology: A Christian Perspective* (Grand Rapids: Eerdmans, 1986), 85, 91.

54. Lynn White, "The Historical Roots of Our Ecologic Crisis," *Science* 155 (1967): 1203–7.

55. Norman J. G. Pounds, *An Historical Geography of Europe, 1800–1914* (Cambridge: Cambridge University Press, 1985), 32.

56. Andrew Walker, *Telling the Story: Gospel, Mission, and Culture* (London: SPCK, 1996), 57.

57. David Wells, *God in the Wasteland: The Reality of Truth in a World of Fading Dreams* (Grand Rapids: Eerdmans, 1994), 7.

58. Walker, *Telling the Story*, 110–11.

59. Mark Poster writes, "From liberal and Marxist perspectives discourses about society have the intention of furthering emancipation. Knowledge promotes freedom. This basic assumption characterizes discourse since the Enlightenment" (*Foucault, Marxism and History: Mode of Production versus Mode of Information* [Cambridge: Polity, 1984], 160).

60. The word *liberalism* is first used in the English language around 1819. But the tenets of this philosophy appear much earlier. Perhaps John Locke can be seen as the father of liberalism. But liberalism as a full-fledged narrative arises in the nineteenth century roughly equivalent to the way David Wells defines capitalism.

61. See Newbigin, *Foolishness to the Greeks*, 106. Newbigin notes concerning these visions that "they are both atheist. The one attempts without success to enforce atheism in the private as well as the public sector. The other permits belief in God as an option for private life but excludes it from any controlling role in public life."

62. Whereas we speak of two forms of humanism, Arthur Holmes speaks of four forms of humanism: scientific, romanticist, existentialist, and Marxist (*Contours of a World View*, Studies in a Christian World View 1 [Grand Rapids: Eerdmans, 1983], 21–27). As already suggested, Marxism is one form that scientific humanism takes. Existentialist humanism is one of the movements that follow in the stream of Romantic humanism.

63. Quoted in Wells, *History through the Eyes of Faith*, 188.

64. From Wordsworth's poem "The Tables Turned."

65. John Keats, *The Letters of John Keats, 1814–1821*, ed. Hyder E. Rollins, 2 vols. (Cambridge, MA: Harvard University Press, 1958), 1:184–85.

66. John Herman Randall, *The Making of the Modern Mind* (Cambridge, MA: Riverside, 1940), 415; cf. Newbigin, *The Other Side of 1984*, 13.

67. This categorization appears in the title of a famous book by C. P. Snow that explores the two cultures of university life—the natural sciences and the arts—spawned by these two forms of humanism (*The Two Cultures and the Scientific Revolution* [Cambridge: Cambridge University Press, 1959]).

68. Carl Jung, *Modern Man in Search of a Soul* (New York: Harcourt and Brace, 1933), 231, 234–35.

69. Wells, *History through the Eyes of Faith*, 218.

70. United Nations Development Programme, *Human Development Report 1992* (New York: Oxford University Press, 1992), 34.

71. United Nations Development Programme, *Human Development Report 1999* (New York: Oxford University Press, 1999), 2.

72. Bob Goudzwaard, Mark Vander Vennen, and David Van Heemst, *Hope in Troubled Times: A New Vision for Confronting Global Crises* (Grand Rapids: Baker Academic, 2007), 153.

73. Compare Stockholm International Peace Research Institute, "Recent Trends in Military Expenditures," http://www.sipri.org/contents/milap/milex/mex_trends.html (accessed April 5, 2008); World Food Programme, "Hunger Facts," http://www.wfp.org/aboutwfp/facts/hunger_facts.asp (accessed April 5, 2008); and Feed the Children, "Hungry and Poor . . . ," http://www.feedthechildren.org/site/PageServer?pagename=org_nicaragua (accessed April 5, 2008).

74. Kenneth J. Gergen, *The Saturated Self: Dilemmas of Identity in Contemporary Life* (New York: Basic Books, 1991), 13.

75. Lesslie Newbigin, "Rapid Social Change and Evangelism" (unpublished paper, 1962), 3.

76. Brian Walsh, *Who Turned out the Lights? The Light of the Gospel in a Post-Enlightenment Culture* (Toronto: Institute for Christian Studies, 1989), 15.

77. Walker, *Telling the Story*, 143 (italics added).

Chapter 7 What Time Is It? Four Signs of Our Time in the Western Story

1. On the earliest uses of the term *postmodern*, see Hans Bertens, *The Idea of the Postmodern: A History* (London: Routledge, 1995), 20; Margaret Rose, *The Post-modern and the Post-industrial: A Critical Analysis* (Cambridge: Cambridge University Press, 1991), 3–20.

2. Jean-François Lyotard, *The Postmodern Condition: A Report on Knowledge*, Theory and History of Literature 10 (Manchester: Manchester University Press, 1984), xxiv.

3. Richard Rorty, *Philosophy and the Mirror of Nature* (Oxford: Blackwell, 1980).

4. Kenneth J. Gergen, *The Saturated Self: Dilemmas of Identity in Contemporary Life* (New York: Basic Books, 1991), 82.

5. See especially, in this respect, the work of Michel Foucault. For an overview of his views, see David Naugle, *Worldview: The History of a Concept* (Grand Rapids: Eerdmans, 2002), 184–86.

6. See Bertens, *The Idea of the Postmodern*, 134–37.

7. Richard Rorty, "Postmodernist Bourgeois Liberalism," *Journal of Philosophy* 80, no. 10 (1983): 585–86.

8. Michel Foucault, *The Order of Things: An Archaeology of the Human Sciences* (London: Tavistock, 1970), xxiii.

9. David Harvey, *The Condition of Postmodernity: An Enquiry into the Origins of Cultural Change* (Oxford: Blackwell, 1990).

10. Alvin Plantinga, "Advice to Christian Philosophers," *Faith and Philosophy* 1, no. 3 (1984): 269.

11. See Lesslie Newbigin's account of the elephants and the blind men in *The Gospel in a Pluralist Society* (Grand Rapids: Eerdmans, 1989), 9–10.

12. Mary Hesse, "How to Be Postmodern Without Being a Feminist," *The Monist* 77, no. 4 (1994): 457.

13. David Lyon, *Postmodernity* (Minneapolis: University of Minnesota Press, 1994), 70.

14. Edward S. Casey, *Getting Back into Place: Toward a Renewed Understanding of the Place-World*, Studies in Continental Thought (Bloomington: Indiana University Press, 1983), 389–90.

15. Peter Heslam, *Globalization: Unravelling the New Capitalism*, Grove Ethics Series E125 (Cambridge: Grove, 2002), 7–8.

16. Richard Bauckham, "Reading Scripture as a Coherent Story," in *The Art of Reading Scripture*, ed. Ellen F. David and Richard B. Hays (Grand Rapids: Eerdmans, 2003), 46.

17. Susan J. White, "A New Story to Live By?" *Transmission* (Spring 1998): 3–4.

18. Don Slater, *Consumer Culture and Modernity* (Oxford: Polity, 1997), 27.

19. See Anthony Bianco, *The Bully of Bentonville: How the High Cost of Wal-Mart's Everyday Low Prices Is Hurting America* (New York: Doubleday, 2007), 166–69.

20. Bianco, *The Bully of Bentonville*, 169.

21. Slater, *Consumer Culture and Modernity*, 29.

22. Rouse is quoted in Jon Pahl, *Shopping Malls and Other Sacred Spaces: Putting God in Place* (Grand Rapids: Brazos, 2003), 70.

23. Pahl, *Shopping Malls*, 79.

24. Joseph E. Stiglitz, *Making Globalization Work* (New York: Norton, 2006), 4.

25. On the connection between globalization and modernity, see Bob Goudzwaard, Mark Vander Vennen, and David Van Heemst, *Hope in Troubled Times: A New Vision for Confronting Global Crises* (Grand Rapids: Baker Academic, 2007), 143–46.

26. Bob Goudzwaard, "Globalization, Economics, and the Modern World-and-Life View" (unpublished paper).

27. In what follows we are deeply indebted to Bob Goudzwaard and Harry M. de Lange, *Beyond Poverty and Affluence: Toward a Canadian Economy of Care* (Toronto: University of Toronto Press, 1995).

28. Goudzwaard and de Lange, *Beyond Poverty and Affluence*, 48.

29. Goudzwaard and de Lange, *Beyond Poverty and Affluence*, 51, 53.

30. Goudzwaard and de Lange, *Beyond Poverty and Affluence*, 61, 65.

31. Stiglitz, *Making Globalization Work*, 62.

32. Stiglitz, *Making Globalization Work*, 78, 79.

33. Stiglitz (*Making Globalization Work*, 11) notes that except for China, poverty has increased in the developing world over the past two decades. About 40 percent of the world's 6.5 billion people live in poverty (up 36 percent from 1981), with about one-sixth (877 million) in extreme poverty (3 percent more than in 1981). Africa is the worst case, where the number of people living in extreme poverty has doubled from 164 million to 316 million.

34. Goudzwaard, Vander Vennen, and Van Heemst, *Hope in Troubled Times*, 191.

35. See, for example, Stephen L. Carter, *The Culture of Disbelief: How American Law and Politics Trivialize Religious Devotion* (New York: Anchor Books, 1993).

36. See, for example, Gianni Vattimo, *Belief*, trans. Luca D'Isanto and David Webb (Stanford, CA: Stanford University Press, 1999); originally published as *Credere di Credere* (Milan: Garzanti, 1996).

37. Philip Jenkins, *The Next Christendom: The Coming of Global Christianity* (Oxford: Oxford University Press, 2002), 1.

38. Jenkins, *The Next Christendom*, 3.

39. Philip Jenkins, *The New Faces of Christianity: Believing the Bible in the Global South* (Oxford: Oxford University Press, 2006), 41.

40. Jenkins, *The Next Christendom*, 181–82.

41. I allude here to the Manila Manifesto's definition of mission. The Manila Manifesto is an elaboration of the evangelical Lausanne Covenant (1974). It was framed by the participants of Lausanne II, the Second International Congress on World Evangelization, held in Manila in 1989.

42. Jenkins, *The New Faces of Christianity,* 141, 142.

43. Karl Barth, *Church Dogmatics*, vol. 3, *The Doctrine of Creation, Part 1* (Edinburgh: T&T Clark, 1958), 21.

44. Samuel P. Huntington, *The Clash of Civilizations and the Remaking of World Order* (New York: Simon & Schuster, 1996).

45. Jenkins, *The Next Christendom*, 166. It is important to note that Jenkins means that the population will be predominantly Muslim or Christian, and not necessarily the state and society as a whole.

46. Khurshid Ahmad, *Islam: Its Meaning and Message* (London: Islamic Foundation, 1975), 37.

47. Paul Marshall, preface to *Radical Islam's Rules: The Worldwide Spread of Extreme Shari'a Law*, ed. Paul Marshall (Lanham, MD: Rowan & Littlefield, 2001), 1.

48. Chaudhry Abdul Qadir, *Philosophy and Science in the Islamic World* (London: Croom Helm, 1988), 1.

49. Qadir, *Philosophy and Science*, 5–6.

50. Akbar S. Ahmed, *Postmodernism and Islam: Predicament and Promise* (London: Routledge, 1992), 264.

51. Ziauddin Sardar, "The Ethical Connection: Christian-Muslim Relations in the Postmodern Age," *Islam and Christian-Muslim Relations* 2, no. 1 (June 1991): 59.

52. Sardar, "Ethical Connection," 59, 68.

53. Sardar, "Ethical Connection," 61–62.

54. Jenkins, *The Next Christendom*, 168.

55. Lesslie Newbigin, "Part Four: A Light to the Nations: Theology in Politics," in *Faith and Power: Christianity and Islam in "Secular" Britain*, by Lesslie Newbigin, Lamin Sanneh, and Jenny Taylor (London: SPCK, 1998), 148–49.

56. Jacques Ellul, *The Subversion of Christianity*, trans. Geoffrey W. Bromiley (Grand Rapids: Eerdmans, 1986), 100.

57. Bernard Lewis, *The Crisis of Islam: Holy War and Unholy Terror* (New York: Random House, 2004), 37.

58. Peter G. Riddell and Peter Cotterell, *Islam in Context: Past, Present, and Future* (Grand Rapids: Baker Academic, 2003), 192.

59. John L. Esposito, *Unholy War: Terror in the Name of Islam* (Oxford: Oxford University Press, 2003), 19.

60. Esposito, *Unholy War,* 24.

61. Colin Chapman, *"Islamic Terrorism": Is There a Christian Response?* Grove Ethics Series E139 (Cambridge: Grove, 2005), 23.

62. Chapman, *"Islamic Terrorism,"* 22. See also the important book by Jimmy Carter, *Palestine: Peace Not Apartheid* (New York: Simon & Schuster, 2006).

Chapter 8 Living at the Crossroads: A Faithful, Relevant Witness

1. David Bosch, *Believing in the Future: Toward a Missiology of Western Culture* (Valley Forge, PA: Trinity Press International, 1995), 34.

2. Carl F. H. Henry, *The Uneasy Conscience of Modern Fundamentalism* (1947; repr., Grand Rapids: Eerdmans, 2003), 30, 33, 42.

3. "Lausanne" refers to the meeting of the International Congress of World Evangelization that met in Lausanne, Switzerland, July 16–25, 1974. Over 2,700 participants from 150 different countries assembled. About half of the participants came from the non-Western world. Lausanne is the largest meeting devoted to the mission of the church in modern history. The gathering

produced a statement of fifteen articles entitled the "Lausanne Covenant," which "intended to define the necessity, responsibilities, and goals of spreading the Gospel." It is one of the most influential documents ever produced by modern-day evangelicals.

4. Lausanne Covenant, "Christian Social Responsibility," paragraph 5.

5. Wheaton '83 Statement, paragraph 26.

6. See Brian J. Walsh and J. Richard Middleton, *The Transforming Vision: Shaping a Christian World View* (Downers Grove, IL: InterVarsity, 1984), 150–51.

7. H. Richard Niebuhr, *Christ and Culture* (New York: Harper, 1951).

8. Missiology is the academic discipline of studying mission. Although it is changing today, in the past it has primarily studied cross-cultural missions.

9. See Paul Tillich, *Theology of Culture*, ed. Robert C. Kimball (New York: Oxford University Press, 1964). We might also include Emil Brunner, *Christianity and Civilisation*, 2 vols. (New York: Scribner, 1948–1949).

10. Lesslie Newbigin, *Foolishness to the Greeks: The Gospel and Western Culture* (Grand Rapids: Eerdmans, 1986), 2–3.

11. See Lesslie Newbigin, *The Other Side of 1984: Questions for the Churches* (Geneva: World Council of Churches, 1983), 31, 47, 54; idem, "Can the West Be Converted?" *Princeton Seminary Bulletin* 6, no. 1 (1985): 25, 36; idem, *Foolishness to the Greeks*, 1.

12. Lesslie Newbigin, "What Is a 'Local Church Truly United'?" *Ecumenical Review* 29 (1977): 119.

13. Abraham Kuyper, *Souvereiniteit in eigen kring: Rede ter inwijding van de Vrije Universiteit den 20sten October 1980 gehouden in het Koor der Nieuwe Kerk te Amsterdam* (Amsterdam: Kruyt, 1880), 32 (our translation).

14. See Lesslie Newbigin, *The Good Shepherd: Meditations on Christian Ministry in Today's World* (Grand Rapids: Eerdmans, 1977), 98.

15. Lesslie Newbigin, *A Word in Season: Perspectives on Christian World Missions* (Grand Rapids: Eerdmans, 1994), 54.

16. Lesslie Newbigin, "Unfaith and Other Faiths" (unpublished lecture given to the Division of Foreign Missions, National Council of the Churches of Christ in the U.S.A., 1962); idem, *The Gospel in a Pluralist Society* (Grand Rapids: Eerdmans, 1989), 15–16.

17. Hendrik Kraemer, *The Communication of the Christian Faith* (Philadelphia: Westminster, 1956), 36.

18. See Michael Goheen, "The Surrender and Recovery of the Unbearable Tension," *Journal of Education and Christian Belief* 11, no. 1 (Spring 2007): 7–21.

19. See Denys Munby, *The Idea of a Secular Society, and Its Significance for Christians* (Oxford: Oxford University Press, 1963).

20. Newbigin, *Foolishness to the Greeks*, 132.

21. T. S. Eliot, *The Idea of a Christian Society* (New York: Harcourt, Brace & World, 1940), 20 (italics added).

22. See Dean Flemming, *Contextualization in the New Testament: Patterns for Theology and Mission* (Downers Grove, IL: InterVarsity, 2005), 146–49, 228–29.

23. Flemming, *Contextualization in the New Testament*, 148, 228.

24. Bosch, *Believing in the Future*, 59.

25. Lesslie Newbigin, "The Work of the Holy Spirit in the Life of the Asian Churches," in *A Decisive Hour for the Christian Mission: The East Asia Christian Conference 1959, and the John R. Mott Memorial Lectures*, by Norman Goodall et al. (London: SCM, 1960), 28.

26. Darrell Guder, ed., *Missional Church: A Vision for the Sending of the Church in North America*, The Gospel and Our Culture (Grand Rapids: Eerdmans, 1998), 115.

27. Lesslie Newbigin, *Truth to Tell: The Gospel as Public Truth* (London: SPCK; Grand Rapids: Eerdmans, 1991), 81.

28. Reformed Ecumenical Synod, *The Church and Its Social Calling* (Grand Rapids: Reformed Ecumenical Synod, 1980), 36.

29. Herman Ridderbos, "The Kingdom of God and Our Life in the World," *International Reformed Bulletin* 28 (January 1967): 11–12.

30. Newbigin, *Truth to Tell*, 85.

31. Lesslie Newbigin, "The Church and the CASA [Christian Agency for Social Action]," *National Christian Council Review* 93 (1973): 546.

32. See Craig G. Bartholomew and Michael W. Goheen, *The Drama of Scripture: Finding Our Place in the Biblical Story* (Grand Rapids: Baker Academic, 2004), 143–45.

33. One thinks here of the ministries of people such as Mother Teresa, Henri Nouwen, and Jean Vanier.

34. See Gary Scott Smith, ed., *God and Politics: Four Views on the Reformation of Civil Government* (Phillipsburg, NJ: Presbyterian & Reformed, 1989), 75–99.

35. Newbigin, *Truth to Tell*, 56–60.

36. See Lesslie Newbigin, *Trinitarian Faith and Today's Mission*, World Council of Churches Commission on World Mission and Evangelism Study Pamphlets 2 (Richmond: John Knox, 1964), 42.

37. Lesslie Newbigin, "Bible Studies: Four Talks on 1 Peter," in *We Were Brought Together: Report of the National Conference of Australian Churches Held at Melbourne University, February 2–11, 1960*, ed. David M. Taylor (Sydney: Australian Council for the World Council of Churches, 1960), 112.

38. N. T. Wright, *New Tasks for a Renewed Church* (London: Hodder & Stoughton, 1992), 86 (italics added).

39. Lesslie Newbigin, *Journey into Joy* (Grand Rapids: Eerdmans, 1972), 112–13.

40. Lesslie Newbigin, "Our Task Today" (a charge given to the fourth meeting of the Diocesan Council, Tirumangalam, India, December 18–20, 1951).

41. Helmut Thielicke, *Life Can Begin Again: Sermons on the Sermon on the Mount*, trans. John W. Doberstein (Philadelphia: Fortress, 1963), 33.

Chapter 9 Life at the Crossroads: Perspectives on Some Areas of Public Life

1. On Old Testament law, see Craig G. Bartholomew and Michael W. Goheen, *The Drama of Scripture: Finding Our Place in the Biblical Story* (Grand Rapids: Baker Academic, 2004), 66–70.

2. In Deuteronomy 25 the condemnation of dishonesty in business transactions is specifically linked to "the LORD." This is quite often the case in the Torah and in Proverbs.

3. Ray van Leeuwen, "Proverbs," in *The New Interpreter's Bible*, ed. Leander E. Keck, 12 vols. (Nashville: Abingdon, 1995–2003), 5:262.

4. Richard Bauckham, *Bible and Mission: Christian Witness in a Postmodern World* (Grand Rapids: Baker Academic, 2003), 107–8.

5. Fairtrade is a product certification system that is designed to help people identify products that meet agreed labor and environmental standards. For further information, see http://www.fairtrade.org.uk and http://www.fairtrade.net.

6. Wendell Berry, *The Unsettling of America: Culture and Agriculture* (San Francisco: Sierra Club Books, 1997). All of Berry's books are worth reading.

7. For an excellent book that surveys various ideologies that are shaping political life today, see David T. Koyzis, *Political Visions and Illusions: A Survey and Christian Critique of Contemporary Ideologies* (Downers Grove, IL: InterVarsity, 2003).

8. An older but still good introduction is Paul Marshall, *Thine Is the Kingdom: A Biblical Perspective on the Nature of Government and Politics Today* (London: Marshall, Morgan & Scott, 1984).

9. Oliver O'Donovan, *The Desire of the Nations: Rediscovering the Roots of Political Theology* (Cambridge: Cambridge University Press, 1996), ix.

10. See Oliver O'Donovan and Joan Lockwood O'Donovan, *From Irenaeus to Grotius: A Sourcebook in Christian Political Thought* (Grand Rapids: Eerdmans, 1999). See also Oliver O'Donovan, *The Just War Revisited* (Cambridge: Cambridge University Press, 2003).

11. See Stanley W. Carlson-Thies and James W. Skillen, eds., *Welfare in America: Christian Perspectives on a Policy in Crisis* (Grand Rapids: Eerdmans, 1996).

12. The genocide in Darfur is the first one of the twenty-first century. See Don Cheadle and John Prendergast, *Not on Our Watch: The Mission to End Genocide in Darfur and Beyond* (New York: Hyperion, 2007).

13. A. Bartlett Giamatti, *Take Time for Paradise: Americans and Their Games* (New York: Summit Books, 1989), 38.

14. Marvin Zuidema, "Athletics from a Christian Perspective," in *Christianity and Leisure: Issues in a Pluralistic Society*, ed. Paul Heintzman, Glen Van Andel, and Thomas Visker (Sioux Center, IA: Dordt College Press, 1994), 185.

15. John Byl, "Coming to Terms with Play, Game, Sport, and Athletics," in Heintzman, Van Andel, and Visker, *Christianity and Leisure*, 155–63.

16. Bradshaw Frey, William Ingram, Thomas McWhertor, and William Romanowski, "Sports and Athletics: Playing to the Glory of God," in *At Work and Play: Biblical Insight to Daily Obedience* (Jordan Station, ON: Paideia, 1986), 46.

17. Zuidema, "Athletics from a Christian Perspective," 185.

18. Henry Russell "Red" Sanders, an American football coach at UCLA and Vanderbilt in the first half of the twentieth century, is credited with coining this phrase. Lombardi popularized it.

19. In fact, some of the ways sports are used for evangelism, even proselytism, are, we believe, invalid. See Frey et al., "Sports and Athletics," 55–56.

20. Edward L. Shaughnessy, "Santayana on Athletics," *Journal of American Studies* 10, no. 2 (1977): 188.

21. Byl, "Coming to Terms with Play," 157.

22. Charles Prebish, "Heavenly Father, Divine Goalie: Sport and Religion," *Antioch Review* 42, no. 3 (1984): 318.

23. Gordon Spykman, "Toward a Christian Perspective in the Leisure Sciences," in Heintzman, Van Andel, and Visker, *Christianity and Leisure*, 54.

24. See Frey et al., "Sports and Athletics," 51–56. We have not stressed the sinful distortions of sports and competition. Our primary purpose in this small section is talk about sports and competition as rooted in Scripture's teaching on creation.

25. Spykman, "Toward a Christian Perspective," 58.

26. For a lovely book in this respect, see Edith Schaeffer, *Hidden Art* (Wheaton: Tyndale, 1972).

27. Hans R. Rookmaker, *Art Needs No Justification* (Downers Grove, IL: InterVarsity, 1978); see also idem, *The Creative Gift: The Arts and the Christian Life* (Leicester, UK: Inter-Varsity, 1981), chap. 6.

28. Abraham Kuyper, *Lectures on Calvinism* (Grand Rapids: Eerdmans, 1931), 142, see footnote.

29. See Bartholomew and Goheen, *Drama of Scripture*, 48, 49.

30. For an accessible introduction to recent approaches to the Psalter that stress the carefully crafted literary shape of the collection as a whole, see Craig G. Bartholomew and Andrew West, eds., *Praying by the Book: Reading the Psalms* (Carlisle: Paternoster, 2001).

31. The purpose of art is complex and controversial. In *Art in Action: Toward a Christian Aesthetic* (Grand Rapids: Eerdmans, 1980), Nicholas Wolterstorff denies that there is such a thing as *the* purpose of art. See also Cal Seerveld, "Cal Looks at Nick: A Response to Nicholas Wolterstorff's *Art in Action*," in *In the Fields of the Lord: A Calvin Seerveld Reader*, ed. Craig Bartholomew (Carlisle: Piquant, 2000), 360–64.

32. Wolterstorff, *Art in Action*, 144.

33. Joseph Conrad, preface to *The Nigger of Narcissus* (New York: Collier, 1962), 19.

34. Leland Ryken, *Culture in Christian Perspective: A Door to Understanding and Enjoying the Arts* (Portland, OR: Multnomah, 1986), 112.

35. Ryken, *Culture in Christian Perspective*, 26.

36. C. S. Lewis, *An Experiment in Criticism* (Cambridge: Cambridge University Press, 1961), 137–39.

37. On science and imagination, see Cheryl Forbes, *Imagination: Embracing a Theology of Wonder* (Portland, OR: Multnomah, 1986), chap. 7.

38. See Carl Jung, *Memories, Dreams, Reflections* (New York: Vintage Books, 1965), 173–75.

39. C. S. Lewis, *Christian Reflections* (Grand Rapids: Eerdmans, 1967), 33–34.

40. Ryken, *Culture in Christian Perspective*, 172.

41. Keith McKean, *The Moral Measure of Literature* (Denver: Swallow, 1961), quoted in Ryken, *Culture in Christian Perspective*, 166.

42. George M. Marsden, *The Outrageous Idea of Christian Scholarship* (Oxford: Oxford University Press, 1997).

43. Charles Habib Malik, *A Christian Critique of the University*, Pascal Lectures on Christianity and the University (Downers Grove, IL: InterVarsity, 1982), 19–20.

44. Albert M. Wolters, *Ideas Have Legs* (Toronto: Institute for Christian Studies, 1987), 5.

45. Wolters, *Ideas Have Legs*, 5.

46. Wolters, *Ideas Have Legs*, 7.

47. Brian J. Walsh and J. Richard Middleton, *The Transforming Vision: Shaping a Christian World View* (Downers Grove, IL: InterVarsity, 1984), 164–66.

48. Sidney Greidanus, "The Use of the Bible in Christian Scholarship," *Christian Scholar's Review* 11, no. 2 (1982): 146–47.

49. Albert M. Wolters, *Creation Regained: Biblical Basics for a Reformational Worldview*, 2nd ed. (Grand Rapids: Eerdmans, 2005), 87–89.

50. See Bob Goudzwaard and Harry M. de Lange, *Beyond Poverty and Affluence: Toward a Canadian Economy of Care* (Toronto: University of Toronto Press, 1995).

51. Lesslie Newbigin, "The Secular-Apostolic Dilemma," in *Not without a Compass: JEA Seminar on Christian Education in the India of Today*, ed. T. A. Matthias et al. (New Delhi: Jesuit Educational Association of India, 1972), 61–71.

52. Brian Walsh, "Education in Precarious Times: Postmodernity and a Christian Worldview," in *The Crumbling Walls of Certainty: Towards a Christian Critique of Postmodernity and Education*, ed. Ian Lambert and Suzanne Mitchell (Sydney: Centre for the Study of Australian Christianity, 1997), 14. Walsh quotes Robin Usher and Richard Edwards, *Postmodernism and Education: Different Voices, Different Worlds* (London: Routledge, 1994), 2.

53. Neil Postman, *The End of Education: Redefining the Value of School* (New York: Vintage Books, 1995), 27–58.

54. Walsh, "Education in Precarious Times," 14–15.

55. Stuart Fowler, "Communities, Organizations, and People," *Pro Rege* 21, no. 4 (June 1993): 24.

56. Some good places to start are David I. Smith and John Shortt, *The Bible and the Task of Teaching* (Stapleford: Stapleford Centre, 2002); Harro Van Brummelen, *Walking with God in the Classroom: Christian Approaches to Learning and Teaching* (Burlington, ON: Welch, 1988); Richard Edlin, *The Cause of Christian Education*, 3rd ed. (Northport, AL: Vision Press, 1999); Ian Lambert and Suzanne Mitchell, eds., *The Crumbling Walls of Certainty: Towards a Christian Critique of Postmodernity and Education* (Sydney: Centre for the Study of Australian Christianity, 1997); John Van Dyk, *The Craft of Christian Teaching: A Classroom Journey* (Sioux Center, IA: Dordt College Press, 2000); idem, *Letters to Lisa: Conversations with a Christian Teacher* (Sioux Center, IA: Dordt College Press, 1997); Albert Greene, *Reclaiming the Future of*

Christian Education: A Transforming Vision (Colorado Springs, CO: Association of Christian Schools International, 1998).

57. John E. Hull, "Aiming for Christian Education, Settling for Christians Educating: The Christian School's Replication of the Public School Paradigm," *Christian Scholar's Review* 32, no. 2 (2003): 203–23.

58. Jack Mechielsen, preface to *No Icing on the Cake: Christian Foundations for Education,* ed. Jack Mechielsen (Melbourne: Brookes-Hall, 1980), vi.

59. Roy Clouser offers a compelling refutation of this in the area of theory formation in *The Myth of Religious Neutrality: An Essay on the Hidden Role of Belief in Theories,* rev. ed. (Notre Dame, IN: University of Notre Dame Press, 2005).

60. Postman, *The End of Education,* 7.

61. Gloria Stronks and Doug Blomberg, *A Vision with a Task: Christian Schooling for Responsive Discipleship* (Grand Rapids: Baker Academic, 1993).

62. Stuart Fowler, Harro Van Brummelen, and John Van Dyk, eds., *Christian Schooling: Education for Freedom* (Potchefstroom: Potchefstroom University for Higher Education, 1990).

63. Nicholas Wolterstorff, *Educating for Responsible Action* (Grand Rapids: CSI Publications; Eerdmans, 1980).

64. Nicholas Wolterstorff, *Educating for Shalom: Essays on Higher Education,* ed. Clarence W. Joldersma and Gloria Goris Stronks (Grand Rapids: Eerdmans, 2004).

65. Elmer J. Thiessen, *Teaching for Commitment: Liberal Education, Indoctrination, and Christian Nurture* (Montreal: McGill's-Queens University Press, 1993).

66. See Ken Badley, "Two 'Cop-Outs' in Faith-Learning Integration: Incarnational Integration and Worldviewish Integration," *Spectrum* 28, no. 2 (Summer 1996): 110.

67. Hull, "Aiming for Christian Education," 208.

68. Hull, "Aiming for Christian Education," 207.

Pastoral Postscript

1. Readers are encouraged to consult Eugene Peterson's excellent corpus of work on spirituality.

2. Eugene H. Peterson, *A Long Obedience in the Same Direction: Discipleship in an Instant Society,* 2nd ed. (Downers Grove, IL: InterVarsity, 2000).

3. See, for example, part 2 of Edward C. Butler, *Western Mysticism: The Teaching of Augustine, Gregory and Bernard on Contemplation and the Contemplative Life,* 2nd ed. (New York: Harper & Row, 1966), 157–223.

4. Congregation for Institutes of Consecrated Life and Societies of Apostolic Life, *Starting Afresh from Christ: A Renewed Commitment to Consecrated Life in the Third Millennium* (Montreal: Médiaspaul, 2002), 49.

5. See David Bosch, *Transforming Mission: Paradigm Shifts in Theology of Mission* (Maryknoll, NY: Orbis, 1991), 389–93.

6. Wendell Berry, "A Poem of Difficult Hope," in *What Are People For? Essays by Wendell Berry* (New York: North Point, 1990), 58–63.

7. Karl Marx, *Theses on Feuerbach,* thesis 11 (1845).

8. James W. Skillen, "Christian Action and the Coming of God's Kingdom," in *Confessing Christ and Doing Politics,* ed. James W. Skillen (Washington, DC: Association for Public Justice Education Fund, 1982), 102–3.

9. Christian Reformed Church, *Our World Belongs to God: A Contemporary Testimony* (Grand Rapids: CRC Publications, 1987), paragraphs 56, 57, 6 [also available at http://www.crcna.org/pages/our_world_main.cfm].

Scripture Index

Subject Index

"Knowing where you have come from is nearly as important as knowing where you want to go. Goheen and Bartholomew trace the deep roots of our contemporary Western worldview in that kind of easy, broad-brush comprehensiveness that makes one exclaim, 'Yes of course, that's exactly the way things are—and why!' But alongside that, they do an equally good job in presenting the biblical worldview as the story that tells it like it really is, for life, the universe, and everything. That's the way things are—but as God sees them. The combination powerfully forces us to see the dissonance between the two and the stark choice that Christians need to make. Which story do we live by? Which road do we travel from the crossroads? But the book is far from all theory. It grounds the challenge of living out the Christian story in a variety of practical, up-to-date, areas of life in the world around us. This is a book filled with eye-opening insight, biblical nourishment, practical challenge, and robust hope. It turns the mission of God into our mission in the world and compels us to make some radical choices."

—**Christopher J. H. Wright**, international director,
Langham Partnership International

"Finally, a worldview text that moves incisively beyond mere theory. *Living at the Crossroads* is profound and practical, intelligent and warmly pastoral as it proceeds from a comprehensive understanding of the biblical story to an insightful engagement with twenty-first-century issues. Goheen and Bartholomew write out of their deep missional commitment with admirable clarity. They beckon us into a faithful and relevant involvement with complex issues, including globalization, postmodernity, consumerism, and the resurgence of Islam. *Living at the Crossroads* will stir you to embrace both unbearable tension and unprecedented opportunities to bring genuine hope to a waiting world. It is a must read for all who long to develop a worldview shaped by God's Word."

—**Rod Thompson**, School of Theology, Laidlaw College

"If you haven't been able to keep up with all the books on a Christian world-view that have appeared in recent years, now is the time to act. Read this book. Goheen and Bartholomew not only have made use of all the other worldview books but also have written a volume that distinguishes itself. Illuminating our times with historical perspective, biblical depth, and social breadth, the authors show what a biblical worldview should mean for us today."

—**James W. Skillen**, president, Center for Public Justice

"As the title implies, this book shows that a Christian worldview is not merely something of intellectual importance, but it has relevance to the whole of life. Clearly written and powerfully argued, *Living at the Crossroads* is rooted in biblical faith but reaches out to engage the contemporary world in a histori-cally informed way. This is essential reading for thoughtful Christians who wish to live out the gospel and love God with all of their being."

—**C. Stephen Evans**, University Professor of Philosophy
and Humanities, Baylor University

"This book means to put genuine *life* back into worldview studies. Bartholo-mew and Goheen present a Reformational world-*and-life* view with missional dynamic. Biblical theology and an evangelizing church enter fully into their reflection on following Jesus in every sphere of human society in today's mixed-up, deteriorating world culture. The authors bring redemptive insight to bear upon Western history, business, politics, art, and spirituality as well as the resurgence of Islam, and they do it in clear, passionate, down-to-earth language. *Living at the Crossroads* is basic, an invigorating challenge to anyone who would become a mature disciple of Jesus Christ."

—**Calvin Seerveld**, Institute for Christian Studies, emeritus